Unknotting the Heart

Unknotting the Heart

Unemployment and Therapeutic Governance in China

Jie Yang

ILR Press

AN IMPRINT OF
Cornell University Press
Ithaca and London

First published 2015 by Cornell University Press
First printing, Cornell Paperbacks, 2015
Printed in the United States of America

Library of Congress Cataloging-in-Publication Data

Yang, Jie, 1970– author.
    Unknotting the heart : unemployment and therapeutic governance in
China / Jie Yang.
        pages cm
    Includes bibliographical references and index.
    ISBN 978-0-8014-5375-5 (cloth : alk. paper)
    ISBN 978-0-8014-5660-2 (pbk. : alk. paper)
    1. Unemployment—China—Beijing—Psychological aspects.
2. Unemployed—Counseling of—China—Beijing.   3. Psychology,
Industrial—Political aspects—China—Beijing.   4. Labor policy—
China—Beijing—Psychological aspects.   5. Counseling psychology—
Government policy—China—Beijing.   6. Changping Qu (Beijing,
China)   I. Title.
    HD5708.2.C5Y36 2015
    331.13'7951019—dc23   2014045634

Cornell University Press strives to use environmentally responsible
suppliers and materials to the fullest extent possible in the publishing
of its books. Such materials include vegetable-based, low-VOC inks
and acid-free papers that are recycled, totally chlorine-free, or partly
composed of nonwood fibers. For further information, visit our website
at www.cornellpress.cornell.edu.

Cloth printing   10   9   8   7   6   5   4   3   2   1
Paperback printing   10   9   8   7   6   5   4   3   2   1

For my parents

Contents

PREFACE

A healthy life starts from the heart.
—CCTV 12, *Psychology Talk Show*

I did not set out to study the psychological dimension of state enterprise restructuring when I first began this project in Changping, Beijing in 2002. In fact, for a long time in my fieldwork, I shied away from examining the psychological and emotional dimensions of mass unemployment. Workers experienced layoffs as traumatic, and their reactions were so drastic that I was afraid I would not be able to find enough informants who wanted to share their personal experiences of being laid off. However, one day in July 2002, I met Li Mei, a woman in her early forties. Li had just been laid off from the factory. Pointing at her gray hair, she asked me to guess her age. Without waiting for me to come up with an answer, she said that she had turned to a *bai mao nu* overnight. (*Bai mao nu*, literally translated as "a gray-haired woman," often refers to Xi'er, the heroine of an old movie about the hard life of peasants before 1949, who was forced to live in a cave in order to escape her landlord's persecution and became gray-haired as a young woman.)

Li Mei continued, "I now understand why Xi'er's hair became gray overnight. It was not because of lack of sunshine in a cave but because of anger and resentment. The feeling of deep hatred and betrayal forces me to want to bomb the factory into a flat ground at any time." Pumping her right fist in the direction of the watch factory where I have conducted research during the last decade, Li said, "I will never go there again until I am ready to bomb it. I was ruthlessly mistreated and need to be vindicated (*shuofa*). I feel something stuck in my throat, very suppressed, very depressed." She bit her lip and tears started to stream down on her face. Seeing my sympathetic puzzlement, she told me that her workshop director's constant fault-finding had led her to make mistakes in processing key watch parts. In front of the whole workshop, she had been scolded and laid off. "I started to work for this factory at 19. They didn't even care to give you some 'face' to let you go decently. Thinking of this, my heart is bleeding," Li said. Ashamed and depressed, Li Mei left the community where she had grown up and had labored for the factory for over twenty years. She rented out her apartment in Changping and moved to downtown Beijing to be near her son, who was attending high school there. I did not see Li Mei again during my fieldwork in 2002 and 2003.

Stories such as Li's highlight the complexity of the process of mass layoffs due to economic restructuring and the depth of the trauma resulting from job loss for former state workers who had once been promised employment for life. These workers who had been mobilized to sacrifice their lives for various nation-building purposes in the past found themselves unable to keep silent and could not help sharing with people their discontent and disappointment and their searing critique of state-led privatization. The intensity of feelings—anger, resentment, and despair—that infused workers' discourses in their demands for a *shuofa* (justice or vindication) and in their bargaining with management for reemployment forced me to go beyond a mere discursive approach by considering how affect also penetrates workers' bodies and hearts and impacts their lives (Ahmed 2004; Yang 2014). The centrality of these affective dynamics compelled me to look into the psychological dimension of privatization.

The book echoes recent calls for continuing support for laid-off workers, including that made by Zhang Meng, director of the 2010 film *gang de qin* [A piano made in a factory]. Zhang laments that over time both government and media have paid less attention to the millions of workers who have been marginalized and impoverished and have paid a tremendous price for economic restructuring. His film focuses on this group of workers and their ongoing struggle to survive in an increasingly competitive job market. This book, from a different angle, demonstrates the breadth and depth of the psychological impact of state enterprise restructuring in China. In particular, I delve into the notion of the heart and the way its flexibility, ambiguity, and potentiality is deployed as a resource for value extraction, social stabilization, and political contestation, specifically, the way factory managers use it to extract value, the state uses it to stabilize society, and workers use it to contest state policies.

In 2008, when I visited a laid-off woman worker from Changping at her rented flat in a shantytown near Yuanmingyuan (the Summer Palace) in the district of Haidian, Beijing, she mentioned that Li Mei lived several blocks away. One Sunday afternoon in August, I finally met Li again. This time she looked more calm and composed. She had been trained in domestic management (*jiazheng fuwu*) and preliminary psychology at a domestic work agency co-sponsored by a local women's organization and an Australian nongovernmental organization. Having worked as a domestic worker for several Qinghua University professors for a few years, she indicated that the process of getting trained and working for people of different backgrounds had helped her gradually recover from her bitterness and depression as a result of her layoff. However, when talking about her last days at the Changping watch factory, her eyes still became wet; she appeared visibly emotional.

When I asked about the efficacy of the psychological training by the domestic work agency, she shook her head and said, "[It's] not even as useful as television counseling. They simply asked you to be strong, cheer you up to start again, then teach you how to see things from a different angle. But one thing the counselor taught us is useful: people appreciate positive company. To be employable as a domestic worker, you have to be happy and positive. Indeed, no one likes negative, unpleasant company. This is something new that helped me get hired because I was so bitter and negative at that moment. Their training for domestic work is more practical." When I asked her why she thought television counseling was more useful, Li said, "Counseling on TV is easier to relate to, for example, the story of Xiao Cui. Xiao Cui's condition sounds like mine. He was probably mistreated by CCTV [China Central Television] and then became depressed. If one day I bump into Xiao Cui, I would tell him, it is not that you are sick but it is that CCTV is sick." Li Mei, based on her own experience, perceived depression to be caused by social and political factors rather than a personal pathology.

Like Li Mei, for many workers in Changping the most effective way to directly confront the seriousness of mental illness is through Cui Yongyuan, a host for a CCTV program called *Say It as It Is* [*shi hua shi shuo*]. Because of his down-to-earth style and humorous and witty speech, he was extremely popular among workers in Changping. Workers called him Xiao Cui (Little Cui). On February 25, 2005, Cui was interviewed on another CCTV program called *yishu rensheng* [Life as art], where he publicly acknowledged that he suffered from depression (*de yiyuzheng*).[1] He discussed the symptoms in accessible language and called for people who suffer depression to seek medical treatment. He seemed to try to destigmatize depression by medicalizing it. For example, Cui said, "You can ask any doctor and they will tell you that this is a real disease. A person who is depressed is different from normal people. He thinks that ending his life will free him from problems. This is what happened to me two years ago. Since then, I've been under the care of a doctor, taking medicine, doing counseling. I feel I am getting better."

Cui Yongyuan's frank public confession of his own depression was startling to Chinese viewers, including workers in Changping. Because of the immense popularity of both Cui Yongyuan and the program *yishu rensheng*, many workers became familiar with the notion of depression. In Changping, workers and psychosocial workers often invoked Cui's depression as an example to destigmatize psychological disorders or legitimate the use of psychotherapy in their daily work. Two weeks after the interview with Cui Yongyuan in 2005, CCTV 12 began to broadcast a new daily counseling program named *Psychology Talk Show* (*xinli fangtan*). This program claims to provide psychological services for viewers who are facing different kinds of difficulty and social pressure.[2]

Accounts from both workers and psychosocial workers in Changping seemed to highlight the efficacy of this daily counseling program in educating the population. Particularly for community psychosocial workers, the counseling offered on the *Psychology Talk Show* often served as an important and accessible resource in their daily work. The professional counselors on the *Psychology Talk Show* were trained by Western clinicians in psychodynamic therapy, structural family therapy, and developmental psychology, all of which are firmly grounded in Euro-American tradition (Krieger 2009). While most community psychosocial workers seemed cautious about the Western origins of these psychotherapeutic traditions, when they switched to their normal model of commonsense psychology, they sometimes assumed that certain principles of these Western traditions were universal.

Although China has a long history of indigenous philosophies and practices that could broadly be considered psychotherapeutic (Jing and Fu 2001), what is generally thought of as Western psychotherapy has been gradually introduced to China over the last two decades (Chang et al. 2005). Psychotherapy has gradually infiltrated into people's daily lives and has even begun to become an appropriate way to deal with individual difficulties and familial conflicts (Ford 2007; Krieger 2009). The *Psychology Talk Show* functions as a way of educating Chinese viewers who have little previous exposure to psychological concepts about what is psychological, what it might mean to think psychologically, and what a psychological expert would do with such knowledge (Krieger 2009).

During my two-month field research in the summer of 2008, I had several conversations with Li Mei. In one of our conversations, she talked about the *Psychology Talk Show* and its impact on the "counseling" she does in her role as a *peiliao* (domestic worker and companion for chatting). She also indicated that she liked the counselors on the show but not the host, who reminded her of the meddling of a typical party secretary. Her remarks on the counseling format of the *Psychology Talk Show* resonate with my observations of the work style of community psychosocial workers, who used a hodgepodge of counseling and traditional communist thought work in their daily work. Li also emphasized how much her embodied knowledge of depression had contributed to her current work as a *peiliao*. She gave an example of the "counseling" she offered to one of her former employers, a professor from Qinghua University. After her application for full professorship had been rejected, this professor seemed to suffer from depression. Li described her diagnosis of the professor:

She often sat there either staring at the walls or at me doing housework, emotionless and speechless. When I tried to comfort her, her tears started to stream down, similar symptoms as mine when I was laid off. I told her if she continued to be like that, her hair would look like mine. Then I told her how my hair became gray and how I suffered from depression and gradually recovered. She started to talk with me more. But after she was promoted the next year, she fired me. *Jiang xin bi xin*, comparing my heart—the way I treated her and contributed to her healing—with her heart, I don't think she is kind [to me]. She appeared kind and promised to refer me to another professor and help my son get a job, but she never did any of these. It's like the factory, which promised to call us back but never did. She paid me by the time, by the hour, not by the depth of the care of my heart [*Jin xin jin Li*].

Li's account demonstrates two types of kindness. Li went all out to be kind to her employer. She even invoked her own embodied suffering to help the professor recover from depression in order to win her heart, approval, and support. The employer promised to be kind and supportive to Li but her promises have never been realized. However, her promises constituted an important impetus for Li Mei to dedicate herself more to her domestic work. In this sense, the employer's kindness operated as a mode of power and control, intensifying the exploitation of Li's physical and emotional labor. This dynamic of kindness resembles the working of the kindly power of the state in its psychotherapeutic intervention for unemployed workers, but the latter is symbolic kindness to compensate for previous unkindness—the destruction caused by state-led economic restructuring.

This form of kindly power is centered on the heart, a ground for cognition, virtue, and bodily sensation in the Chinese context. The heart, an ambiguous concept, refers to people's minds, emotions, attitudes, desires, morality, potential, and imaginations (Worm 2010). The ambiguity of the notion of the heart and its moral and psychological agency allows it to be framed to serve various purposes, including as a medium of sustaining social and political order and as a site for regulation and value extraction. It constitutes a resource that government projects can mobilize. For example, some of the state-led reemployment and poverty-relief programs are called *minxin gongcheng* (the Hearts of the People Project), a name that highlights the willingness of the party to win the hearts of the people as it seeks to manage mass unemployment.

Such "kindness" in the power of the government that delivered the destruction in the first place becomes necessary because it serves to open the hearts of workers, making them more tolerant of their misery and less resistant to state-led privatization. Kindness in the form of psychological "care" and other symbolic benevolent measures sometimes brings emotional relief and other positive change to workers. This kind of appeasement is partly responsible for the overall "peacefulness" of the privatization process. In this sense, kindly power did work to some degree. However, kindly power also creates new vulnerabilities for the marginalized. For example, psychological care not only fails to offer real solutions for workers' economic difficulties, it also generates new forms of exploitation and intensifies social stratification, as in the case of Li Mei and her employer.

Other dimensions of this form of kindly power include "kindness" as unfreedom and a mode of social control. For example, the Changping factory's prioritization of reemploying *falungong* practitioners is actually a way of scrutinizing them more closely and more efficiently. Kindly power can also be exercised through an emphasis on the positive potential of the workers while downplaying their perceived negative potential in order to avoid direct antagonism and confrontation. For example, in order to appease laid-off workers who attack the legitimacy of the ruling party and the aridity and hypocrisy of shifting state policies, community psychosocial workers have prioritized the development of workers' *qianli* (hidden capacities or positive potential) as a way of enhancing their productivity and "entrepreneurship."[3] This is because this same group of people also harbors *yinhuan* (hidden risks and dangers) that pose potential threats to governance.

In this book, I investigate both people's subjective experiences and psychological governing as the state interacts in the lives of its people. Intertwining these two, I employ a notion of therapeutic governance as it intersects with psychotherapy, mental health, and other sociopolitical issues including unemployment, urban poverty, and social anger in China. I define therapeutic governance as a loosely connected set of psychological expertise, representations, and governing technologies applied to the management of social problems from the perspective of therapy. In addressing the mental health "crisis" to save the nation, China is reacting by constructing new forms of governance designed to control as much as to heal its populace in order to harness the potential of its citizens for economic development. However, therapeutic ethos makes such control appear to be benevolent care and humanizes China's growth-oriented market development and its negative consequences.

Li Mei's story not only exemplifies the notion of kindly power but also mirrors the general trend toward psychologization in China. While Josh Krieger (2009) uses psychological understanding—a framework that uses psychological concepts to support individuals in thinking about their own and others' schemas—to interpret psychological education and psychological self-help in China, in this book I examine a more complex process of psychologization. More than interpreting non-psychological issues in "psychological" modes of thinking, it is a process of hybridization and distortion that encompasses economic, moral, psychological, and political dimensions. It is culturally and historically specific. For example, in Changping, workers often talked about their experiences of being mobilized to sacrifice for various nation-building projects. Examples include what has been asked of workers during waves of unemployment in contemporary China: in 1962, factory workers with rural roots returned to the countryside in order to relieve the pressures of unemployment at urban state enterprises. Unlike before, today the discontent and anger of laid-off workers can no longer be suppressed, and this poses a threat to governance. It is in this context that psychologization or kindly power through psychological care is carried out. It aims to win back the hearts of the people through channeling their desires after their hearts—their happiness, hope, and trust in the party—were broken by state-led privatization. It is a unity of contradictory practices.

In fact, this working-class community has a unique connection with one of the most prominent psychologists and counselors in China, Dr. Shi Kan, a professor at the Psychology Institute of the Chinese Academy of Sciences. In the late 1980s, he conducted a psychological research project to enhance workers' efficiency and productivity at the watch factory. Dr. Shi has founded and frequented several popular television counseling programs in China. This community's attention and emphasis on psychology is partly attributable to Dr. Shi's work. One day in early 2003, when I was still at Beibiao, the director of the factory's Reemployment Service Center showed me a clip he recorded from a CCTV program where Dr. Shi was counseling a group of laid-off workers. In his interactions with a laid-off woman worker, he emphasized the legitimacy of the job of traffic warden (*jiaotong xieguan*)—one type of replacement job offered to laid-off workers (Yang 2010). Over the years, many informants in Changping told me that they had seen Dr. Shi counseling laid-off workers and earthquake victims on television. Others heard him lecturing on the radio about psychological adjustment to Olympic volunteers before the 2008 Summer Olympic Games in Beijing. The impact of psychology on workers through Dr. Shi's public work seems persistent. In summer 2008, I finally met Dr. Shi and conducted a three-hour interview at his suburban house. He later sent me his book on job counseling for laid-off workers, emphasizing that psychology is the key to resolving the problems of mass unemployment.

The cumulative effect on viewers of media portrayals of psychology and mental illness creates stereotypes of what psychology and psychotherapy are and what psychotherapists do (see Gabbard and Gabbard 1999). The ubiquity of such narratives through Dr. Shi's counseling and on the *Psychology Talk Show* has meant that they have stopped being psychological for most people; they are a definitive series of facts about how people should relate, express themselves, and negotiate conflict (Ward 2002). In this sense, the psychologization trend in China constitutes a (political) process for manipulating and regulating how people think, interpret, and imagine.

In this book, I develop the relationship between power, psychology, and subjectivity in order to conceptualize the therapeutic mode of governance that emerges during psychologization. I suggest that even though psychology may offer a quick-fix solution in a difficult period, using psychology to manage social and economic issues obscures the possibility of more complex, responsible approaches to socioeconomic change. I argue that psychology is now part of a new language in China that is designed to encourage people to rebuild their identities around an emotional core that obfuscates the effects of socioeconomic dislocation they experience. The book highlights the connections between psychology, imagination, and potential that emerges in contemporary postsocialist contexts, contributing to new forms of governance, subject formation, and knowledge production.

The book is divided into two parts. Part I (Chapters 1–4) explores psychologization and state-led psychotherapeutic interventions, especially those that target laid-off workers, whom psychosocial workers view as embodying both *qianli* and *yinhuan*. I examine the pushes and pulls psychosocial workers (party staff and members of local residents' committees) experience who apply both psychological knowledge and traditional thought work in their daily management of marginalized individuals in their efforts to actualize their *qianli* while preempting the realization of *yinhuan*. I stress the different strategies counselors draw from the principle of *biantong* (change with continuity) and from neoliberalism as they use "psychotherapy" in their management of different groups of workers.

In Chapter 1, I examine how reemployment counseling programs encourage unemployed workers to undergo self-reflection as part of state-offered "therapy" that promotes happiness, productivity, and harmony. I explore three modes of self-reflection and a happiness-triggered notion of potential that highlight the role of the self in coping with the pressure of being laid off. This shift to self-management enables the government to shirk its responsibility and reshape the privatization of the economy. The analysis focuses on happiness as therapeutic and on the dialectic relationship between positive and negative potential: the highlighting of happiness preempts the realization of negative potential. In Chapter 2, I analyze the role of community residents' committees in psychologizing unemployment and other related issues in order to maximize the positive potential of the unemployed. I trace the professionalization process that has turned residents' committees (party staff in particular) into psychosocial workers and the effects of this change on larger-scale postsocialist governance in China. In their psychotherapeutic training these party members abandon the legacy of Leifeng, the figure of wholehearted communist service, to adopt "scientific" approaches to helping people help themselves. In this chapter I trace the trajectory of the notion of self-reliance since Mao's era, showing that contradictions between old and new forms of self-reliance have resulted in a proliferation of ironies and criticism from the intended subjects of therapy and counseling. This is a consequence of adopting the Maoist dialectics of *biantong* in a neoliberal context.

In Chapter 3, I broaden the ethnographic scope of the book by investigating the community poverty relief program of *song wennuan* (sending warmth), through which psychotherapeutic (counseling) and affective measures (including gift-giving and *renqing*, or sharing "human feelings") contribute to pacifying unemployed men in order to promote stability and renew socialist ethics. I examine the implications of the gendered notion of potentiality in prioritizing men over women for reemployment assistance and welfare distribution. I attend to a shift in *song wennuan* programs from the provision of daily necessities by state employers to delivery of psychology-infused processes intended to problematize dependency and "empower" those in poverty to help themselves. As an ideological and affective nexus, *song wennuan* highlights the government's strategic "care" for the marginalized, offering a non-Western approach to the therapeutic state that minimizes the state's responsibilities for the individual. *Song wennuan* constructs the image of a nurturing state.

In Chapter 4, I explore the distinct therapeutic relations emerging in postsocialist China through an analysis of the role of talk therapy in constructing new therapeutic subjects. Unlike traditional communist thought work, which married individual concerns to collective interests, current counseling highlights individual desire and personal responsibility. The chapter traces the transformation of speaking subjectivity from its role in thought work to its conception in talk therapy. In the past, party authorities combined the three communication roles distinguished by Goffman (1979)—animator, author, and principal—in thought work to align people's consciousness with official ideologies. Today, counselors, often following Carl Rogers, are allotted minimal speaking agency, instead emphasizing the self of the client, which putatively sets the condition for maximizing positive potential. Also, even though counselors adopt Rogers's nondirective approach, which calls on clients to draw upon their own resources to find solutions to their problems while developing inner authority in the healing process, clients still expect direction, guidance, and even quick-fix solutions to their problems from therapists. This chapter explores some of the distinct features of psychotherapeutic encounters and new technologies of self in China.

While Part I maps the increasing focus on psychology and its role in harnessing the positive potential of the unemployed through psychotherapeutic intervention, Part II (Chapters 5 and 6) offers a critical analysis of the political ramifications of this therapeutic governance and traces the role of class and gender in shaping new therapeutic strategies and the consequences of those therapeutic strategies for the politics of class and gender. To address this I focus on laid-off men and women who are retrained as informal "counselors" in their new capacity as domestic workers and taxi drivers.

Chapter 5 examines the psychological labor performed by laid-off workers who are reemployed as *peiliao* (companions for chatting), a new "profession" that has been particularly promoted among women since the mid-1990s. Unlike other psychological caregivers, who empathize or sympathize with clients through imagining the suffering of another, job counselors encourage *peiliao* to appropriate their embodied knowledge in their efforts to help others overcome difficulty and depression. *Peiliao*, who are perceived to embody boundless *qianli*, are expected to produce care and companionship through embodied knowledge and performativity in exchange for meager payment in a grim job market. This strategy not only reinscribes the pain these women originally encountered when they lost their jobs in state-owned factories; it also naturalizes their psychological care labor as part of their moral virtue instead of framing their companionship as a working relationship that is established and maintained with effort. This downplays the social and economic value of their care. I show that as a result, *peiliao* are vulnerable to discrimination and exploitation.

In Chapter 6, I look at laid-off men who presumably embody *yinhuan* and are targeted for preemptive measures, including counseling. I pay particular attention to laid-off workers turned taxi drivers, most of whom are male. Since the mid-1990s, taxi driving has become the most "popular" job for laid-off men in Changping. Often labeled as unaccustomed to diminishing job prospects and a declining standard of living, these men have been targeted for counseling as part of their job training to help them cope with burnout. However, the state misjudges the causes of drivers' burnout, or *xiangpi ren*. For taxi drivers in Changping, burnout often derives from the contrast between their present employment conditions and their previous experiences in state enterprises. The chapter suggests that the phenomenon of *xiangpi ren* is a form of suppressed anger. Frustration over their inability to change current employment patterns and the hefty franchise fees levied against them by taxi companies lie at the root of their dismay. Yet these structural conditions are ignored, and drivers are encouraged in their job training to manage productive lives as taxi drivers while simultaneously acting as the "windows" on the capital, transmitting happiness and "counseling" to passengers who appear depressed or dejected by the turn of events in their lives. I also address how these drivers and community psychosocial workers manage a burgeoning and complex "crisis of masculinity" and how the government mobilizes both gender and psychotherapy to defuse intensified class tension.

Acknowledgments

These acknowledgments are a form of affective expression of my gratitude toward those who have invested in the writing of the manuscript. Here I want to thank the many individuals and institutions who have enabled me to complete the long process of producing this manuscript. First, thanks are due to Hy Van Luong, Bonnie McElhinny, Monic Heller, and Jesook Song at the University of Toronto. Their encouragement and intellectual support sustained me throughout my fieldwork in China and the writing stage, although the manuscript must look foreign to them by now. Lisa Rofel's penetrating comments on my manuscript and her continued inspiration, support, and intellectual guidance have been an important impetus for me to finish this book.

A Wadsworth Fellowship from the Wenner-Gren Foundation generously funded my study at the University of Toronto. I also want to thank the Department of Anthropology at the University of Toronto, the Social Sciences and Humanities of Research Council of Canada, and Simon Fraser University for funding my field research since 2002.

My informants and friends in Changping deserve my deepest gratitude. Although I cannot thank most of them publically, their wisdom and voices imbue the following pages. Some of my informants have become long-term friends, including He Jianhua, Li Haizeng, Xu Xuewen, Yin Xiaoqiang, Liu Jie and Zhang Ailing. I feel very fortunate to know them and very much appreciate their strong support during the last decade. Particularly He Jianhua, who is like my sister, nurtures me with her warmth and delicious food during my field trips to Changping, and helps me tirelessly whenever I need an extra image or extra interview. She has opened so many doors for me in Changping. I cannot imagine how this project could have been completed without her. I am grateful for excellent research assistance from George Zhao, Ryan Brown, Craig MacKie, Hye Jin Kim, Wang Linan, Liu Enqian, Ci Jianfang, Yu Pingping, Li You, Sui Yang, and Joney Yujiao Shang.

Dr. Shi Kan has generously shared his time and expertise with me. His books on job counseling and the psychological approach to reemployment have opened my eyes to see the state-led psychotherapeutic intervention for unemployed workers and have transformed my perspective on solutions to the problems associated with mass layoffs of workers. His pioneering work on employee assistance programs has led me to see the gradual deepening of the psychological modes of governance in China. Dr. Zhang Mo and her lectures on social work have inspired me to compare social work with thought work and social workers with Lei Feng and to pay more attention to the general trend of indigenizing the Western psychotherapeutic tradition in China. I am grateful to my psychotherapist friends in Beijing, Guo Jiyuan, Guo Lifang, Wang Lilin, Xu Qinglin and many others, for their generosity with their time and insights on counseling. Many of them opened their counseling rooms to me so I could do participant observation. Ha Si who invited me to visit her counseling clinic and her social work diploma class. Her insights forced me to historicize psychological governance in China and her critical comments enriched this project tremendously. Professor Xiao Mei and Xiao Hua played a crucial role in connecting me with several psychotherapists in Beijing.

The book has benefited greatly from conversations with and written comments from Andrew Kipnis, Li Zhang, Mun Young Cho, Hans Steinmuller, Lisa Hoffman, Amy Hanser, Alan Smart, Alison Bailey, Timothy Cheek, Deborah Tooker, Warwick Tie, Teresa Kuan, Hsuan-Ying Huang, Zhang Wenyi, Delia Lin, Ellen Lanlan Lu, Borge Bakken,

Trent Bax, Sun Wanning, Jonathan Unger, Elisabeth Engebretsen, Zhao Yuezhi, Zhang Yanhua, Kong Shuyu, Xing Guoxin, Hu Xinying, and Sha Yao. Nancy Chen, Andrew Kipnis, Roy Richard Grinker, and Jesook Song acted as discussants at panels I co-organized in 2009 and 2010. Their comments opened new pathways in my conceptualization of the notion of therapy and its relationship to power and agency in the Chinese context.

I presented materials drawn from this project at various conferences and institutions. I thank the organizers of and participants at these events: the conference China Inside Out: Modernity and the Individual Psyche, organized by Andrew Kipnis and Tamara Jacka at the Australian National University; the conference Irony and the Chinese State, organized by Hans Steinmuller and Susanne Brandtstadter at the London School of Economics; the David Lam Center at Simon Fraser University; and the Department of Social Anthropology at Edinburgh University. I particularly appreciate comments from Andrew Kipnis, Tamara Jacka, Hans Steinmuller, Francesca Bray, Stefan Ecks, Stephan Feutchwang, Charles Stafford, Nikolai Ssorin-Chaikov, and Michael Hezfeld.

Byron Good's comments on a conference paper based on Chapter 6 compelled me to rethink the relationship between so-called *xiangpi ren* (job burnout) and suppressed anger and the importance of the topic of anger in China. At a crucial moment in my writing of this manuscript, Stephan Feuchtwang referred me to the work of Robin Munro and his notion of psychiatriation during the Cultural Revolution, which forced me to historicize the emerging psychologization in the Chinese context and its differences from the Western "psychological complex." The monthly meetings of China Studies Group at the University of British Columbia of 2007–2009 were a place where I tested the very first ideas of this book. I am particularly grateful for comments from Amy Hanser, Alison Bailey, Timothy Cheek, Timothy Brook, Huang Xin, and Christopher Rae.

The intellectual and emotional support of my close friends George Zhao, He Ying, Zhu Aixin, Gao Xiang, Xu Hong, Tong Min, Selina Tang, Jill Joyce, Wang Aiwu, and Anne-Marie Broudhoux were crucial for sustaining my sanity and well-being during the ups and downs of researching and writing this manuscript. I thank Tan Ying and Dan Abramson for long-term intellectual support and companionship.

My colleagues at SFU, Parin Dossa, Dany Lacombe, Jeremy Brown, Janice Matsumura, Bidisha Ray, and Michael Kenny, have offered intellectual and moral support, especially Wendy Chan and Bob Menzies, whose kindness, intellectual guidance, and generosity with their time and expertise, have sustained me over the last seven years. I am grateful for a publication grant from Simon Fraser University, which helped defray the cost of publishing this book.

Janet Dixon Keller read every word of this manuscript twice. Her criticism, insights, and reference guidance transformed and improved the manuscript in many ways. She helped title the book. Marguerite Pigeon is a close China observer and true intellectual. Her insights and superb editorial suggestions were very useful.

At Cornell University Press, I am very grateful to Fran Benson for her competence, insights, vision, and sympathy, which sustained me in the final stage of the writing process. Her enthusiasm, professionalism, and thoughtful guidance made it possible to bring this book to completion. Peter Potter was the first person to identify the potential of this work; I very much appreciate his encouragement and kind support. I am grateful to Cornell University Press for finding capable anonymous reviewers. Their truly insightful suggestions and very helpful reference guidance have greatly improved the manuscript. Thanks also to Karen Laun, Kate Babbitt, Susan Barnett, and Emily Powers for their patience, warm encouragement, and meticulous and brilliant editorial guidance.

My family has always provided a home base for me as I venture into my various research and personal endeavors. It is where I can return at any time to get necessary rest and perspectives and to get refilled and refreshed whenever I feel exhausted during my adventure. My sister's dedication, spiritual strength, and great accomplishment constantly reminds me of how to actualize one's potential and what a strong woman looks like. The sunshine personalities of my two brothers teach me how to appreciate everyday happiness and enjoy life. My four nieces, Yangyang, Shuxin, Ao'ao, and Qiqi, are the joy of my life; they are the leaders of our growing family in terms of fashion, technological innovation, and academic/entrepreneurial endeavors. My parents have dedicated their lives to nurturing my curiosity about the world and helping me manage my study and research agenda since my childhood. I thank them for allowing me to be in the diaspora. Their insights and critique have deepened my understanding of many issues covered in this book and enabled me to gain a greater appreciation for the lessons I learned during the research and writing of this book. It is to my parents that I dedicate this book.

Several chapters originated as articles and book chapters. These include "*Song Wennuan* 'Sending Warmth': Unemployment, New Urban Poverty, and the Affective State in China," *Ethnography* 14, no. 1 (2013): 104–125; "*Peiliao*: Gender, Psychologization and Psychological Labor in China," *Social Analysis* 57, no. 2 (2013): 41–58; and "The Happiness of the Marginalized: Affect, Counseling and Self-Reflexivity in China," in *The Political Economy of Affect and Emotion in East Asia*, edited by Jie Yang (London and New York: Routledge, 2014), 45–62.

UNKNOTTING THE HEART

The "Heart" of China's Economy

The key to reemployment is psychology.

—Shi Kan, *Job Guidance: Theory and Practice*

Without a correct political standpoint, one has no soul.

—Mao Zedong, "On the Correct Handling
of Contradictions among the People"

When those at the top are sick, why must those at the bottom
be given medicine?

—Popular Chinese saying

There is no power relation without the correlative constitution of a
field of knowledge, nor any knowledge that does not presuppose
and constitute at the same time power relations.

—Michel Foucault, *Discipline and Punish*

The therapeutic paradigm effectively reduces the human subject to the
idea of the vulnerable depoliticized inner child and its flipside of
primordial violence, and is instinctly drawn to images and
instances, which seem to affirm this dualistic model.

—Vanessa Pupavac, "Pathologizing Populations and Colonizing Minds"

In Changping, Beijing, in July 2011, Zhang Yi, director and party secretary of *juweihui* (the residents' committee) knocked on an anti-theft iron door to an apartment, looking for Wei Rubao, a laid-off male worker, so he could invite him to one of the biggest counseling sessions the community had organized. This community is the former residential compound for workers at the Beibiao watch factory. I have conducted research there since 2002. Beibiao was once a state-owned enterprise, but when it was privatized in 2004, residents changed their primary affiliation from the factory to the community residents' committee, the lowest level of the administrative hierarchy in urban China. This committee is the administrative and political core of the current urban self-governance system. Because of the gradual collapse of the urban work-unit system, community residents' committees were established as part of the self-governance system to deal with social functions that used to be fulfilled by work units such as Beibiao before and during the early period of the post-Mao reform era. Such functions include maintaining community order and security, caring for the needy, and providing basic social welfare and community services at the grassroots level (Ministry of Civil Affairs of the People's Republic of China 2000).[1] When no one answered, Zhang knocked a second time, but still no answer. Zhang suggested that I slide a poster announcing the counseling session into the side of the door.

We went downstairs, where we found two of Wei's neighbors chatting at the entrance to the building as they parked their bicycles. Zhang greeted them and asked whether Wei had a job now. One of them said, "No. He should be home." It was around 4:30 in the afternoon. Zhang and I went up and knocked at the door again. This time we heard noise inside and Wei opened the door with his hair disarranged, looking as though he had just gotten out of bed. Zhang smiled and said, "Lao Wei, ya, sorry. [We] woke you up? The sun has already set; it's time for supper [jokingly]. I came here to invite you to a job session [handing him the poster]. There will be souvenirs. Do come." Wei shook his head and murmured, "I don't want souvenirs; I need a job." Zhang replied, "You come; there will be jobs. See you there." We had barely stepped out of the apartment when the iron door shut behind us loudly and abruptly. Zhang shook his head and sighed, "I know, I know, he would use that door to show us his temper. Who owes you? These workers are being spoiled too much. I bet capitalist countries manage unemployment differently, right? I have no other choice; otherwise, I wouldn't do this community job facing unreasonable, disgruntled workers daily." Zhang constantly tells people that he has unrecognized talents and deserves a lecturer's job at the Central Party School, given his rich knowledge of Marxism, Leninism, and Mao Zedong's thought.

Zhang used to be president of the workers' union at Beibiao and knows Wei well. According to Zhang, the motive for inviting Wei to the counseling session in person is *ganhua*, "to touch, warm, and melt" him, a practice typically used to reach out in an effort to rehabilitate criminals and bring them back into their communities. In this case the expression refers to a personal appeal intended to soften Wei's anger and open the potential to curb his alleged violence against his wife, a behavior that disrupts the harmony of his home and neighborhood. Since his layoff from Beibiao in 2004, domestic violence at Wei's residence has reportedly increased. At night, loud noise and screaming often awaken those living nearby. However, when neighbors come to check on the safety of Wei's wife, much to their surprise, both husband and wife open the door, smiling and pretending that nothing has happened. To save this former co-worker's face, neighbors complained to the residents' committee and asked for intervention instead of calling the police.

Zhang and I then sent out invitations to other so-called *xiansan renyuan*, or idle and loose people, like Wei, particularly unemployed or underemployed male workers, whom the residents' committee perceived to harbor *yinhuan* (hidden dangers or risks or negative potential). Negative potential refers to the future harm an agent or force is capable of producing (Canetti 1984, 15; Vigh 2011, 74). *Yinhuan* is a keyword in Chinese propaganda about maintaining sociopolitical stability. It can refer to objects, practices, or people, including organized groups the party categorizes as hostile and likely to pose direct threats to the government and groups of people who share a common trait such as the experience of drastic downward social mobility because of ongoing economic restructuring. This latter group includes urban workers, once the ideological representatives and cornerstone of Mao's socialism, who have been displaced and impoverished since the mid-1990s, when much of the economy is privatized (Solinger 2001, 2006, 2009; Wang 2003; C. K. Lee 2007; Yang 2007, 2010; Cho 2012, 2013).

The Chinese working class has a history of radical politics (Blecher 2004; Hurst and O'Brian 2004; C.K. Lee 2007; Hurst 2009). Because of this, a fear of harmful reactions against the government is a constant undercurrent in urban China. This fear encourages government officials to take preemptive measures to avoid social unrest, for example, targeting those who presumably harbor *yinhuan* for psychological "care" and other benevolent governance in the form of reemployment or poverty-relief programs

(Solinger 2006; Yang 2007). Care via psychotherapeutic intervention and reemployment assistance combines two tasks: a state effort to maintain sociopolitical stability by forestalling negative actions by those who harbor *yinhuan* and an effort to expand the market economy by harnessing the *qianli* (hidden strength or positive potential) of the disaffected.

Both *qianli* and *yinhuan* are elusive and subjective concepts that include a spectrum of manifestations by different objects and people. *Qianli* is associated with individual creativity and productivity, qualities that can be enhanced through *peixun* (training) or self-cultivation. Government officials presume that those who were previously employed by state-owned enterprises, are open to reconstruction and reformulation because of their impoverishment. Even though these individuals are thought to embody the negative potential designated as *yinhuan*, both local residents' committees and the national reemployment project believe that they also embody boundless *qianli* for a large variety of reemployment possibilities and for generating entrepreneurial capital. For example, many unemployed workers are given training in the basics of counseling and can be reemployed as *peiliao*, or "companions for chatting," a category that includes housemaid-counselors (typically a woman's position) and taxi-driver counselors, or "counselors on wheels" (predominantly positions for men). These reemployed workers promote the psychotherapy industry in China by filling the market niche created by a shortage of professional counselors.[2] In this way, potential "enemies" of the state, those who may harbor *yinhuan* as a result of economic restructuring, become subjects and advocates of psychotherapy.[3]

The gendered distinctions entailed in these categorizations and new jobs and the related attention to gender in China's emerging economy are the result of gender stereotypes about workers' abilities to cope with changes caused by socioeconomic dislocation. Men are widely viewed as more stoic than women but also more negatively affected by the challenge of processing and internalizing change. This stereotyped understanding of character and potentiality leads state-trained counselors to prioritize laid-off men over women in reemployment counseling and welfare distribution, even though women suffer unemployment and poverty to a greater degree.

According to Zhang Yi, each individual harbors good and bad sides, positive and negative potential that is fluid. Similarly, at the community level, the Beibiao residents' committee imaginatively categorizes workers into two loosely defined groups: those with *qianli*, who can adapt to changes and actualize their positive potential to become entrepreneurs (laid-off women in particular), and those who embody *yinhuan*, disgruntled and confrontational workers who cannot easily cope with change and are unwilling to be counseled (predominantly laid-off men). A tendency to pathologize working-class masculinity as a potential source of social unrest effectively privileges male workers over the female counterparts as failing state enterprises redistribute increasingly meager resources. In general, state-led reemployment programs have sought to accommodate laid-off workers, especially women, to a new economic and social reality, for example, by calling upon these women to literally use their own hardship and trauma as a resource for self-entrepreneurship. Such programs even glorify these women's self-sacrifice. These imputed differences in embodied potential guided the community residents' committee's daily work.

In Changping, after the counseling session, Wei was seen wearing a hat—the souvenir—with four Chinese characters on it: *wo bu bao yuan*, "I do not complain." The purpose of giving out hats with positive messages is to help trainees such as Wei acquire an emotional framework in which they can actualize their positive potential while controlling manifestations of their negative feelings. This dialectical social imagining of *qianli* and *yinhuan* mirrors China's broader political vision of stability and development.

The central thread of this study is the complex role potentiality plays in managing and reorienting the newly impoverished working class and steering them toward the market economy. On the one hand, potentiality is positive, a boundless resource for entrepreneurial capital. It shows the "rise" of the innate and the biological; individuals need to perpetually look inward for moral, therapeutic, and spiritual sustenance, forever reflecting, diagnosing, and adjusting, emphasizing the positive while downplaying the negative. This positive potential is *qianli*, which is more oriented to the hidden capacity of the individual, while *yinhuan* is more often associated with the collective. Indeed, both the government and grassroots institutions are concerned about the threat to the government, organized collective protests by workers would pose. The highlighting of *qianli* also resonates with the government's emphasis on the individual and the psychological over the collective and the state's responsibility for the wrenching effects of economic restructuring.

The official construction of *qianli* and *yinhuan* is not a binary structure; it is an optimizing and reorienting strategy for reconfiguring the forms of the self and the relationship between self and society. The discourse of *qianli* and *yinhuan* serves as a governing technology that shapes people's conduct and reconstructs subjectivity. These are not new concepts; for example *qianli* has been widely used in the booming *peixun* (training) culture and the discourse of *suzhi* (quality) (Yan H. 2003; Anagnost 2004), but they have acquired new social and political significance in the context of mass unemployment since the mid-1990s.

The integration of *qianli* and *yinhuan* in state-led psychotherapeutic interventions for the unemployed is part of a larger trend in China that began in the mid-1990s that I call *psychologization* in which socioeconomic issues are managed in "psychological" modes of thinking. This trend is tied to China's "psycho-boom" (Kleinman 2010)—an awakening interest in books about psychology, psychological terms, and training in counseling associated with an increasing use of psychology in governing social life (see also Shi 1999; Bi 2008; Ng 2009; Kipnis 2012; Zhang 2014; Huang 2014). Psychologization as governance builds upon a social trend that is seen as useful in resolving social disorder created by socioeconomic dislocation. With its focus on marginalized groups, especially unemployed workers, psychologization aims to achieve social balance by reconstructing or reinserting happiness or harmony into workers' lives after economic restructuring has compromised or destroyed them. In the same process the government mobilizes these victims of state enterprise restructuring as resources for creating entrepreneurial capital and for achieving new social, political, and economic forms of equilibrium.

In the name of caring for those who have been displaced and impoverished by state-supported privatization, reemployment program managers and community residents' committees transform these workers to objects of care, thus translating the exercise of power into an activity of therapy and using therapy to regulate them and harness their potential for the new economy. This psychotherapeutic form of governance masks the government's inability to provide for its people with structural remedies. It is rooted in class differences. Government programs for psychological care and economic rehabilitation are primarily implemented among underprivileged groups, especially those unemployed or underemployed workers, while private therapy is available to those of the middle and upper classes who can afford it.

In Changping, inviting those who presumably harbor *yinhuan* to at-tend counseling is an effort aimed at transforming them into people who embody *zhengnengliang* (positive energy) that will enable them to enhance their *xin nengliang* (heart's capacity) and actualize their *qianli*.[4] Maximiz-ing the *qianli* of the unemployed and underemployed (i.e., those who are perceived to harbor *yinhuan*) constitutes the primary task of Beibiao Com-munity Residents' Committee within its larger project of building a safe community.[5] As Zhang Yi said, "People like Wei represent *yinhuan* in this community, but we don't pigeonhole people. We *ganhua* [touch, warm, and melt] them and help them. We see people from a developing perspec-tive. This is *biantong* [change through continuity]." That is, *qianli* and *yin-huan* are not fixed, but fluid and dialectical.

In China both official discourse and people's everyday interactions in-corporate a dialectic of *biantong*. A Chinese version of Marxian dialectics, *biantong* adopts Marx's terminology but its doctrines are derived from *Yijing* (*The Book of Changes*), written 3,000 years ago. This dialectic was de-veloped and popularized by Mao Zedong (Schram 1989; Tian 2005; Worm 2010) as the constant process of becoming. *Bian* signifies becoming in light of differences and varieties. *Tong* indicates becoming in light of continu-ity. *Biantong* in general means change with continuity (Tian 2005; Worm 2010). Mao illustrated the dialectical process through his notion of *yi fen wei er*, or the concept that everything has two sides or polarities. One ex-ample is *yin* (shaded, inactive, negative) and *yang* (bright, active, positive): their interaction—not dichotomous but correlative, appearing contradic-tory yet complementary—creates change. This is what Mao emphasized as *duili tongyi*, the unity of opposites (Mao 1968; Schram 1989; Tian 2005). Reflecting the premise that everything has two aspects, or *yi wu liang ti* (Feng 1956, 854), *biantong* refers to the process of becoming from one event to another, comprehending one thing through other things, through the interaction between the two polar elements implicated in them (Tian 2005, 36). For example, the phrase *weiji* (crisis), includes both *wei*, or dangers, and *ji*, or opportunities. It implies that even in a crisis opportunities are still lurking.[6] The correlative pairing and conceptual interactions of comple-mentary contrasts define *biantong*, which in everyday life often means flex-ibility, fluidity, or gentleness in contrast to being rigid or stoic.

The notion of *biantong* highlights the potential for the seemingly op-posed forces of *yinhuan* and *qianli* to influence or transform one another such that positive potential diminishes the actualization of negative potential. In this dialectical interaction, psychology plays a crucial role in optimizing peoples' aptitudes and their lives in general while making governance and the transition to a market economy easier. State-led psychotherapy also uses *biantong* to highlight the historical continuity of Mao's socialism and the importance of invoking preexisting categories and knowledge in new practices. For example, recent attention to psychology in China, where 90 percent of the available self-help literature is translated from foreign books, appears to contradict the official socialist dismissal of psychology in Mao's era, yet in practice it is the traditional Chinese notion of the heart as the seat of cognition, virtue and bodily sensation (Ots 1994; Hall and Ames 1998), rather than the Western psyche, that is widely invoked.[7] This kind of reimagining of traditional wisdom is instrumental in efforts to reconfigure the community since privatization and in efforts to optimize people and their potential as social resources.

For example, despite his recent training in both counseling and social work, Zhang Yi adopted the dialectics of *biantong*. To illustrate his perspective on change, he cited how Beibiao managers used Spencer Johnson's 1998 book *Who Moved My Cheese?* as part of the self-help offerings that were available to laid-off employees before 2003, when reemployment service centers were closed at state-owned enterprises (Solinger 2001, 675n15; Yang 2007). The Beibiao factory delivered copies of this book to managers and laid-off workers.[8] Johnson's book delineates the different reactions of four characters who are living in a maze after the cheese they have habitually fed on is removed. The parable suggests that instead of complaining about change, people should adjust: "They just moved our cheese. Let's look for the new cheese." The central claim is that one can actualize one's potential by leaving one's comfort zone, overcoming fear, and then enjoying the adventure triggered by change. Despite his positive psychological outlook, Johnson sees danger in imposed change. He points out that people fear change imposed from above and will resist it.

Many workers at Beibiao were dismissive about the book. As one worker said, "It's okay to move the cheese—I don't have cheese anyway, but don't move my pancake [*laobing*], okay?"[9] Although Zhang saw advantages in using this book to manage change, he did not agree that Johnson's analysis of imposed change was applicable in the Chinese context. For Zhang, what happened in China was not imposed or absolute change but change that was implemented through reappropriating and repoliticizing socialist ethics or categories or through the principle of *biantong*. Such change is hegemonic because it emphasizes the continuity of socialism and its collective ethics while downplaying neoliberal policies and initiatives that highlight emerging individual-centered ethics and call on individuals rather than the state for resolving their difficulties and problems. Indeed, in *biantong* dialectics, change involves spatial and temporal continuity that entails difference, complementarity, and contradiction. Transformations in space and time converge in an imagined spiral moving forward (Schram 1989; Tian 2005; Worm 2010): *yin* to *yang, yang* to *yin*, and back again. Change is conceived not from the ontological viewpoint that separates time and space but rather in light of ceaseless transformations of holistic "events" (Tian 2005, 35).

A key element of the tasks of psychosocial workers who are drawn from members of the residents' committee is helping people cope with two interrelated processes of change: macrolevel external changes caused by socioeconomic dislocation and microlevel processes through which a subject internalizes macrolevel change and triggers hidden capacities for externalization and self-actualization. The emphasis on actualizing potential through expert training also downplays the fact that subjective potential in this therapeutic mode is identified with a particular potential to "improve" that psychosocial workers impose on their clients, echoing broader political visions of the Chinese state.

In this book, I explore this dialectical imagination of potential and the culturally and historically specific nature of changes in China's exploitation of human capacities. This form of potential is particularly relevant now in China, especially with the new leadership established in March 2013. President Xi Jinping has announced "China's Dream" (*zhongguo meng*) as a new governing technology that will propel current socialist projects. This vision encourages the release of positive energy and efforts to mobilize people to identify with and fulfill state interests.[10] This dream reconfigures Chinese society in a way that emphasizes both continuity and new knowledge; together these elements are intended to transform subjectivities. I trace the transformation in China from faith in communism and collective socialist labor in Mao's era to the current mobilization of psychology with the goal of releasing the positive potential of individuals. I argue that the government's psychotherapeutic intervention in managing unemployment provides new knowledge and new forms of expertise that emphasize the role of individual agency in harnessing human potential for nation building and that create profit via new forms of commodities in an emerging psycho-political economy. In the hands of state-trained psychosocial workers, psychology provides tools for reimagining social life and social groups through expertly guided work that articulates and actualizes subjective potential. This potential further articulates the government's political visions. This book thus explores the role of psychology in contemporary Chinese governance. It presents new technologies of self, new practices of postsocialist governance, and a new psycho-political economy.

Psychologizing "Socialist" Unemployment and the Heart

I ground this book in ethnography conducted in a working-class community in Changping and in training sessions in Beijing on counseling, social work, and employee assistance programs. This fieldwork was conducted from 2002 to 2013.[11] I cover two periods of the management of unemployment in the Beibiao community: one is the implementation of the national reemployment project at state-owned enterprises through reemployment service centers from 1998 to 2003 (see Solinger 2001; Yang 2007); the other is the management of unemployment by the Beibiao residents' committee from 2004 to 2013, after the factory was privatized. Changping, previously a county seat with a population of 620,000, was promoted to a district of Beijing in September 1999. This administrative change made Changping's development part of Beijing's master plan. Designated as Beijing's "backyard garden" since 1999,[12] Changping has been prioritizing development of a knowledge-based and "green" economy over traditional heavy industries and other sunset industries represented by state-owned enterprises. This development has triggered waves of restructuring and privatization of state enterprises, processes that have created mass layoffs.

Changping is not alone in this change. Since the mid-1990s, the downscaling and privatization of state-owned enterprises in China has resulted in layoffs of over 35 million workers and has transformed millions of them into a "new" class of urban poor (Hu et al. 2002; Wang and Zheng 2008; Cho 2013).[13] Being laid off from a state-owned enterprise, where employment was supposedly guaranteed for life, means more than loss of income.

Its consequences can include emotional trauma, identity crises, and labor unrest. Indeed, the drastic downward mobility of workers from Mao's elite to a marginalized group has precipitated significant labor unrest. In Changping, waves of vandalism, demonstrations, and strikes have forced the local government to prioritize sociopolitical stability. In 1994, in an effort to relieve the threat to stability posed by the masses of laid-off workers across China, the Department of Labor initiated a pilot Reemployment Project in thirty cities; in 1995, the program went nationwide. State-owned enterprises also established reemployment service centers as transitional measures to train the unemployed and arrange jobs for them (Solinger 2001; Yang 2007). These centers were closed in 2003. Nonetheless, assisting with reemployment has remained a priority for local governments and grassroots institutions, particularly residents' committees and street agencies. Such social welfare programs relate, in part, to the ruling party's continued desire to pay homage to socialism and their desire to renew and repoliticize socialist ethics or categories in order to develop the market.

Instead of focusing on creating a greater supply of meaningful employment, the new reemployment framework focuses on the psychology of individuals. This approach reconfigures unemployment as the failure of individuals to adapt to the market or as a consequence of self-maladjustment. Key to this reemployment framework is job training, part of the mushrooming *peixun* culture. *Peixun*, roughly translated as training, teaching, or cultivating, presumably offers practical knowledge or skills that give people an advantage in the job market (see Urciuoli 2008 for a comparative case). In the fields of counseling and psychology, *peixun* is particularly appealing not only to those who intend to become licensed counselors but also to those who have regular jobs and seek such training to enhance their work and social relationships (Zhang 2014). One of the common goals this type of *peixun* claims to achieve is awakening and maximizing human potential through *xintai peixun* (training of the heart attitude). This provides trainees with attitudes, emotions, and thought processes that create favorable psychological conditions for actualizing their positive potential or for self-fulfillment.[14]

Although *xintai*, or heart attitude, is not a neologism, it has recently gained new significance within the political project of constructing a harmonious society. Liu Yuli (2008), a lecturer at China's Central Party School, published a popular psychological self-help teaching video titled *xintai gaibian mingyun* (Heart attitude changes one's destiny). In it, Liu illustrates how and why "both a happy life and a harmonious society begin with one's heart attitude." For Liu, a positive *xintai* encompassing gratitude (to society) is necessary for a happy and productive life. In this framing, *xintai* is not only private and part of the self but is also public and part of the world. It is relational, and its impact or affective bearing is oriented toward the world. The heart is not a being but a becoming in relational perspectives. Further, Liu's deployment of *xintai* as a combination of attitude and psychology and as key to a harmonious society illustrates the dynamic relationship between ideological commitments and epistemological practice in China.[15]

The heart is a fundamental component of being and a key precept in traditional Chinese medicine. As the seat of cognition, virtue and bodily sensation, the heart is the origin of all emotions and the grounding space for all aspects of bodily and social well-being (Ots 1994; Hall and Ames 1998; Tian 2005).[16] Unlike the Western formation of personhood, which is based on a psyche that is separate from soma (the body), Chinese psychologists adopt a more embodied and holistic approach to psychological problems that are referred to, for example, as *xinbing* (heartache) or *xinjie* (heart knots). Indeed, psychology is translated in Chinese as *xinlixue* (the study of the heart's reasoning).[17] This holistic approach is significant not just because of its therapeutic consequences for subjects; it also serves to broaden the power of the government and psychological experts to intrude into people's lives more thoroughly than a psyche-based Western psychology would.

Both *qianli* and *yinhuan* are anchored in the heart. Community psychosocial workers believe that *qianli* is mainly based on happiness, hope, and a positive heart attitude and that *yinhuan* often derives from discontent, anger, and negativity. The focus on the heart and the emphasis on embodied and performative features of psychology resonate with the rise of "soft skills" such as leadership, intuition, vision, and affect in management (Thrift 2005, 11; Rudnyckyj 2010). In this book, I follow Sara Ahmed (2004) and Sianne Ngai (2005), who see affect and emotion as interchangeable and distinctions between the two as a matter of degree. Both emotion and affect include a combination of cognition and bodily sensation. That is, both cannot be entirely cognitive or captured by language; both have a sensual dimension that cannot be entirely narrated verbally but must also be experienced bodily (see Yang 2014 for a review of affect and emotion). In Changping, the attention to affect in psychotherapy and job training is also a way of reenchanting work by restoring or rejuvenating what socialist work units had repressed: emotions, personal responsibility, and the possibility of self-realization.[18]

Apart from the loss of income, unemployment has often affected workers' attitudes and morale. Many took their layoffs personally, even seeing their unemployment as a reason for cutting all ties with the Communist Party. The traumatic impact of layoffs stems from deep-rooted assumptions of employment for life in the work-unit system and from the draconian ways workers experienced layoffs (Solinger 2001, 2006; Yang 2007). Some have characterized the latest wave of layoffs in medical terms as something that produced *shiye zonghezheng* (unemployment complex syndrome) (Wang 2008, 166), which involves both psychological disorders (e.g., depression, alcoholism, suicide) and physical problems (e.g., headaches, stomachaches, hair loss). In the context of the grim job market in China, the constant pressure to look for reemployment exacerbates these symptoms. Many workers I spoke to in Changping have conveyed stories of layoff trauma and its impact on their emotions and bodies with extraordinary acuity. Suicide has become more common. Eight people have committed suicide since layoffs were initiated at Beibiao because of the downsizing of the work force triggered by the Asian financial crisis of 1997. Most were men. Several left suicide notes indicating that layoffs were to blame.[19] Others have returned to the factory to vandalize it or "make a fuss" (*daoluan*); these actions are one reason why these male workers are viewed as *yinhuan*.

This wave of Chinese unemployment parallels and contributes to a general mental health "crisis" (e.g., depression, schizophrenia, stress, suicide) spawned by widespread socioeconomic dislocation (Phillips et al. 2002; Bi 2008) that reportedly affects over one hundred million Chinese (Chen 2010). Like the "unemployment complex syndrome," this mental health crisis has manifested as both a material condition and as a state- and expert-sponsored discourse that legitimizes psychotherapy as a solution to social problems. This discourse persists despite the fact that the therapy offered through job training and reemployment schemes does not address mental health directly but invokes mental illness to pathologize unemployment and unemployed workers and transform their attitudes and thought processes in order to help them adapt to the market economy. The logic of psychologization that emphasizes the self and self-fulfillment presents the breakdown of the work-unit system that was once a source of emotional and communal support for workers as "empowering" for the individual.[20] This discourse informs and compels the development and commodification of psychotherapy, accentuating the complicity between the state and market.

The development of psychotherapy was uneven in China during the twentieth century. Western psychotherapy first arrived in the early 1900s, marked by two significant events: the establishment of the Beijing Psychology Institute in 1917 and the founding of the Chinese Psychological Society in 1921 (Han and Zhang 2007). Over the next three decades, training courses in Freudian psychoanalysis were developed, then Soviet-influenced Pavlovian rapid comprehensive therapy emerged in the mid-1950s. During the Cultural Revolution, however, psychology and psychiatry were deemed to be bourgeois, counterrevolutionary disciplines that were "spiritual opiates," numbing and exploiting the masses. Both the development and the delivery of psychotherapy were halted (Munro 2002). By the 1980s, political changes and economic reform had yielded a more favorable environment, and psychotherapy reemerged as a legitimate scientific discipline.

Psychological services are now available in large cities in China. Yet even with this progress, the ratio of counselors to the population in China remains low, at 2.4 per 1 million people—a stark contrast with the United States, where there are 3,000 counselors for every 1 million people (Han and Zhang 2007). Formal counseling training in China was initiated in 2002 (Higgins et al. 2008, 102), and since then, private counseling has begun by serving mainly the well-to-do middle class. For the rest of the population, community-based mental health interventions (along with psycho-education media and self-help literature) have become important bearers of therapeutic messages and psychological knowledge.

The continuing shortage of formal counselors to address people's stress and anxiety about change and socioeconomic dislocation has allowed (former) party staff to retrain in various modes of therapy. In the Chinese language, the word for "ideology" and "mentality" is the same, *sixiang* (Munro 2002, 7). Since the early days of Chinese communist rule, there has been a presumed dialectical relationship between ideology and mentality, including mental illness; correcting one's political ideology in Mao's era would allow one to recover from mental illness. The putative reason people became mentally ill was that their heads were filled with an excess of selfish ideas and personal concerns (Munro 2002, 9) that could be eradicated through thought work.[21]

With this historical backdrop in mind, one can see why one solution to the shortage of counselors in China has been to retrain party staff as psychosocial workers. Those in the party are presumably best positioned to weed out all manners of problems because of their superior knowledge of Marxism, Leninism, and Mao Zedong's thought. This knowledge is now fused with psychological precepts, and with these tools party workers are deployed to help others. This is particularly true of community-based social workers, who are often retrained party staff the government has paid to take part in training sessions in social work or counseling and use their new knowledge and skills in psychological interventions for workers (Shi 2011).[22] In the process, not only Communist thought work but also Chinese cultural traditions, including Confucianism, have also been revitalized as resources of psychological care and self-help.[23]

In this book, I analyze the counseling methods and work styles of three types of counselors—professional counselors who are occasionally employed by community residents' committees to counsel residents, community-based psychosocial workers, and laid-off workers turned informal counselors. I focus on the latter two groups. Community psychosocial workers are often retrained party staff and members of residents' committees; they take advantage of their skills in thought work to transform themselves directly into psychosocial workers. Because of their deep embeddedness in the community where they work, these psychosocial workers not only adopt a psychological approach but can also embed their work in the social and cultural context to address people's problems and psychological distress holistically. They psychologize social issues and also perceive emotional and psychological disorders as social and moral issues.[24] These psychosocial workers also train laid-off workers as informal counselors.

With preliminary training in counseling and psychology, laid-off workers are reemployed to do domestic work *and* "counsel" those who are lonely and depressed and those who are experiencing similar difficulties and stress following job loss. In the training laid-off workers are given for their new roles as informal counselors, they are encouraged to invoke their own suffering and their experience of overcoming stress and difficulties as they empathize and sympathize with those whom they "counsel." In this sense, through the reformulation of their own suffering, these workers' reemployment as psychological care givers constitutes a way of regulating at least a fraction of the dispossessed, who then act in service of others. Basic psychological knowledge has been integrated in job training and reemployment counseling programs in Beibiao and then into the community job center, because over 75 percent of the trainees are women who are often reemployed as domestic workers, nurses, cleaners, and *yue sao* (maternity matrons) and in other (care-related) jobs where a psychological perspective can be helpful.[25]

Despite the link made between psychologization and the Chinese notion of heart, in practice, new psychological knowledge does not always align with people's existing frameworks of knowledge. Thus, it often fails to provide them with a familiar base of concepts that are helpful in grounding productive reflection and in rethinking premises for action. The psychologization process instead introduces into the lives of millions of Chinese a new politics of unequal therapeutic interchange based on class and gender. I argue that current practices of psychotherapy in China can obstruct the healing of and further marginalize those whom psychosocial workers purport to treat. Therefore, this book also illustrates the possibility of subversive responses and resistance. I show that values, styles, and domains of psychological knowledge that have been developing and gathering strength at the margins of society are beginning to penetrate and reconstruct dominant modes of thought in China.

Psychologization, Potentiality, and the Psychological Imaginary

The discourses of government-sponsored psychotherapy function not only to minimize structural forces that produce mass unemployment but also to constitute a medium that mobilizes the psychological and moral traits of the unemployed in order to nurture their potential and growth for the purpose of extracting value. In the context of China's massive growth through neoliberal enterprises and policies, psychology advances market development, for example, by creating new employment opportunities and constructing entrepreneurial subjects. In general, the psychologization trend in China is not a departure from authoritarian political rule; rather, it facilitates both economic development and political legitimacy, for example, through building a harmonious society for the state. It is a kind of political (mis)use of psychology that entangles subjective perspectives with state power (Rose 1996; Gordo and De Vos 2010; McLaughlin 2010; De Vos 2011; Yang 2013a) through notions of happiness and potential that combine both personal desire and state interests. This form of psychologization encompasses two interrelated dimensions. The first renders nonpsychological issues in "psychological" terms. In China, this does not always mean a systematic application of state policy with regard to psychology; more often, it is a hegemonic psychological discourse that creeps into the process of managing social issues and groups, for example, by imagining them in terms of their potential. It is exercised by both governmental and nongovernmental agencies. The other dimension emphasizes affect and therapeutic governance. This therapeutic governance is not only based on pathologization or problematization but also relies on precepts of positive psychology. For example, by promoting the happiness and positive potential of the marginalized through counseling, the therapeutic strategy appears to be constructive while its goal is also to be preemptive. This echoes Pupavac's (2002) observation that the pill of counselling is often coated with the sugar of other activities. Examples include providing community, women's, or youth centers as a way of establishing points of contact with locals to entice them into counseling programs. This strategy also demonstrates the importance of politics in mediating the experience of trauma (499).

I see psychology not only as a knowledge system but also as a culturally specific way of understanding and ordering actions (Foucault 1998, 249) and a way of imagining reality. Brinkman (2011) suggests that psychology, as an array of practical modes of understanding and acting in everyday life, can be seen as having penetrated the social imaginary of the West to the extent that people have problems seeing that social life can be imagined in nonpsychological terms in contemporary Western societies (2011, 18). Illouz (2008, 15) further points out that modern imaginings are likely to be formulated at sites where expert knowledge systems, media technologies, and emotions intersect. The notions of therapy and psychological self-help contribute to a new way of thinking about the relationship of self to others, imagining new potential, and implementing them in practice. I focus on new ways of imagining social relationships and groups in China triggered by the integration of psychology with governing social life.

Although the new psychotherapy in China is mainly sponsored by the state, it is also associated with a shift from a notion of discipline from above to discipline that should ideally come from within the individual. It is also associated with a shift from the government's calls for the people to sacrifice their lives for the nation-state to calls for people to value life—an example of kindly power and the "deepening of governmentality" (Zhang 2011a). At its core is the possibility of imagination, which includes the capacity to represent what does not exist. However, it is not limited to this function. It also informs images of existing and non-existing objects (Bottici and Challand 2010, 3). Without this merging of the extant and the novel there could be no utopia or ideology in the sense of false consciousness. Because psychology promises that individuals will achieve certain goals if they behave in certain ways, it can be used to construct idealistic or utopian situations that parallel or identify with social goals and, in China, communist ideals.

Bottici and Challand (2011, 4) define politics as "a struggle for people's imaginations." Indeed, as Hippler (2011) observes, those who hold power often see imagination and passion as causes of social disharmony. Hippler (2011) identifies hope and fear as the passions that powerful authorities use most often to pacify societies: hope for a better life in the future and fear of punishment. However, since human nature will not submit to absolute repression, it is more useful for political powers to rely on hope than fear. Imagination provides the link between the social creation of hope and the stability of the state. When states use imagination in this way, power is felt indirectly, through the intensity of an affective experience, such as the power of hope. Bugliani (2011) further suggests that instead of looking for power in terms of its location (who wields it), researchers should look for power in the limits placed on peoples' faculties of imagining and in how these limitations are imposed.

The notion of imagination is closely related to potential. Potential is the possible actualization of a hidden capacity (Munn 1986; Strathern 1999; Bateson 2000). In a social context, this means that a present figure, force, or formation is experienced or imagined as containing hidden states that have not yet materialized. The future is thus experienced as a specific configuration of potentiality (Agamben 1999). As Vigh (2011) argues, the influence of the potential is not restricted to the ideational dimension of lives. People not only reflect on potential; they also act on it. Despite the lack of physical or concrete presence, potential is capable of influencing social and physical bodies and current governing processes. In other words, people act both habitually and innovatively based on their sense of possibilities (Hirsch 1995, 4).

Scholars have begun to view people's potential to act and their potential to withhold action as parameters of politics (Hardt 1999; Massumi 2007; Venn 2007). Mette N. Svendsen (2011) proposes an anthropological approach to the study of potential that "addresses the cultural context as well as the material conditions of that seen as incomplete yet with a power—a potency—to develop into something else" (416). While this approach emphasizes the power of potentiality to transform social networks and relations, it neglects a politics in which constituting, animating, actualizing, and preempting potential falls under the purview of the sovereign power of experts and the government (Yang 2013a, 2014). In China, although the psychotherapeutic intervention emphasizes the self and personal responsibility, the conditions under which individuals can access psychological resources are governed by experts and the state.

Here it is important to understand both facets of potential; the potential to do or become something and the potential not to do or become something. Opposing the claim that potential exists only in an act, Agamben (1998, 45) endorses Aristotle's insistence on the idea that potential has an autonomous existence; human beings are capable of an act even if they are not doing it. For example, a builder retains his ability to build even when he does not build. Some scholars have criticized this notion of potential, which they see as emphasizing the power to suspend the passage of potential into actuality because they see in this the construction of promissory subjects—subjects that are not realized and only potential—and inactivity that appears to reduce individual agency (Power 2010). In the Chinese context, however, notions of both positive and negative potential in reemployment counseling maximize individual agency, because individual potential is mobilized to contribute to the metamorphosis of broader political possibilities.

As Agamben (1998, 47) points out, when sovereign powers politicize potential, some possible worlds never pass into actuality while others become manifest. In China, both the state and psychosocial workers encourage the unemployed to actualize their potential to become entrepreneurs, to adopt new morals, or to enjoy a better life. However, these same groups of people also embody negative potential, and government-sponsored psychother-apy is designed to encourage them *not* to actualize negative potential, such as engaging in alcohol abuse, physical violence, or social unrest. Through its programs of sponsored therapy, the Chinese government relies on the notion of a subject who can act or choose not to act as the basis for healing and moving forward on both the personal and social level. I thus empha-size the dialectic interaction between two loosely configured processes of becoming that workers embody as *qianli* and *yinhuan*. These can be actual-ized or constrained by external relations or triggers—in this case, the new psychology in China and its cognates such as counseling and social work. In addition to subjective potential, the notion of potential in Changping appears as an embedded part of the future, reframing space-time as a series of possible worlds.

The definition, actualization, and preemption of potential in China are historically and culturally specific. For example, Confucius made the statement that *junzi bu qi*, meaning that virtuous men are not machines or vessels but have creativity and potential that can be achieved through self-cultivation (Worm 2010, 223). In Mao's era, individual potential was putatively released through collective socialist labor. This resonates with Marx's (1977) idea that the human potential for rational understanding and freedom is derived from labor or production. For Marx, production is not the mechanical and manipulative use of domination but the free flow of potential life. With the power of imagination a subject can visualize things not yet existing; he or she can plan and begin to create (Fromm 1947, 94–95).[26] Both communism and Mao's thought gave people the re-sources for social imagination; that is, *xinnian* (faith) in communism drove people in Mao's era to imagine the collective and work together to build socialism.

However, when promises of communism failed (particularly work-ers) in China, a new politics of potentiality based on the self (or psycho-logical imaginary) came into being. Now in the context of the boom in psychology in China and the current rampant development of the *peixun* culture, the public and government officials presume that human potential is released through psychological or heart-attitude training and through self-reflection and self-adjustment. These new modes of social imagina-tion divert people from focusing on a present demarcated by intensified social stratification to focusing on something forthcoming that gives hope.

The potentiality Changping psychosocial workers promote in their management of unemployment is oriented toward the future, informed by history, and mediated by psychology as a new mode for imagining society. For example, in recent training of *peiliao*, or housemaid counselors, characteristics associated with ethics in former work units such as *laoshi*, or being honest and down to earth, are psychologized as new moral attributes that enhance the *peiliao*'s potential in the new job market (see Chapter 5). These women serve as pioneers who bridge the old planned economy and the new market economy; they are encouraged to internalize change in order to externalize or release potential into the market economy that is dormant or suppressed by the planned economy.

Chinese counselors widely adopt Carl Rogers's (1951) client-centered therapy, which also emphasizes the agency and potential of the client in the therapeutic process. Rogers's therapeutic process is based on a positive perspective of human nature and potential.[27] The core therapeutic conditions are congruence, acceptance, and empathy. This therapeutic process is designed to lead to new knowledge about the self and to fuller actualization of the client's potential. While Rogers adopts a nondirective approach that proposes minimum intervention by the therapist in order to allow clients to find their own solutions to their problems, Chinese people are often socialized to heed direction from authority figures and to expect external guidance and approval (Qian et al. 2002). In addition to the uniqueness of such microlevel therapeutic processes, I also explore the cultural imaginings of members of the Chinese working class, the counselors drawn from their ranks, and the state that governs the therapeutic interactions that bring them together.

Therapeutic Governance and Kindly Power

Psychosocial intervention in unemployment is a new mode of therapeutic governance in China. Indeed, a therapeutic ethos—the ideas and practices of therapeutic expertise (Nolan 1998) and other sociocultural practices of healing—pervades policies on reemployment with its diagnosis of traumatized identities of the unemployed. The idea that unemployment renders workers traumatized and dysfunctional problematizes their capacity for self-governance. The perception that traumatized workers cannot govern themselves legitimizes indefinite supervision and therapeutic intervention.

To look more closely at the efficacy of governing by psychology, I build on theories of state use of therapeutic modes of social control and the competition between new expertise and historical knowledge within types of governance. The notion of the therapeutic state was first proposed by Thomas Szasz in the 1960s. Szasz (1963) examines society's orientation toward systems of therapy for dealing with deviant behavior, arguing that the state has an interest in directing the behavior of its citizens. While Szasz's work focused on medicine and mental health, China's recent psychotherapeutic interventions have targeted social and economic issues such as urban poverty, labor unrest, and unemployment.[28] For example, the psychological approach to reemployment implies that layoffs are the result of workers' norms and attitudes such as a habitual dependence on the state that is now deemed deviant. Unemployed workers who have internalized these characteristics are putatively unable to adjust to the demands of the market economy. It is then the state's (and psychotherapists') responsibility to redirect unemployed individuals toward the market (Beijing Reemployment Project Leadership Office 2002).

Since Szasz, other scholars have expanded on the notion of the state's usurpation of therapy. James Nolan (1998) argues that the logic of the therapeutic state is one of governmentality that focuses on citizens' sense of self and emphasizes emotions as a source of truth.[29] In line with this argument, unlike in Mao's era, when personal emotion and mental illness were considered bourgeois or ideologically undesirable (Munro 2002), in China's current reform era, public culture emphasizes individual feelings and autonomy (Yan Y. 2003). Popular media are saturated with terms such as *yali* (stress), *xinqing* (mood), *youyu* (depressed), and *xinli* (psychological) (Feng 1996). Yet psychologization in China not only disseminates the language of psychology into everyday life; it also renders social and economic life as the life of the heart or mind-body that is oriented by individual responsibility and productivity particularly in the management of mass unemployment.

Andrew Polsky (1991) extends the notion of therapy to the study of the contemporary welfare state, which incorporates aspects of therapy to deal with marginalized populations. This move is predicated on pathologizing lower classes and labeling them as incapable of adjusting to the demands of normal, everyday life and therefore in need of therapeutic assistance. Polsky regards such normalizing interventions as violations of the autonomy of the individual citizen. Miller and Rose (1994, 331) go beyond seeing the therapeutic state as a force that represses marginal populations. They argue that therapeutic governmentality is subtle, akin to a new style of power that endows individuals with new competencies, aptitudes, and qualities that can be mobilized to generate new knowledge and surplus value. Along this line, but diverging from the Western literature that emphasizes the power of psychology professionals and the state over individual life, I examine the dialectic interaction between therapeutic governance and the experience, emotions, and agency of those who are subjected to such governance in China. The form of governance in China—the promotion of governmental reason through fostering lives and channeling people's desire by both governmental and nongovernmental agencies—constructs a unique role for psychology in maximizing individual agency and potential in the context of the current economic transformation.

Also, in the Western literature of the therapeutic state, forms of local knowledge that are embedded in society and rooted in history are not typically recognized, even as expert knowledge comes directly into conflict with them or tries to invoke them. However, the dialogic emergence of new forms of knowing and being that result from new expertise understood in conjunction with a historical canon is crucial to fully grasping the power and pragmatics of contemporary psychotherapy in China. In the strands of China's history of psychology that have come together in current psychologization, China's diverse and local forms of psychological knowledge are integrated into the new governance that is implemented in diverse locales. I explore in what follows how informal and local psychological knowledge in Changping (including the heart, the dialectics of *biantong*) confronts the hegemony of norms of human consciousness, potentiality, and identity that are established in Western counseling and social work (see Chapter 4). In China, experts and their knowledge cannot operate successfully without the localized perspectives. In interactions between experts and clients and within the clients, newly introduced psychology and historically rooted values and perspectives are brought into dialectical engagement.

To redress the lack of attention to a dynamic role for local, historical, and culturally specific knowledge, in this book, I combine an analysis of the therapeutic state with context-specific ethnographic data, investigating first how the Chinese therapeutic governing, as exemplified in psychologization, differs from manifestations in the West. I argue that while Western therapeutic states seek to *normalize* the marginalized, in China, differently situated unemployed workers are treated disparately by the government and psychosocial workers: some are normalized, others are pathologized, others are nurtured, and still others are glorified because of their putative embodiment of different potentialities. Indeed, newly marginalized workers are perceived to harbor multiple potentialities, both positive and negative. Diverging greatly from previous attempts in China to achieve social control via therapeutic or medicalized strategies, such as in the misuse of psychiatry under Mao, this differential treatment of marginalized subjects is unique to the moment that began in the mid-1990s with China's economic restructuring. Echoing Solinger (2001), such differential treatment of laid-off workers prevents them from getting united and organized, posing threats to the government. This form of therapeutic governance is a unity of contradictory practices: the government "cares" for those who have been displaced and impoverished by its own policy of privatization. It is contextualized in the notions of *minsheng* (the people's livelihood) and *renzheng* (benevolent government). I call this mode of governance kindly power (Yang 2010).

When China's new state leadership took power in 2002, it ushered in new governing styles to strengthen its affinity with the masses. Invoking Mencius's doctrine of benevolence (*ren*), the government claimed that the people and their livelihoods would be the basis of its rule (*yi min wen ben; minsheng wei ben*). Mencius (371–289 BCE), who is widely endorsed as the authentic interpreter of Confucius, emphasized benevolent rule and moralizing politics in empire building. He believed that if a ruler loves benevolence, he should have no enemy in the world (Mencius 2004).[30] However, unlike Mencius's emphasis on *ren* as a virtue that is anchored in the intrinsic goodness of human nature, kindly power is not genuine; it is often translated into symbolic kind gestures or tokenistic welfare programs, particularly those that target underprivileged groups. It is a show of symbolic kindness after unkind state policies destroy the livelihood and wellbeing of the people. Such a show of "kindness" can be operated through psychotherapeutic techniques and other programs (i.e., those that focus on poverty relief).

Factory managers claim that their kind acts of providing psychological self-help and psychological care highlight the key feature of socialist unemployment. However, workers asked rhetorically who delivered the damage in the first place. Through such psychological "care," the state and its arms were trying to induce a false sense of well-being by shifting responsibility to suffering individuals while continuing its destructive impulse. In other words, this type of psychological counseling and other welfare programs—psychological care, symbolic reemployment and emphasis on positive potential—are only a trick of kindness that is intended to disguise the unkindness of the state—control, regulation, and exploitation. The discourse of *qianli* and *yinhuan* that laid-off workers embody also exemplifies the notion of kindly power. Emphasizing the positive potential and productivity of these workers while downplaying the potential risks and threats these workers harbor is both a form of kindness and a mode of regulation.

Indeed, this kindly power is part of the shift in governance. The current government views the people's wealth, health, and value as the legitimating framework for governing (Kleinman 2011, xiv). Zhang (2011a, 2) renders such shifting governance as "the deepening of governmentality," that is, elevating life from the survival of living beings to a level of adequacy and human flourishing, from ensuring biological being to ensuring well-being.

Drawing on Foucault's notions of biopower or governmentality (fostering and extending life or the power over life) and sovereignty (killing or the power of death), Zhang (2011a, 11) argues that the two modes of power have often been inseparable in China since 1949. China's lack of or underdevelopment of a liberalism that would check sovereignty and promote freedom renders the rule of benevolence a pretension of the sovereign government or as mere tentative measures the sovereign government has taken to survive rebellions and turbulences. *Minsheng* (the people's livelihood) directly appeals to the concerns and desires of the people in everyday living. The increasing official attention to *minsheng* without fully developing *minquan* (the rights of the people) can constitute an obstacle to the deepening of governmentality in China. That is, China's move toward an adequate life is just the beginning of fully developed governmentality, and if this is not ensured, the deepening of governmentality can be stalled (Zhang 2011a, 22).

While the popular use of Western theories of psychotherapy may impact therapeutic practices in the rest of the world, including China, disease and illness categories are not universal. They are constituted by culture, experienced and articulated differently in culturally and historically specific contexts (Kleinman and Good 1985; Kleinman 1986, 1991, 2000; Good et al. 2008). It is also important to situate the current psychotherapeutic interventions in

China in relation to other forms of therapeutic politics, for example, through sociocultural practices such as affective or literary measures to heal various forms of "victimhood" and "illness." An example is the so-called scar literature that emerged in the wake of the Cultural Revolution. Through "speaking bitterness,"[31] people who suffered from the violence and disturbance of that period reconciled themselves with their memory and suffering (Rofel 1999). In addition, the popular practices in China of *ganqing* or *renqing* (sharing human feelings or compassion) also have a therapeutic function. According to Andrew Kipnis (1997, 29), the *ganqing* created through visits to the sick by fellow villagers in rural North China was considered to contribute to curing the sick, making an otherwise depressing situation somewhat positive. In my observations of the poverty relief program of *song wennuan*, which is not that different from home visits to the sick, the practice of both *renqing* and counseling performed the (superficial) therapeutic function of "healing" the poor. In this therapeutic framework, party staff problematized the urban poor and their difficulties and distress as issues to be addressed, modified, or cured. This new form of "sickness visits" skews the popular memory of the traditional (literal) kind of illness visits in terms of practices of *renqing*, turning it toward the political (see Chapter 3).

To capture how and why Chinese therapeutic governance approaches various classes of marginalized subjects differently, I treat the therapeutic strategies used in managing unemployment as loosely connected sets of expertise, representations, and governing technologies through the perspective of therapy (Miller and Rose 2008). This therapeutic strategy centers on the application, transaction, and performance of psychological knowledge and other sociocultural healing practices by unemployed workers or former party staff (cf. M. Harris 2007). Targeted by such therapeutic interventions, these psychosocial workers have become the embodied vehicle for transmitting and promoting psychotherapy for the state. This mode of therapeutic governance emphasizes self-regulation and indirect control. For example, to explain the difference between today's psychosocial work and Mao's traditional "thought work," a Changping party secretary turned social worker, Shao Wen, invoked one of Aesop's fables, about a contest of strength between the sun and the wind:

> When they saw a man walking on the street, the wind said that he could get the man's coat off. The wind blew, but the man held on tightly to his coat.

The more the wind blew, the tighter he held. When it was the sun's turn, he used his energy to create warm sunshine, and soon the man took off his coat.

The moral of the tale is that indirect interventions are more effective than direct ones. Shao Wen implied that self-regulation and self-governance are more efficient than direct control imposed from above, a control that was long exerted in the thought work of Mao's era.

In thought work, party staff reframed individual consciousness and imposed on it party ideologies or visions (Rofel 1999; Brady 2008). From 1949 to the mid-1990s, this played a key role in scrutinizing and regulating urban workers at work units. In addition to reading and interpreting ideologies disseminated in newspapers and during political study sessions, thought work was a one-on-one ideological ritual for workers. Many in Changping indicated that they despised thought work as a coercive mode of control that twisted individual psychology. Yet they also professed nostalgia about certain aspects of thought work, for example, the "intimate" relationship between the party and workers and the party's power to solve their problems. This nostalgia has arisen in the context of their judgment of current psychosocial work to which they have been subjected. Some fondly remember the time when they could go to the party committee at their former work units whenever they faced difficulties (even those related to family, marriage, or other private issues), an openness reflected in the slogan *you shi zhao dang wei* (Come to the party whenever you have problems). Such close contact has become rare with party staff turned psychosocial workers today, who claim to be scientific and professional and widely adopt Rogers's (1951) non-directive approach in client-centered therapy. Psychosocial workers in Changping say they are no longer like the ranks of party staff who served people wholeheartedly and sacrificially in Mao's era. They now use professional knowledge to help people help themselves (see Chapter 2). The shift in focus from ideological orientation to epistemological practice in China is manifested in the rapid development of the *peixun* culture.[32]

However, although the state is now rehabilitating psychotherapy, the psychologization trend does not replace traditional communist thought work. Rather, the new rejuvenates the old by infusing ideological reorientation with the scientism and professionalism now associated with psychotherapy. Traditional ideological orientation through thought work thus takes a new form in psychological counseling in which the psychological, the political, and the therapeutic are hybridized. This hybridity—a hodge-podge of thought work and psychotherapy—defines current psychosocial work in Changping. This work, which on the surface is depoliticized, carries the authority of the party state and its new ideology. In other words, psychotherapy is adapted to the logic of politics in order to alleviate the effects of unfolding economic restructuring.

Gender, Potential, and Informal Counseling

The book explores how gender naturalizes inequality between men and women and masks class inequalities that marginalize working-class women in the labor market and pathologize working-class men's frustration and despair about their downward mobility in status.

Despite a general tendency of public discourse in China to pathologize social issues or individual dependence on the state, in practice, psychosocial work prioritizes positive potential over deficits and pathology. Dangers and risks are viewed as subversions or distortions of human potential rather than as evidence of an inherent and inevitable human condition. The gendered notion of potential at Beibiao portrayed women as embodying boundless positive potential that could be maximally harnessed by entrepreneurial capital. Although women have largely borne the brunt of economic restructuring in China (Yang 1999; Wang 2003; Dai 2004),[33] they are glorified and glamorized as entrepreneurs or "re-employment stars" and are mobilized as informal "counselors" who play a vanguard role in performing and promoting psychotherapy by helping others manage mental health.[34] They bridge the former "stagnant" planned economy and current "dynamic" market economy (Lee 2006). It is women who must negotiate the gap between the public and the private. They embody and negotiate the contradictions between market and non-market structures by engaging in part-time work, housework, and casual or illegitimate labor and by stretching fewer resources to meet more needs (see Kingfisher 2002).

Recent literature shows a current trend across cultures toward gender as the primary construct of social difference. Joan Scott emphasizes the constructed or constitutive nature of class, arguing that class is deeply gendered and that gender provides a way of articulating and legitimating class (inequalities) (Scott 1988, 60; Ortner 1991; Dai 2004; Yang 2007, 2010; Hanser 2008). In China, as Arif Dirlik (2007) observes, because of the failures of class politics, class as an analytical and political concept has often been replaced by gender (and race). Instead of replacing class with gender, I examine both class and gender and the way gender expresses class tension, for example, by the state's feminization of work or gendering of unemployment. Retraining laid-off women to hold the middle-class positions of informal "counselors" symbolically narrows class gaps, but in actuality the subject formation of the dislocated class converges with historical biases that intensify the exploitation of and discrimination against these women in a grim job market.

Scholars have focused on the fact that disadvantaged women have become central to China's bid to become a key player in the global economy (Rosen 1994; Yang 1999; Dai 2004; Lee 2006). Researchers have examined how the perceived boundless potential of laid-off female workers has been called upon to expand the service industry (Sun 2000; Yang 2007), advance transnational capitalism (Lee 2006), and launch the beauty economy in China (Xu and Feiner 2007; Yang 2011a). However, the role of unemployed women in providing psychological therapy has not been addressed. This neglect minimizes the importance of women's "hearts" and their psychological labor as (new) sites where the party can legitimate its continued existence and both regulate and extract value from these marginalized individuals through therapeutic intervention.

The media often glorifies laid-off women workers as ideal, psychologically healthy, and entrepreneurial subjects who with preliminary training are able to perform "psychotherapy." These women are perceived through popular stereotypes to be caring subjects with a lived experience of painful unemployment to draw from, subjects who therefore embody the therapeutic ethos. As informal counselors these women become conduits of knowledge and a bridge between the population and the expertise of psychotherapy. The government advocates happiness and positive psychology as a means through which these women can animate and release their potential to live a life of which they have only dreamed. Indeed, there is an aura about these women of becoming, of moving into a future with limitless potentialities. They construct a potential self based on and regulated by imagination. While these subaltern women are in general constructed in media as role models for entrepreneurship, my ethnographic data demonstrate that the actual experience of female workers is complex: they use new opportunities to empower themselves psychologically and financially but in the process suffer intensified exploitation and status decline.

Unlike laid-off women who presumably embody positive potential, laid-off men are perceived to embody negative potential; they are disgruntled and violent, predisposed to serious crimes, vandalism, and labor unrest that destabilize the community. Their working-class masculinity is pathologized as a potential source of social unrest.[35] While most men are not so violent, the discontent and anger of workers presumably can smolder for a while and then erupt suddenly into major strikes, protests, and other disruptions (see Chapter 6). At Beibiao, members of the residents' committee scrutinized unemployed or underemployed men, seeking to identify symptoms of mental disorders and negative potential. Psychosocial workers anticipate the potential effects of social events and future unfolding, gaining what they perceive as clarity over invisible dimensions and people's potential. Because this scrutiny constitutes part of security measures, it is designed to yield the knowledge that will enable authorities to predict people's attitudes and actions.

Part I

THERAPEUTIC GOVERNANCE

1

HAPPINESS AND SELF-REFLEXIVITY
AS THERAPY

Psychology is a science; it gives people knowledge, perspective,
and happiness.

—SHAO WEN, A PARTY SECRETARY TURNED SOCIAL WORKER IN CHANGPING

Emotional maladjustment breeds dissatisfaction and thwarts the
search for happiness and success.

—PETER MILLER, "PSYCHOTHERAPY OF WORK AND UNEMPLOYMENT"

When I first arrived in the Beijing district of Changping in 2002 to conduct field research, the Beibiao watch factory, my primary field site, was
in the process of being privatized through a joint venture with a Swiss
company. This process involved downsizing the work force and laying off
state workers.[1] When I discussed my research topic of the effect of privatization on workers with the factory's director of quality control, she took
me directly to the Reemployment Service Center, the most eventful place
at the factory in her view. Passing a noisy production building and then a
huge statue of Chairman Mao, a reminder of the factory's state ownership
and its glorious socialist history, we followed a newly paved cobblestone
path to the foyer of an office building. On the second floor was the Reemployment Service Center, close to the factory director's office; its central
location signaled its significance for the factory at that moment. There,

1.1. The factory ground with a Mao statue. Photo by He Jianhua.

I saw the impact of privatization; laid-off workers went there not only for information about retraining and new jobs, but also to complain, cry, fight, and bargain with the director for reemployment and other benefits.

At the reemployment service center, the director, Zheng Ming, was preparing two men for an interview for a new type of job created specifically for laid-off workers like them. A *jiaotong xieguan* (traffic warden) assists traffic police at busy intersections by waving a red flag and using both body and words to prevent traffic infractions. Seeing that the two workers were having trouble viewing themselves in this role, Zheng showed a clip from a China Central Television (CCTV) program called *Contemporary Workers*, in which the famous Chinese psychologist Dr. Shi Kan instructed a woman traffic warden about the dignity of laid-off workers who fill that position. "It is a *job*," said Dr. Shi. "You just do it; waving the flag, shouting at those who don't stop at red lights. Shout loudly and shout out the dignity of our workers. No matter in the past or now, we are all proud workers." Afterward, Zheng Ming told the two workers, "You two all know Dr. Shi from when he was here for his research. I recorded this clip also because I knew Shi Kan.[2] He is a serious scholar. *It* is *gongzuo* (a job), a new type of *job*. Nowadays, any work that gives you income, even five cents, is a job."

"Counseling" at the Beibiao community encourages laid-off workers to undertake roughly two types of jobs. One consists of new positions created specifically for laid-off workers to compensate for the fact that there are not enough formal positions to absorb all of the workers who have been laid off. These include *peiliao* (housemaid counselors) and taxi counselors, who fill a niche caused by the shortage of counselors in China, and traffic wardens, who complement the inadequacy of traffic police. These positions do not usually generate legitimate identities for workers. The other type of employment consists of self-employment in "entrepreneurial" jobs such as small food businesses, fruit stands, and laundry stalls. This type of job allows workers to become "entrepreneurs" and their own boss. The government offered small loans and other beneficial policies to help workers start such businesses.

In addition to providing workers with a new notion of *job*, the reemployment service center (1998–2003) targets workers to create change in their emotions and heart attitudes. Promoting the "happiness" of the unemployed or underemployed has been central in state-led reemployment programs since the mid-1990s. One main reason is perhaps what a taxi driver in Changping indicated to me in 2010:

> Recent propaganda promotes *qiongren de kuaile* [the happiness of the poor]. You can see how TV series, movies focus on the unemployed, migrants, and urban poor and their ordinary but happy life. Why? Because these people are not happy. Not happy, they will *naoshi* [make a fuss]. The government is afraid of *luan* [chaos].

The recent focus of the Chinese media on everyday life and disadvantaged groups reflects new guidelines for propaganda work issued under Hu Jintao's leadership since 2003. These guidelines emphasize building "a harmonious society" and "three closenesses": the propaganda should be close to reality, close to life, and close to the masses (Kong 2014). A slogan in recent propaganda is that "People's interests are the highest!" (*renmin liyi zuigao*); policies and practices should be oriented to making people happy and satisfied (Zhao 2008). Through emotional management or appropriate positioning of one's heart, counselors and community residents' committee members anticipate that workers will be able to tap into a new notion of human potential, motivated by a promise of happiness. Indeed, positive psychology putatively gives people new social horizons for imagination and deters them from reacting too negatively to their current economic struggles.

China has recently witnessed the emergence of numerous counseling programs, self-help literature, self-reflexive projects, and confessional TV talk shows that promote happiness and positive psychology. There are dozens of programs and series at the nationally viewed China Central Television and on local cable television stations. Counselors on these programs use Chinese terms such as *xingfu, kuaile, huanle*, and *kaixin*, all of which roughly translate as "happiness."[3] Since 2006, happiness has been adopted as an index in China to evaluate economic growth and governing efficiency, particularly in relation to the new political project of constructing a harmonious society, one that claims to be people centered and socially and economically sustainable. Happiness has become a governing technology for maintaining social harmony.

These instances of happiness promotion are evidence that the so-called happiness turn has taken place in China.[4] To better understand this turn, it is useful to examine what Chinese people are turning toward when they turn to happiness (Ahmed 2008) and which notions of happiness are most appealing to workers and to the ruling party. Lisa Blackman (2008) suggests that the happiness turn is a way of using various traditions of psychology to think through affect, life, power over life, or personal control over life's directions. Promotions of happiness in China through counseling and media campaigns are directed to all of China's citizens, but they are especially associated with newly marginalized workers who have been laid off from state-owned enterprises since the mid-1990s.[5] These newly displaced and impoverished workers, once the prestigious proletariats and the founding class of the Communist Party, have experienced drastic downward mobility in status. They are *not* happy. The widespread happiness campaigns are evidence of their lack of happiness and harmony (Sun Wanning, professor of Chinese media and cultural studies, University of Technology, Sydney, August 2010, personal communication).

In the context of recent socioeconomic dislocations, mass unemployment, and the mental health complications associated with unemployment, precepts loosely identified with positive psychology have been invoked to instill happiness and optimism in people (especially the unemployed and the urban poor) to help them endure poverty and despair. Instead of happiness conceived as part of a broad cultural turn (Ahmed 2008), happiness promotions targeting the unemployed in Changping represent a governing technology that delivers "therapy" to the unemployed. These happiness promotions not only attempt to enhance human productivity and actualize people's positive potential but also aim to preempt potential threats posed by the unemployed or underemployed. Promoting the happiness of the underprivileged is part of the psychologization trend that is emerging in China to manage social, economic, and political issues through "psychological" modes of thinking or psychotherapeutic approaches.

In this chapter I focus on one set of practices in China's psychologization trend: state-led reemployment counseling programs for underemployed workers and those who have been laid off from state-owned enterprises since the mid-1990s.[6] These programs, which feature psychologically infused ideologies and practices, encourage the unemployed to pursue happiness and positive thinking even in the most difficult and unfair situations caused by job loss as a result of economic restructuring. One way of achieving happiness, according to these programs, is for individuals to turn inward and manage their relationship with their self through "proper" self-reflexivity. By tapping into an individual's desire for happiness and fulfillment, these programs attempt to provide psychological solutions to social issues (i.e., unemployment and mental illness). Counselors encouraged trainees to learn how to *ziwo tiaozheng* (adjust themselves in terms of attitude, lifestyles, and expectations) and *ziji xiangkai* (open their minds and sort out things on their own). Indeed, what better way for the government to legitimate crippling economic restructuring and intensified social stratification than to deploy programs that suggest that these processes are actually an opening for people that could lead to their happiness?

My analysis in this chapter centers on how happiness and self-reflection are promoted as therapeutic strategies for the unemployed to reposition or adapt themselves to the market economy, which, in turn, maintains stability and advances market development. I first lay out the sociopolitical background for contemporary uses of happiness and psychology, highlighting state-promoted happiness that is designed to optimize individual desires for contentment and fulfillment and ties these desires to political and economic ends prioritized by the government. By examining the role of happiness in actualizing and preempting potentiality, I then discuss the promotion of happiness through self-reflexivity as a therapeutic strategy for helping workers transcend, enhance, and realize their selves. The final section focuses on workers' contestations of happiness campaigns and the psychologization trend. This chapter provides a foundation for subsequent chapters in which I explore specific counseling programs in more detail. Before turning to the discussion of the kind of happiness "therapy" in Changping, I first contextualize the development of workers' unhappiness in the history and political economy of the Beibiao factory.

The History and Political Economy of the Watch Factory

This factory's development parallels the history of Chinese manufacturing industry. Three historical periods can be identified in the factory's economic performance: from 1958 to the late 1960s, from the 1970s to 1991, and from 1992 till now. During the first period, the factory's development stagnated because of its strong political orientation and the outbreak of the Cultural Revolution. But in general, this period constituted a major source of workers' proud socialist memory. During the second period there were upheavals in factory production due to the impact of the market. Since 1991, the factory has been greatly impacted by shifting state policies and the world economy, first by the relaxed policy on imports of foreign watches from Japan and Switzerland and then by the 1997 Asian financial crisis. These external changes forced the factory to reduce the price of its products and downsize its work force in order to survive in an increasingly competitive market. During this period, the factory had to be privatized, in response to both market imperatives and a political mandate.

Together with sewing machines and bicycles, watches were one of *san da jian* (the three luxuries) in China in the 1980s. The price of a watch was then 120 yuan, while the salary of the working class averaged 40.10 yuan per month (institutional wage). Although workers were not paid well, they enjoyed high honor and prestige because the factory, which was referred to as "Beijing's Money Box," contributed to the capital's finance significantly. During its early years, leaders from the central government and Beijing's municipal government paid great attention to this factory and inspected it several times. For example, according to the factory's "history book," on one of his visits, Mayor Peng Zhen mobilized workers to improve the quality of the watches with these words: "All the watches produced by [the Beibiao factory] should be based on the Swiss watch standards; otherwise, they shouldn't be dispatched from the factory." The past glories of such events constitute an essential part of workers' identities as proud socialist laborers and are a source of their cherished memory, forming a stark contrast to their marginalization since 1997.

Watch manufacturing in China began in 1956. Beibiao was established in 1958, the first year of the second five-year plan for China's national economy. The first seventeen watches—a small run because of the low number of employees at Beibiao at the time—imitated a Swiss watch called "Rome"; the level of craftsmanship demonstrated the determination of the factory management to excel in quality. But later, factory officials rebranded these watches as "Beijing" in Chinese characters in the style of Mao's calligraphy in order to show their political loyalty. The design and production of watches were centrally planned during this period. During the early 1970s, the Ministry of Light Industry organized technicians and experts from all over the country to design a national standard watch movement called *Z1 tongji biao* (standard watch) at Beibiao. This standard watch was then put into mass production; people from all over China wore the same type of watch at that time.

Factory employees were proud of their contributions to China's watch industry and many mentioned to me that the money they had made for Beibiao could have established thirteen watch factories of the size of this one. They were nostalgic about the security and peace they enjoyed in the old days when life was simpler, easier, and more carefree than the tumultuous reform era. The supposedly all-encompassing welfare state and the "iron rice bowl" (lifetime employment) provided workers with everything they needed daily. They could buy cheap and good-quality food from the factory's dining hall. Their children could go to the factory's kindergarten and then the factory's technical schools without paying any fees. They knew all the doctors in the factory clinic and could get free medicine, free acupuncture, or even fake sickness notes. Many women nostalgically narrated how much they enjoyed the "freedom" and slow work tempo. There were no quotas in those days, so that they could easily integrate housework and child care with their formal work.

The transition to a market economy involved both opportunities and challenges for Chinese enterprises. The watch industry was among the first group to be streamlined and marketed both domestically and abroad. The influx of cheap and high-quality electronic watches imported from Japan or smuggled from Hong Kong or Taiwan were a heavy blow for domestic watch production. All Chinese watch factories had to make great efforts to adapt to the market economy by reducing prices in order to cut down on production backlogs. By 1984, factories had been forced to reduce the price of domestically manufactured mechanical watches three times. After China entered the market economy, its sales system had to be changed. Under the planned economy, sales were managed by the state. No matter how many watches were produced, the wholesale station would guarantee that they would be sold. But in a market economy, there were no guaranteed sales any more. The Beibiao factory had to set up its own sales department in downtown Beijing and manage sales on its own.

In 1998, the factory subcontracted its workshops as a way to implement market mechanism and stimulate production. While this did not improve the factory's profit margin, management turned to its real estate and rented out most of the buildings to a neighbor, a university, to increase its revenue. Many workers were dismayed when university students and faculty overtook the grounds of the factory complex. However, the real estate business has increased the factory's revenue by 4,500,000 yuan each year while income from the watch parts production remains very low (and the factory sometimes operates at a loss). The goal of operating the factory was to maintain *shehui xiaoyi* (social effects)—social stabilization—and avoid laying off too many people in one locale rather than making a profit.

In 1997, Beibiao laid off large numbers of workers for "an extended holiday," but this downsizing did not improve the factory's efficiency or profit margin. In 2000, following a trip to Switzerland, the factory director began a two-year negotiation for a joint venture with a Swiss company. In Changping, the ideal model for privatizing state-owned enterprises is through joint ventures with foreign companies. This joint-venture pattern not only transforms property rights, it also increases foreign direct investment. However, negotiations to form an international joint venture with the Hong Kong–based Swiss watch company were unsuccessful (Yang 2013b). In July 2003, Beibiao and 103 other state enterprises in Beijing advertised in three major Chinese newspapers (the *Workers' Daily*, the *Beijing Daily*, and the

Beijing Youth Daily) in order to attract investment from home and abroad. This piece of news finally smashed the dreams of workers that the factory would revive (Yang 2013b). Workers constantly asked me for information about the negotiation of the proposed joint venture because I sometimes acted as a note-taker at factory board meetings. One worker said, "Doc, we workers are so easily contented. With a little sunlight, we will shine brilliantly [*geidian'er yangguang, women jiu cailan*]. But we didn't see any trace of light in this project. It's doomed. Management is wasting money and energy, dragging us into a bottomless hole." Finally in 2004, a Chinese real estate tycoon purchased the factory. One condition of this purchase was that the factory be allowed to continue manufacturing watches. The work force of 2,500 workers was then downsized to about 500 that year.

Beibiao's overemphasis on privatization through an international joint venture took resources away from its investment in social welfare. It invested more than 1,000,000 yuan to improve the appearance of the factory (installing a luxurious automatic gate, renovating and painting all the factory buildings, purchasing new work uniforms, etc.). But these image construction projects were done at the expense of workers' welfare. Management even refused to pay women the five-yuan one-child subsidy and cancelled the state-prescribed annual medical examination for women workers. These were examples of why workers feel betrayed and angry. Management was fully aware of the price workers paid during the state enterprise restructuring. It is in this context that positive psychology through various government programs was offered to underemployed and laid-off workers in order to reconstruct their happiness.

Happiness and Positive Psychology

In the wake of mass layoffs, state enterprise leaders and newly trained counselors have advocated optimism and positive psychology as key in the search for new jobs. In the context of the recent boom in psychology, these authorities point to these emotions as moral norms to which the unemployed should aspire. Leaders of state enterprises, for example, suggest that there is no efficient way to deal with unemployment other than helping laid-off workers acquire the value structure that leads to positive self-esteem and self-sufficiency for the market economy (Blecher 2002).

Indeed, psychology orients clients toward goals that resonate with what Charles Taylor (2004) defines as a social imaginary: "the ways people imagine their social existence, how they fit together with others, how things go on between them and their fellows, the expectations that are normally met, and the deeper normative notions and images that underlie these expectations" (23). Today in Changping, psychologists and counselors construe unemployment less as a result of economic restructuring than as an opportunity for a client to orient him or herself toward "entrepreneurship" and self-realization (Shi 1999). Counseling has thus been used to regulate "irrational" psychological reactions to unemployment and to redirect the attitudes and energy of workers to the market economy—a process of psychologizing unemployment.

While psychologization practices are often associated with Western liberal societies (Rose 1996; Gordo and De Vos 2010), Eghigian (2004, 183) points out that psychological sciences also flourished in former communist societies such as East Germany and the former Soviet Union in the 1940s. In his study of the role of forensic psychology in preventing youth crimes in East Germany, Eghigian argues that while the agendas and methods of policy makers, researchers, and psychologists cross-pollinated, prompting a psycho-pedagogical turn in the East German approach to delinquency, this development was not a departure from authoritarian political rule but was "an extension of the socialist utopian project" (184). In China, at the most general level, psychologization legitimates and facilitates current socialist projects, including building a harmonious society. The party uses psychology or psychotherapy to construct idealistic or utopian situations that parallel or can be associated with socialist ideals.

This vision is implicitly manifested in Premier Wen Jiabao's 2011 government report that claims to prioritize the promotion of people's happiness and well-being over economic development. Various forms of happiness promotions have thus been carried out throughout the country. In this context *happiness* seems to become a floating signifier without fixed referents. The power of this term does not derive from its capacity to describe an emotional, political, or social reality that already exists but from its semantic openness and flexibility, which enables it to become a site where investments may accrue. Thus, calling on this emotion in therapeutic contexts is sufficient, those in authority surmise, to rally, mobilize, and produce the political contingency it appears to represent (see Butler 1993,

199, for a fuller account of this dynamic). However, the promotion of happiness among the underprivileged by the Chinese government is designed mainly to address two issues: people's self-reported low happiness and the so-called mental health crisis. Government and business leaders view these current characteristics of the people and the society as threatening social stability and the party's political legitimacy. Post-Mao eudaemonic politics channeled public interest toward tangible gains and led people to link their assessment of the government to their personal material advancement. The government explicitly offered material goods in exchange for public support (Chen 1997, 423). However, in recent years, the government's capacity to deliver goods and services has diminished in the face of people's increased expectations, resulting in widespread dissatisfaction. Workers have expressed resentment toward the government for casting off millions from the state sector. The unemployed and the urban poor who have been subject to this disregard often report low levels of happiness (Dolan et al. 2008; Smyth and Qian 2008).

Also, despite a massive improvement in living standards in China since the 1990s, people's self-reported happiness and life satisfaction have declined. The growing commodification of a number of areas of life, including housing and education, has resulted in greater financial dissatisfaction, which affects people's overall feeling of well-being. When happiness is monetized, money means happiness (Brockmann et al. 2008). The combination of competitive consumption and rapid expansion of the market has intensified economic inequality. This has led some to conclude that people's sense of happiness will continue to deteriorate as society continues on its market course (Ng and Ho 2006). In addition to offering socioeconomic solutions that have been unfortunately inefficient, the government has turned to psychological or affective intervention, a strategy that promotes happiness and positive psychology and downplays economic inequalities (Shi 1999).

The "mental health crisis" also contributes to the promotion of happiness and the trend toward psychologization in China. This refers to the increasing numbers of people who are experiencing depression, anxiety, schizophrenia, and suicide; these illnesses and disorders currently impact over one billion people in China (Chen 2010).[7] At the Beibiao community, the suicide rate has risen since late 1990s, when layoffs began (Yang 2010). Yet China's public support for mental health care has been inadequate:

only 2 percent of the national health budget is allocated for treatment of mental ailments, which account for about one-fifth of China's public health burden (People's Daily 2001). Private counseling is available but targets mainly the well-to-do middle class. Formal counseling training was initiated in this context in 2002 (Higgins et al. 2008, 102), and state-sponsored counseling has been implemented in reemployment programs to assist the unemployed.

The famous psychologist Shi Kan (1999) argues that psychology is key to reemployment at this historical moment in China. Since the mid-1990s, counseling has been integrated in reemployment and poverty-relief programs for laid-off workers. However, instead of offering sensitive counseling for those who have experienced the trauma of unemployment in the context of a transition away from guaranteed lifetime employment, the therapeutic programs focus on reshaping workers' behaviors, attitudes, and emotions in the direction of self-reliance and self-governance.[8] The counseling programs often adopt methods that are loosely identified with rational emotive behavior therapy, which aims to help people overcome "unrealistic" and "irrational" feelings or actions and put them in perspective (Ellis 1973). Rational emotive behavior therapy is designed to apply to specific problems and is easily adapted to the fragmented format of reemployment counseling programs. According to many counselors in Beijing, this therapeutic method, which focuses on identifying and addressing "incorrect" or "irrational" elements in clients' lives, resembles traditional thought work. The therapeutic ideals of these counseling programs are happiness, harmony, and growth.

Scholars have characterized the loss of employment as a source of extreme psychological deprivation (Miller 1986, 155; Roberman 2013). These scholars, while not ignoring economic consequences, construe job loss primarily in terms of its effects on the mental health of an individual. Stress, depression, and the disruption of family life follow. These psychologized definitions of the aftermath of unemployment are very apparent in Beibiao. The fact that two mental hospitals are located nearby in a region of Changping called Huilongguan has facilitated the development of discourses that conceptualize unemployment as psychologically detrimental. Hospital staff and enterprise leaders invoke the language of mental illness to stigmatize and regulate unemployed workers who have "made trouble." Factory managers have also labeled laid-off workers who refuse to sever their relationship with the state enterprise or who return to vandalize the factory or protest their treatment as "mentally ill."

Indeed, in recent years, with the gradual breakdown of the socialist work-unit system as a "positive" basis for supporting workers and a venue of ideological control, community-based psychosocial workers are the ones who have managed residents and helped sustain stability in urban communities. They disseminate positive psychology through their counseling and psychosocial work, and this platform is extended to education, business, and government sectors in China (see Sundararajan 2005 for a Confucian critique of positive psychology).[9] For example, the books and videos of the famous Chinese writer and counselor Bi Shumin have played a significant role in the media's campaign to educate the public about psychology. Bi's 2007 bestseller, *nu xinli shi* (The female psychologist), triggered the feverish reading of psychology books in China. Two short plays on psychological counseling broadcast at the 2000 and 2005 Chinese New Year's Eve Galas on CCTV, China's most important annual entertainment programs, also played a pivotal role in promoting psychology. The 2000 skit delineates a laid-off woman worker who has been successfully retrained to be a housemaid counselor. In the 2005 play, a party secretary who failed to get re-elected turned himself into a psychological counselor and set up his own "talk therapy clinic." Magazines run special columns on psychology and counseling, and books have been published on school counseling, practical psychological self-help, and mental health. The increasing attention to personal biography in interviews and talk shows on TV highlights the importance of self-reflection.

The "rise" of psychology also resonates with the interests of the government. In a report by the Chinese Congress of its Twelfth Five-Year Plan period (2011–2015), which was released in 2011, Premier Wen Jiabao set a lower goal for GDP growth while focusing more on improving people's lives and well-being. This political vision initiated a torrent of happiness campaigns, happiness surveys, and well-being promotion measures in the country. In fact, 2011 became China's "Year of Well-Being." This emphasis on well-being contributes to the national project of building a harmonious society, signaling the deepening of governmentality—channeling people's desire and valuing life (Zhang 2011a, 2). China observers have suggested that happiness has become the new mantra that fuels China's economy (Richburg 2010). However, instead of lumping these instances of happiness promotion into an economic mantra (Hochschild 1983; Hardt 1999; Richburg 2010) or designating them as part of a broad cultural "happiness turn" (Ahmed 2008), in this book, I view the notion of happiness as a form of psychologization with Chinese characteristics; it is part of the therapeutic governance and management of socioeconomic issues in "psychological" terms.

Happiness, Potentiality, and Kindly Power

In her challenge to rationalist readings of power and governance in the political and social sciences, Judith Butler (1997) suggests that political rationalities have a psychic dimension. In Warwick Tie's (2004, 169) framework for understanding the psychic life of governmentality, governments design programs that use affect or psychic phenomena to assist in their hold on subjects. These programs resonate, often at an unconscious level, with popular, pleasurable fantasies or imaginations caused by the kind of happiness and hope that state-funded counseling and reemployment programs promote. Similarly, Slavoj Zizek (1994, 56–57) examines governmental manipulation of subjects' unconscious desires to supplement official power, which, he claims, provides subjective enjoyment as unacknowledged support of meaning and authority. For example, in their interactions with state programs, subjects in the making can be interpellated, that is, called forth, as appropriate recipients for a given program when they are seduced by discourses, emotions, and strategies that resonate with their particular economies of pleasure, as in the case of aspirations for happiness. By maximizing the potential impact of positive feelings for individuals, such counseling aims to produce *jouissance* (meaningful enjoyment); once happiness is associated with particular social norms or ideals, these norms or ideals can take root in the minds of the masses. Similarly, in purveying happiness, Chinese counseling programs for the unemployed connect with people's desire for well-being and place this desire in the service of state goals, for example, the goal of a harmonious and productive society. The pleasurable fantasies offered by the Chinese reemployment counselors enable subjects to be interpellated at an emotional level, rendering power more affective and hegemonic (Tie 2004, 163).

However, the strategy of promoting happiness is rooted in contradiction. The same government responsible for the new therapy programs that aim to reconstruct happiness or harmony is also held responsible by the people for dismantling the social balance achieved through socialist job security and public welfare that once sustained people's happiness in work units. Simply put, such state-sponsored psychotherapy aims to reconstruct happiness in a context in which laid-off workers are predisposed to negative feelings and potentially disruptive actions.

Therefore, the happiness promoted by those reemployment projects, in addition to releasing positive potential, preempts negative potentialities. For the unemployed, the potential to be actualized encompasses "positive" elements such as entrepreneurship, the adoption of new morals, and the enjoyment of life. However, these same groups also embody the potential *not* to; the potential threats, or *yinhuan*, posed by the unemployed include alcohol abuse, physical violence, or social unrest, things they are capable of but have not yet actualized. The emphasis on preempting *yinhuan* resonates with the party's call for *ju'an si wei*, or "thinking of danger in times of safety" (i.e., being vigilant in peacetime) and *fang huan yu wei ran*, or "pre-empting hidden dangers or risks before they materialize." Encouraging the unemployed to focus on happiness is an attempt to preempt these future threats. Indeed, preemption of this kind is a form of potential politics; it operates on the basis of a future threat (Massumi 2007; Vigh 2011).

In China, classic Marxist analysis holds that human potential derives from labor and production. Indeed, in Mao's socialist era, human potential was often released through a belief in communism and collective socialist labor and was exploited ostensibly for the collective good. However, current psycho-politics aim to maximize human potential by addressing the psychological capacity to imagine oneself in better circumstances through self-reflection and self-adjustment—a positive heart-attitude (Liu 2008).

Self-Reflexivity and the Regime of the Self

Self-reflexivity in China is closely related to the Confucian notion of self-cultivation. Confucius stated, "What the superior man seeks is in himself and what the petty man seeks is in others." People in China in general believe that they can improve themselves and their social position through studying hard or through self-cultivation (Worm 2010, 223). One type of self-reflection in Mao's era was *sixiang douzheng* (thought struggle) to get rid of selfish ideas that were not in line with public or collective interests. For example, blood donation in Mao's era was a political mission, and every work unit was given a certain quota to meet. Whenever the factory could not meet the quota, the party committee had to do thought work with people to secure more volunteers. The former party secretary at Beibiao stated:

> The best candidates were those who wanted to join the party. Then I would go to those party activists [*rudang jiji fenzi*]. I simply told them, "Donate blood, and I will prioritize your application." And sometimes, I even directly promised them party membership if they [would] donate. A woman worker didn't want to donate and told me that she was planning to get pregnant. I simply let her reflect on which was more important, your selfish desire and personal concerns or the party's interest. That was a quite easy decision to make in the context of "politics commands" [*zhengzhi guashuai*]; after some self-reflection, she definitely had to agree. The party was then still attractive and had power in everything in the factory. Workers were longing to join the party. Now it's the opposite; no one wants to join the party.

Even mentally ill people were subjected to reeducation by medical staff and ordered to dig out the ideological roots of their illness (Munro 2002, 10). Probably like the self-absorbed individual happiness promoted by American self-help ideology, happiness promotion in China encourages people to focus on the self and realize one's true self. Indeed, one of the political effects of such happiness campaigns is the inculcation of new values such as self-care, self-realization, and self-enterprise.[10] However, diverging from such self-absorbed happiness, the goals of state-sponsored happiness campaigns that target the unemployed are to tie individual desires for happiness and self-realization to broader social, economic, and political objectives—for example, advancing market development and maintaining stability. These nationalist goals not only make the self more other-oriented and intersubjective, but also promote the spiritual and idealistic aspects of happiness to be derived from reemployment counseling programs.

Within the current boom in psychological thinking in China, self-reflection means turning inward by internalizing the insights psychology offers. Roger Smith (1997) sees psychologization as popularizing and encouraging the internalization of psychological knowledge in advanced Western countries. He writes that psychologization involves the "internalization of belief in psychological knowledge so that it acquire[s] a taken-for-granted quality, alter[s] everyone's subjective world and recreate[s] experience and expectations about what it is to be a person" (Smith 1997, 575). My use of the term psychologization is similar to this with the added dimension that such internalizing processes are a critical part of current governance in China.

Counseling constructs self-cultivating and self-reflective subjects. Self-reflexivity is often considered a mode of self-making and subject formation and is predicated on the fact that individuals have been initiated into the process of self-concern and self-regulation. As Anthony Giddens (1991) states, "Reflexivity is a defining characteristic of all human action. All human beings routinely 'keep in touch' with the grounds of what they do as an integral element of doing it" (36). But not all people are self-reflexive all the time or reflect "correctly"—that is, self-centric. In fact, this is a skill that requires nurturing in Changping.

The factory's former trade union leader, Zhang Yi, once commented on the trauma of layoffs: "If there is ever to be healing, there must be reflecting. People are trying to sweep things under the carpet, but they have to face what has happened because it involves tremendous change and causes great trauma." Adopting a positive attitude and routines of self-reflection (*ziwo tiaozheng*, or self-adjustment, and *ziji xiangkai*, or opening one's mind to sort things out on one's own) is assumed to be therapeutic and to guarantee personal success over adverse circumstances. Self-reflexivity is key to establishing a "correct" self-image. According to the director of the reemployment service center at Beibiao,[11] the self-image within one's heart is the core of one's self. To discover that self-image, one needs a mirror, and self-reflection creates that mirror. Through it, the individual sees his or her self, then transcends, enhances, and realizes his or her "correct" or "true" self.

I want to focus on three modes of self-reflexivity that Beibiao management promoted as a way of nurturing personal happiness and growth. These modes of reflexivity did not render individuals passive or docile. Rather, they claimed to endow them with new competencies and qualities. But in exercising such officially promoted self-scrutiny, the subject unwittingly reproduced the same systems of limitation and exclusion through which they came into being as subjects in the current moment in China. The three modes of reflection are also therapeutic in the sense that they were designed to make people feel better by increasing their self-confidence and bringing them immediate relief so they could get through life more easily. All posit a self that is responsive; each responds to different types of stimuli. In general, self-reflexivity attempts to orient people away from the sociopolitical structure and toward their inner selves for happiness and salvation.

The first mode of self-reflexivity is a form of self-transcendence. At Beibiao in January 2003, the trade union leader used this mode of reflexivity to pacify underemployed workers who demanded a higher work quota and an increase in salary:

> When I started to work at the factory, we only made 41.10 *yuan* [per month]. We had this salary for many years. We were content and happy then [because people were equally poor, communizing poverty]. Now we make one hundred times more than this, and we're not happy. But we should be satisfied and grateful. Don't compare yourself with other people, compare yourself with yourself, with your own past—what you ate, where you lived twenty years ago. Look at what we eat and where we live now! Then you feel grateful and at peace with life.

This is a kind of transcendental happiness, the result of considering the totality of life experience. This transcendental attitude seems to be in direct conflict with economic principles of maximization but is explained as a natural development as one becomes more spiritual over time. To enhance happiness, one needs to resolve conflicts, both internally within one's mind and externally in terms of relating harmoniously to other individuals (Ho 2006)—both self-centric and other-oriented. This self-transcendence can also be realized by comparing oneself with those who are less fortunate and less able. Bi Shumin, a famous writer and counselor who advocates enjoying the happiness of everyday life through her television lecture entitled *tixing xingfu* (celebrating happiness),[12] uses an example from her sixteen years as a soldier in Tibet to explain that her happiness and satisfaction are derived from her reflections on her life at that time, when she saw many of her comrades sacrifice their lives.[13] Indeed, according to Mikhail Bakhtin (1986), one gains an identity only across a boundary; it takes a minimum of two consciousnesses to guarantee an authentic image of any given self.

When we do as Bi does and compare ourselves to those who are less fortunate than us, a feeling of gratitude can result. In fact, management at Beibiao have invoked the notion of gratitude (toward life or society) to promote happiness and optimism among downtrodden workers and lead them to act in a virtuous way. But as Arlie R. Hochschild (2003, 104–118) suggests, gratitude involves not only feelings of appreciation, warmth, and a desire to return a favor but also indebtedness. In this case, nurturing attitudes of gratitude suggests an indebtedness to the life and society offered (or governed) by the ruling party.

The second mode of self-reflection is a process of self-affirmation: affirming one's existence and one's power to affect the environment through strategically selecting a sounding board. In this mode, the self is seen as a reflected object who exists primarily in others. Nature is one such sounding board. It provides psychological relief, for example, through the practice of eco-psychology. Seemingly depoliticized and neutral, the practice of eco-psychology temporarily detaches people from socioeconomic structures. At Beibiao in 2003, the trade union leader claimed that many workers felt distressed and had lost an awareness of their true selves in the privatization process. To help workers relieve their anxiety about layoffs and rediscover their identities, he organized mountain-climbing contests that included climbing and shouting as forms of both physical and psychological exercise. One component of the competitions was "shouting at mountains" (*hanshan*). This involved an inward-focused version of outdoor activities. The union leader encouraged workers to shout as loud as possible, shouting out whatever was in their hearts:

> Simply shout at the top of your lungs and shout out all your anxiety and concerns, cursing and calling names. When you hear your echo resounding, you realize the very existence of yourself, your voice, and your strength. You come back, refreshed and re-energized.

According to Zhang Yi, mountain shouting has significant implications for workers' identities. The echo aggrandizes or enhances the self: the self becomes the source of power and strength. Some workers did feel relaxed on top of the mountain and temporarily forgot their difficulties. But others labeled such activities as *qiong huanle*, roughly "happiness despite poverty" or "fake happiness" that ignores the reality of poverty and difficulties. This is an acoustic, proprioceptive self that is derived from bodily sensations and perception (Vitz 1994, xxii). It is the reduced or subdued self that is aware of its basic existence. Feeling one's aggrandized existence in one's echo is a way of counteracting the stress caused by economic restructuring. Moreover, the affective and energetic exchange between nature and human beings has long had a therapeutic connection, assisting in the production of happy and healthy subjects. According to Zhang, exercise is good for the health of the heart and the body and is more enjoyable than taking medicine.

However, these mountain-climbing contests involved prizes such as soap, towels, mugs, soft drinks, and cookies. The majority of the participants attended the event for the prizes. One worker told me that after working at the factory during the day and riding a pedicab at night, he was not in the mood and did not have the energy to climb mountains. This was a luxury for the elite (factory management) who do not need to labor hard to make a living. There was nothing new about mountain climbing or mountain shouting, but promoting such practices in the rhetoric of the therapeutics of the body and soul and in terms of eco-psychology was unprecedented: it signified the emergence of a therapeutic ethos of governance in China.[14]

The third mode of self-reflexivity is performed through an official narrative structure, which implies that conforming to dominant ideologies can lead to healing, self-realization, and even entrepreneurship. A salient example is the media discourse of reemployment. Since the mid-1990s, the Chinese media have been saturated with images and stories of "re-employment stars." These are predominantly female workers who have been laid off and then reemployed in the service sector. To be designated a reemployment star, an official government designation, is considered an honor. The women are then "invited" to reflect upon and narrate their reemployment experiences in official media outlets. The narrative line of these self-reflections is usually a three-stage flashback: first, unemployment and its negative impact on the narrator's life and psychology—anxiety, depression, and frustration; second, empowerment through job training and the counseling offered by state enterprises, social programs, or women's organizations; and third, the marked improvement in quality of life and psychology after reemployment (Yang 2007). This discourse constitutes more than a happiness campaign. It becomes a site for subject formation: the reemployment stars' happiness and success demonstrate fulfillment from having overcome the crippling effects of unemployment; they are happy, psychologically "healthy." More than normalization, this discourse glorifies these reemployed women. As both ideological and affective subjects, they speak for the state and defend economic restructuring.

For example, in December 2002, on the CCTV program *Contemporary Workers*, a woman who was beaming with confidence narrated her reemployment story. She had been laid off from a fabric factory and then reemployed at a laundry stall. She then became an "entrepreneur" and managed several laundries in Beijing. She described her work trajectory and emotional transformation:

> I was very depressed after [my] layoff. I didn't want to see people, and sometimes felt ashamed. I remember one day bumping into a neighbor at a market; I pretended not to see her. But she saw me, and I told her I was on vacation. . . . Then I started to attend reemployment training sessions and job counseling and finally got hired at a laundry. . . . They noticed how hard I worked and trusted me. The next year, they allowed me to contract the laundry stall. Then I had more confidence and contracted to do all the laundry for a nearby hospital. . . . Now I wish I had come out earlier and embraced the change earlier rather than feeling so bitter and depressed for so long. Nothing can really beat you if you don't beat yourself.

Watching this woman on TV, it was easy to see the affective charge of her discourse and its capacity to move people at emotional, ideological, and sensory levels. The notion of happiness is constructed through conforming to dominant ideologies and state mobilization—through reemployment and a renewed sense of self-sufficiency (Wang 2003). Here happiness is achieved through efforts that demand patience, diligence, and perseverance. In the context of intensified inequality in China, happiness or optimism involves thinking that one can achieve recognition for remaking the self—recognition of one's ability to endure the crippling effects of economic restructuring, adapt to social change and maximize one's potential. This discourse of "reemployment stars" employs an old communist practice of using the voices of female subalterns to legitimate state policies. By seeming to extend political agency to women, the party constructs an illusion of its continued commitments to "women's liberation" and renews the communist narrative on the women's movement, through which the state produces an ideal entrepreneurial subject position for people to recognize and fit in in order to serve its rapid market development.

This new laundry entrepreneur realized her potential through reemployment. She claimed to have experienced a process of self-actualization and an affirmation of her true self. The self that was previously repressed under the planned economy was actualized in the market economy. The woman described herself as becoming better integrated, more productive, and more confident. She celebrated reemployment as a therapeutic process of renegotiating her emotional state and reconstructing her selfhood—a process for changing and growing the self in order to create ideal affective and ideological subjects authorized by both the state and psychological professionals to promote the psychotherapy industry and market development. That is, the "unexpected" achievement of newly reemployed women who overcome depression or devastation because of job loss and actualize their potential within a psychology-enabled emotional framework for success serves as both testimony of the efficacy of psychosocial work and as a pedagogy for job training that prepares laid-off women to undertake service jobs, for example, to become housemaids or informal counselors.

Reemployment stars are ideal subjects and role models for state propaganda. However, the emphasis on the positive feelings and happiness of the reemployment stars at official media outlets renders their own subjectivities invisible. This emphasis also illustrates how subalterns are targeted and mobilized to play the role of the vanguard in promoting happiness and psychotherapy.

In this discourse of reemployment, happiness and optimism are emotions that are more valuable and more suitable to the "liberating" market economy than depression or anxiety. This emotionality is dependent on relations of power that endow some feelings with more value than others; the hierarchy of emotions is thus translated into, and reinforced by, the current social hierarchy (Ahmed 2008, 10–11). Within the culture of psychology in China, the market economy and happiness and satisfaction with entrepreneurial productivity are preferred over the planned economy and the security and complacency it provided.

Counseling and Happiness Promotions as *Huyou*

I end this chapter with attention to contestation and criticism on the part of the marginalized group, many of whom perceive the recent rise of counseling as a form of *huyou* (hoodwinking), a hegemony that capitalizes on the pain and suffering of the disadvantaged through psychotherapy intended to create social stabilization and expand the market economy. As mentioned, the factory had a special connection with the famous psychologist Dr. Shi Kan. Because of this, management paid special attention to Shi's work and his TV counseling of unemployed workers. For example, in interviews with me, Zheng Ming, the director of the reemployment service center at Beibiao (who is now a licensed counselor) emphasized the importance of optimism for instilling in workers an alternative interpretation of layoffs:

> If you think of unemployment as a crisis; crisis [in Chinese, *wei ji*] has two meanings; *wei* means "in danger;" *ji* means "opportunity." Unemployment offers opportunities to start something new. Those who beam with optimism and smile will get hired first. That's why you need to be optimistic. No employer likes a person who is bitter or grumpy.

This positive illustration seems to come directly from one of Dr. Shi's counseling sessions. Shi (1999) also taught unemployed workers how to present themselves for job interviews—how to dress, smile, shake hands, and so forth, to create a plastic and transient self to impress employers. Many workers felt challenged to perform the plasticity of the self in the market economy because even though *biaoxian*, or performance, was required for promotion at the factory in the reform era (Walder 1986), it differs greatly from the performance required in the new job market, which is more competitive and is key to one's survival. Optimism has been advocated as a strategy for reemployment. One worker who attended a training session considered this teaching useless. "Most jobs we can apply for are dirty labor work. No one wants to shake hands with you or see how big your smile is. It's hard to smile, considering the way we have been treated [laid off]. It's like *xie mo sha lu* [killing the mule immediately after it finishes work]." Despite this kind of doubt and real pain, those who lead the new psychotherapeutic programs see workers' misery as an opportunity for them to start anew.

Indeed, members of management have found many opportunities to transform themselves into therapeutic practitioners. Several former managers from Beibiao have become community counselors or social workers since 2006. However, their training was largely based on Western counseling and social work, and its application was not always culturally appropriate.[15] For example, one newly trained counselor indicated that the Chinese way of counseling should pay more attention to *qing*, human feelings, compassion or commiseration, because *qing* can not only open up the client's heart, it can also lead to understanding of what a client has experienced in life that caused his or her mental problems (see also Lee H. 2007). This local notion of *qing* has different connotations than those of the notion of compassion in Carl Rogers's client-centered therapy. This *qing* is above rationality and law. The order of attending to things in Changping is first *renqing* (human feelings or personal relations), then *li* (rationality or reasoning), and finally *fa* (law), an implicit mandate that plays a central role in the local social order. This notion of *renqing* suggests that counseling in Changping draws on basic human feelings, a practice that nevertheless dovetails with the agenda of the local power hierarchy. The lack or misuse of *qing* in managing unemployment was believed by workers to trigger emotions that lead to the violence and unrest that both Beibiao management and the Chinese government want to control or the suicides that have followed state enterprise restructuring.

Popular critique of the new psychotherapeutics, however, is not always welcome. The discourse of mental illness is often evoked to label workers for whom psychological strategies fail. However, workers also appropriate this strategy for their own purposes, as when they act "mentally ill" to show resistance. For example, one male worker vandalized several pieces of equipment in the workshop where he had been laid off. He was interrogated by the Beibiao security office but released without being penalized. In his interview with me, this worker said, "How could they deal with a crazy person like me? The factory director had already diagnosed me as crazy. Yes, since I'm crazy, I can do whatever; I fear nothing. What can they do with me?! Send me to Huilongguan? They'll have to use a rope to bind me. But who would dare to bind me, one of the damned?" Quite a few workers at Beibiao acted crazy in order to vent their anger and gain their own benefits (Yang 2010).

Workers resist government-proffered happiness programs and counseling in other ways. During my fieldwork, they often criticized counseling as a kind of *huyou*; the person who is counseled is seduced into pleasantly accepting the ideologies or concepts counselors offer. *Huyou* is not a neologism but has recently acquired new significance after comedian Zhao Benshan's successful TV skits in 2001 and 2003. For example, in the comedy of *maiguai* (selling crutches) at CCTV's Chinese New Year Gala of 2001, Zhao Benshan successfully convinced Fan Wei that he would suffer serious illness if he did not purchase a pair of crutches. Actually, he is totally healthy but a little stupid. Fan is lured into buying the crutches. He is even grateful to Zhao for helping him identify his potential health problem and preventing it from getting worse. These comedies were such a success that *huyou* became a household term in China. *Huyou* creates a scheme that makes the target feel appreciated and cared for, after which he or she easily and pleasantly falls into a trap—a folk understanding of Zizek's unconscious supplement.

For many workers in Changping, counseling works in the same way by tapping into individual desires for happiness and a good life and tying them to sociopolitical objectives that force people to rely on themselves to solve "their own" problems. Both counseling and *huyou* identify personal problems, diagnose them, and then prescribe solutions. Like *huyou*, which is premised on the strategy of creating a problem for someone in order to achieve a certain goal (often to cheat them), counseling uses the language of psychology to identify or impose a psychological problem and encourage people to rely on themselves to cure their ills and adapt to social change. By tapping into individuals' concerns for their well-being (health, security, and other interests), the practice of *huyou* is often affective and impactful; the person who is *huyou*ed (*bei huyou*) goes so far as to express gratitude to the person who practices *huyou*, as in Zhao's play.

Some people have bought into psychology, but I have not seen any convincing cases that prove the efficacy of state-sponsored psychologization. One woman, the former director in charge of family planning and women's affairs at Beibiao, had been really involved in psychotherapy, partly because her own daughter suffers from depression. She even suggested that the residents' committee subscribe to the magazine *xinli yuekan* [Psychologies], a German magazine adapted to the Chinese context that is a popular addition to the growing literature of psychological self-help in Beijing. But her case did not promote psychology in a positive way because despite all her efforts (except hospitalization), her daughter's depression had not lifted.

Conclusion

The recent turn to happiness in China is a turn toward psychology and affective life. By promoting happiness and self-reflexivity, state-led reemployment programs manage socioeconomic issues (i.e., unemployment) in psychological terms. Therapy promises that belief in the adoption of a "positive attitude" and the routines of self-reflection will guarantee personal happiness and success even in adverse circumstances. Like communism or socialism, happiness reflects a hope and a promise, creating a personal and political horizon that enables people to envision a good life (Ahmed 2008, 12). China's new psychotherapy promises that happiness will give meaning and order to life and seeks to convince people that adjusting to certain forms of living and thinking will bring them contentment (Berlant 2008). The goals psychology claims to achieve are in line with ideals or utopias that socialism or communism promise. Yet the therapeutic process is also aimed at helping people maximize their positive potential and at constructing subjects who are fit for the current development of the market in China. However, the real control that occurs through happiness promotions or therapeutic governance often operates at an unconscious level for clients. As therapists optimize individuals' pleasurable fantasies and ally them with political and economic objectives, clients may unconsciously associate their fantasies with the political and economic objectives put before them.

Promoting happiness for the underprivileged while they have little to be happy about is a strategy for preempting potential threats and alleviating the crippling effects of socioeconomic dislocation (Yang 2013a). By turning economic stratification into personal, emotional, and psychological conditions, happiness promotions downplay structural inequalities. Analysis of the process shows how subjects' attention and emotions are diverted from an everyday reality that is demarcated by the effects of economic restructuring and toward an unknown inner world or imagined future.

Enacting psychotherapy oriented to the production of happiness constitutes a process through which pain and suffering caused by socioeconomic dislocation become tolerable and counselors open their clients to opportunities for "entrepreneurship" that putatively benefits both the emerging market economy and the clients. Such counseling programs create conversations between representatives of the party-state and marginalized groups that are diagnostic and prescriptive. These conversations, mediated by psychotherapists, are part of a therapeutic mode of control and kindly power.

Although subjectivity might appear to be the most intimate sphere of experience, its contemporary intensification as a political and ethical commodity is intrinsically correlated with the growth of expert discourses that enable individuals to render relations with the self and others into words and articulate thoughts using techniques that promise to enable subjects to transform themselves in the direction of happiness and fulfillment (Rose 1996, 157). The promotion of psychology in the form of self-help and happiness campaigns in China has ushered in a new body of therapeutic expertise and new ways of construing, evaluating, and actualizing relations. The government uses psychology not only to provide a language or framework for people to interpret socioeconomic changes, it also integrates psychological forces into socioeconomic processes. One example is a book on job counseling by psychologist Dr. Shi Kan (1999) that uses expert discourses to direct those who have been laid off to readjust themselves and get re-employed. This kind of psychologization apparently satisfies the needs, interests, and aspirations of a certain class in China (i.e., entrepreneurs, psychotherapists, the state), but it betrays the vast majority.

Indeed, these efforts are largely unsuccessful among Chinese workers. Their contestations arise even as China continues to promote happiness as the measure of a good life. The odd parallel here demonstrates that happiness has become a nexus promoted by the government for contending with social and political change while it is equally an analytical tool workers use for social critique. This book contributes to the growing anthropological literature on happiness (Mathews 2006; Thin 2008; Johnston 2012) by engaging with this emotion as it is embedded within a governing technology based on psychologization and as a force for both the government and underprivileged people to rally resources for their respective causes.

In the next chapter, I extend my ethnography to the residential community and explore the complex role of the community residents' committee and party staff turned psychosocial workers in this trend of psychologization.

2

"WE HELP YOU HELP YOURSELF"

Leifeng sacrificially served people, but we help people help
themselves (*bang ren zizhu*).
—PARTY SECRETARY AND SOCIAL WORKER IN CHANGPING, 2010

In 2005, the Chinese New Year Gala, the most important live broadcast of the year on China Central Television, featured a skit in which the famous Chinese comedian Zhao Benshan played a village party secretary who has failed at reelection and sets up his own "talk therapy clinic," transforming himself into a psychological counselor. The skit shows him counseling a fellow villager who has won three lotteries in a row within a short time and is suffering from anxiety over this windfall. The skit transmits multiple messages, each of which dovetails with the interests of the state, including the value the government places on counseling and psychotherapy and the vanguard role party authorities play in performing and promoting this therapy.[1] Talk therapy is represented in this skit as a way to make full use of the skills of party ideological workers and help people adapt to new circumstances in a market economy. In this sense, traditional thought work has taken on the new form of psychological counseling, shifting the exercise of power to therapeutic activities.

The skit parallels an important process that has been happening in China since 2006 in which members of urban community residents' committees (especially party staff) have been receiving training in counseling or social work as part of a national program called *xinlixue jin shequ* (Psychology Enters Communities). As a result, Shao Wen, the former party secretary at the Beibiao factory and the current director of a residential community next to Beibiao, identified herself more as a social worker than as a traditional party secretary. To impress upon residents that she was creative, up to date, and actively seeking improvements, Shao often highlighted her psychological knowledge and training in counseling and social work. However, preliminary training in counseling is inadequate for the psychotherapy demanded of her, and Shao Wen drew upon her sociocultural knowledge of the residents and the community to perform a type of thought work blended with counseling. She preferred that people view her as "the President of the Lane." She claimed that instead of directly intervening in people's lives, she now helps people help themselves achieve their goals and potential.

To shed the stereotypical image of the stern and political party secretary, she claimed to serve people with a smile (*weixiao fuwu*), to remind people of their duties with warmth and sweetness (*wenxin tixing*), and to implement rules and regulations with gentleness (*rouqing zhifa*). (Workers refer to these tactics in a folk rhyme that ridicules the recent transformation of the work style of party organizations and community residents' committees.) Instead of exuding the type of professionalism and aloofness professional counselors embody (as represented by counselors on CCTV's *Psychology Talk Show*), party staff turned counselors in Changping assume an informal and emotional persona in their psychosocial work. Their physical expressions—for example, the constant smiles, friendly attitudes, and patting that Zhao Bensham exhibited as the village party secretary turned counselor in the CCTV skit—are expressions of training in positive psychology and social work. They play a mediating role in the production of psychological knowledge by simplifying it and transmitting it to the rank and file.

Residents' committees were established in China in the 1950s.[2] Before the reform era, the government treated this system as secondary to work units and used the committees to perform "trivial and routine tasks" such as helping work units implement policies, controlling and monitoring the population, and delivering basic social welfare to residents (Benewick et al. 2004). Residents' committees were supposed to be elected and regularly held to account by the residents and were responsible for administering local socioeconomic and political affairs.[3] However, in practice, the committees were not autonomous residents' organization. Instead, they acted mostly as "nasty and meddlesome agents of the government" (Derleth and Koldyk 2004, 752). Also, the residents' committees were by and large inefficient in fulfilling critical functions the central government expected them to perform. To deal with these problems, in the early 1990s the Ministry of Civil Affairs launched a campaign known as "community construction" (*shequ jianshe*) that was designed to create a new urban system of self-government. After a series of pilot tests, in 2000, the Ministry of Civil Affairs issued a decree,[4] calling for the establishment of a new grassroots self-governing organization, the community residents' committees, to replace the old residents' committees.

These new organizations were given two important tasks. First, they are to serve as the foundation of a new social welfare system whose job is to fulfill the roles and perform the duties previously fulfilled by work units. They are to assume the following social functions: expand welfare services, including special services to the elderly, disabled persons, and the poor (see Cho 2013 on the role of residents' committees in governing urban poverty); provide basic services to community residents in general; provide training and job fairs for laid-off residents; improve community sanitation; enrich community cultural life; beautify the environment; and strengthen community security. Second, community residents' committees are expected to become the linchpin of a more autonomous system of self-government in cities. That is, the government expects residents to manage local affairs with more autonomy (Ministry of Civil Affairs of the People's Republic of China 2000).

Within this context, in 2000, the Beijing Municipal Civil Affairs Bureau began to regroup urban residential areas and households within the new structure of community residents' committees.[5] The new committees control more households than the old residents' committees did, averaging about 15,000 households per committee (Zhou 2003). In 2003, the bureau called for the first elections of leaders in the new committees; they were supposed to be directly nominated and elected by community residents.

However, in the Changping community, the residents' committee leaders, which were directly appointed by the Beibiao factory management, automatically became the new leaders of the community residents' committee.

The community residents' committee seems to be part of the shift in governance in China since the mid-1990s. Unlike government (*zhengfu*), which deals with the party-state apparatus and operates top-down through orders, bureaucracy, and coercion, governance (*zhili*) refers to the relationships between the government, corporations, and institutions, operating both top-down and bottom-up through collaboration, coordination, negotiation, and consensus (Yu 2002, 195). This echoes Rose's (1999, 174) notion of "government *through* community." When citizens govern themselves and community does not oppose government but willingly partners with the state, the state can shun its responsibility for providing order, security, health, and productivity (Rose 1999, 174; see also Yu 2002; Sigley 2006; Hoffman 2006).

The community residents' committee plays seemingly contradictory roles as both a mechanism for promoting grassroots democracy and a mode of social control—a tool for maintaining social stability and at the same time mobilizing the masses (Ngeow 2012).[6] Indeed, there are two trends in the study of residents' committee in China: one focuses on the democratic dimension of the institution (Gui et al. 2006; Chen et al. 2007) and the other on the community residents' committee as an arm of the party-state to exercise control over urban populations (Wong and Poon 2005; Cho 2013). Such apparently contradictory roles are reflected in the ambiguous and ambivalent practices of community residents' committee members in Changping. This chapter explores the multifaceted nature of the community residents' committee and the ambivalence of community psychosocial workers in their counseling.

Beibiao's community residents' committee is composed of a party secretary, a director, four staff, and sixteen doorkeepers. It is in charge of 948 households in eight residential compounds. The community residents' committee assigns two doorkeepers to each compound to look after public facilities and the personal belongings of residents, such as bicycles, cars, tricycles, and clothing or bedding placed outside. The committee supervises disabled people, unemployed individuals, and retirees and seeks to maintain order and prevent crimes. It also conducts various political missions such as blood donation and obtaining temporary security volunteers.

Unlike the community in northeast China where residents' committee members or cadres were predominantly laid-off workers (Cho 2013), in the Beibiao community residents' committee, there is a social hierarchy. Cadres are members of the former party committee or union leaders at the factory while doorkeepers are retired party secretaries or reemployed laid-off workers. In the wake of mass layoffs, the community residents' committee also oversees the task of helping the unemployed find reemployment through job training using the new *xiaoshigong jieshao suo* (the center that introduces jobs paid by the hour). This training usually involves working short stints for an hourly wage.

By integrating psychosocial counseling in their daily work, community residents' committee members and party staff like Shao Wen took pains to show that they were current and had expertise. These efforts both legitimize the continued presence of the party in people's daily lives and rebrand them differently from party staff of the past, whose bureaucratic skills have been devalued in the market economy. As a consequence, behaviors that would have previously been deemed "wrong" or "bad" ("irrational

2.1. Members of CRC standing in a small square talking.

thinking" or alternative sexuality) are now viewed as different kinds of sickness, as deviance, or as characteristics that are generally associated with various forms of victimhood (i.e., because of abuse or oppression) that can be remedied with psychotherapeutic interventions (Nolan 1998).

In this chapter, I explore the tensions in the subjectivity of newly retrained party staff, who, despite their position as "experts," view themselves less as professionals and more as *xinli shehui gongzuozhe*, or psychosocial workers. These new psychosocial workers experience a series of pushes and pulls in their new jobs. On the one hand, their training encourages them to use and promote techniques of counseling and precepts of positive psychology. On the other hand, their status as representatives of the party's bureaucracy "depsychologizes" their position; they are responsible not only for paying lip service to socialism in order to legitimate the continued relevance of the party in the market economy but also reappropriate and repoliticize socialist categories for current psychosocial work.[7]

They also have to be part of a much bigger nation-rebuilding project in the face of large-scale change; they are responsible for preempting people's enactment of their negative potential, particularly those who may cause social unrest. Yet they are conscious of distancing themselves from the "old party ways," especially ideological work, including thought work. Thought work took place at Beibiao for decades either in group political studies or in one-on-one interactions between party staff and workers through *tanxin*, or heart-to-heart talk. These efforts were designed to reorient workers' thinking toward party interests and were based on criticism, self-criticism, and harsh punishment that might entail the insertion of damaging results in one's *dang'an* (personal dossier) (Yang 2011b).[8] However, the people who are served by counselors today sometimes nostalgically want thought work to return because of its association with a party that was willing to take on their personal problems. This nostalgia amplified their unhappiness about the current emphasis on self-reliance in reemployment counseling and their recent downward mobility.

Party staff turned psychosocial workers navigate these competing demands and roles. Unlike the propaganda designed to mobilize people to learn from the spirit of Leifeng, a wholehearted and sacrificial communist do-gooder and soldier who lived a life of service to the people and socialist causes in Mao's era,[9] psychosocial workers claim that they help people help themselves grow and realize their potential. This is part of the shift in governance from the call for people to sacrifice their lives for the socialist cause of Mao's era to mobilizing them to value life and fulfill themselves (Zhang 2011a). One of the common ways trainees are introduced to current modes of social work is through comparing their work with the work of Leifeng; this is an example of *biantong*, or continuity amid change. In their work, they are also responsible for staving off negative potential. Yet even in this context, people contest this governance, particularly in their responses to counseling and job retraining.

In what follows, I first examine the local forces of psychologization and the trajectory of the time-honored principle of self-reliance (*zili gengsheng*). I then examine the unique development of counseling in China, the role of community psychosocial workers in psychologization, and the ironies both workers and counselors experience in relation to the present forms of psychotherapy on offer. I illustrate how psychologization can be integrated into authoritarian societies such as China to repoliticize subjects and legitimate the continued existence of the party. The chapter also examines the local theory of psychological dysfunction that is used to justify therapeutic techniques and assesses how effective these techniques are in managing unemployed workers. The chapter ends with an expanded ethnographic account of workers' contestation of psychologization that uses the strategy of *huyou* (trickery).

Gender and the Politics of Self-Reliance

Many residents' committee members and psychosocial workers preach self-reliance and problematize or even pathologize forms of dependence, especially dependence on former state enterprises. In Changping, this occurs in the context of a formerly close-knit working-class community. The breakdown of the work-unit system due to privatization and marketization and the reemployment of workers in various locations have gradually detached many individuals from familiar networks. This process began in the mid-1990s, when the privatization of state-owned enterprises was initiated. Most adults in their 40s and 50s grew up with the perception of the work unit as the source of identification and support, which makes counseling that criticizes dependence particularly difficult for them.

One story from Changping illustrates the change from a time when dependence on the state was encouraged to the present when it is pathologized. Fang Li, a former state worker, was laid off from the watch factory in 1999. In 2004, she discovered that her husband, then a police officer, was having an affair with one of his colleagues. Fang was outraged. Despite her best efforts, she could not get her husband back. So she wrote a letter to the local police bureau disclosing her husband's extramarital affair and other corrupt behaviors on his part. At first, the police bureau did not respond. Fang then asked the party committee of the watch factory for help. It was normal, from the time of Mao's era, for people at work units to take their personal problems, including marital problems, to the party. After the party committee intervened, the police bureau took Fang's accusations seriously and removed her husband from his job. While Fang appreciated the powerful intervention, she was shocked by its heavy-handedness. Fang had only wanted her husband to come back to her; she never expected him to lose his job. The jobless husband resented her so much that he refused to speak to her, even though they continued to live in the same household. Instead, he surfed the Internet and talked to women online. After trying for reconciliation for several years without success, in the summer of 2009, Fang returned to the party committee for help. By then, however, the watch factory had been privatized and there was no on-site party organization. It had been restructured into the residents' committee. Fang spoke to Shao Wen, now a retrained residents' committee director in a community next to Beibiao.

In my interview with her later, Fang recalled: "Shao said something like, 'It was inhumane to simply bind two people together through punitive measures. How can you discipline him now when he interacts with people online? The party committee cannot make a final say on people's private lives anymore; it has stopped working that way in this age.'" Shao counseled Fang to do some soul-searching and to be more like a "good wife and wise mother" in order to win her husband's heart back. She also suggested that Fang and her husband go for counseling on TV through one of the CCTV shows devoted to on-air counseling. Fang replied with irony, "If I go, I will make sure to invite you to join me on TV." Fang's comment was a reminder to Shao Wen of the past role the party committee had played in contributing to her marital problem and a condemnation of its abdication of responsibility in the present by simply advising her to seek professional counseling. In essence, the party asked her to draw on her own resources to overcome her difficulties.

The new notion of self-reliance, in which individuals call upon their own resources, differs from the time-honored principle of "self-reliance" that Chairman Mao promoted in the late 1950s and early 1960s. That version of self-reliance was based on the collective. It mobilized people to be united as a whole in order to modernize the country rather than relying on foreign assistance or cooperation with foreign powers (after China's breakup with the Soviet Union). In other words, Mao used the concept of self-reliance to construct a collective people-subject. In the second half of the 1970s, when the Soviet threat was perceived to be increasing, China changed course. Instead of strictly adhering to the principle of national self-reliance, the leadership adopted a program of economic and technological modernization that greatly increased links with foreign countries. Mao's concept of national self-reliance was gradually abandoned, and China entered an era of international bank loans, joint ventures, and a panoply of once-abhorred capitalist economic practices that required coordination among different peoples.

This was not the end of self-reliance, however. In the 1980s, as the state gradually renounced the principle of the old self-reliance, it reworked self-reliance as a signifier. The state grafted the concept onto three other principles that constitute the concept of *sizi*, or the four selfs: *zi zun* (self-respect), *zi ai* (self-love), *zi qiang* (self-striving), and *zi li* (self-reliance) (Zhang and Luo 1996). Official discourses now explicitly use these four selfs to convict or call forth people (women in particular) in the context of a market ideology. Members of China's senior leadership promote these ideas as vital principles in a transitional era. For example, in 2003, at the National Women's Job Creation and Re-Employment Conference, China Political Bureau member Wang Zhaoguo called upon laid-off women to continue the good tradition of the "four selfs" in their search for reemployment. As the source and momentum of women's development, the principle of the "four selfs" encourages women "not to rely on external forces, but first of all, [to] rely on their own consciousness and struggle" (Gu 2001, 25). Motivated by the "four selfs," contemporary women should devote themselves to economic reform and to pushing social development forward. According to Zhang Guihua and Luo Zhaohong (1996), the spirit of the four selfs should motivate contemporary women to devote themselves to improving their *suzhi* (quality) in three ways[10]: first, by improving their scientific and cultural *suzhi* and enhancing the nation's capacity to compete; second, by enhancing their ideological and spiritual *suzhi* in order to increase their awareness of modernity and foster a noble character in the context of socialist ethics, including a civilized lifestyle and healthy attitudes about marriage and family; and finally, by improving their psychological *suzhi*, to train in order to build a strong personality that will help them overcome the psychological disadvantages of women. This agenda partly explains why Shao Wen encouraged Fang Li to search her soul, act like a good wife and wise mother, and seek professional counseling.

The principle of "self-reliance," which in Mao's time was designed to homogenize *renmin* (the people) as a whole, is now reshaped to influence new female subjects, a process that sharpens reform-era social polarization and essentializes gender. In other words, the self-reliance of the 1960s and 1970s, which was constructed to form a collective people-subject in order to cope with an increasing Soviet threat, has been converted into a tool that uses market ideology to construct (neoliberal) individual identity. This strategy is most often used with women. The market economy thus shapes both gender identity and national interests. Women not only pay the highest price for economic restructuring (they suffer more from cuts to education, health, child care, and other subsidies), but they are also pushed hardest to achieve self-sufficiency without state support. Multitasking psychosocial workers are the agents to push this partial reformulation (or partial continuity) of the concept of self-reliance—another example of *bi-antong*. Not only do social workers enact this concept in the therapy they offer, these historically specific processes and sociocultural transformations are also embodied in their own experiences.

According to Moore (1994), the subject in poststructuralist thinking is actually a site of multiple and contradictory positionings and subjectivities. In addition to the subjective experience of identity and the physical fact of being an embodied subject, there is the historical continuity of the subject. Past subject positions tend to overdetermine present subject positions. These multiple subjectivities are held together and constitute agents in the world. That is, the subject position of collectivity that was constructed via the Maoist notion of self-reliance is being converted, through psychologization, into a mechanism for incorporating individuals (especially women) into market ideology. However, old social structures and concepts are still shaping current therapeutic practices. For example, the idea of self-reliance plays a central role in the new therapies targeting vulnerable groups, even though the "subject" has changed from the group to the individual. The current emphasis on self-help echoes the government's call for the individual rather than the state to be responsible for their lives. In bringing about this transformation, the system has produced its best allies in the push to psychologize citizens. This is another example of the principle of *biantong*, or continuity amid change.

"Psychosocial Work" with Chinese Characteristics

In my field research, both counselors who got their counseling licenses from the Ministry of Health (i.e., clinical counselors at hospitals) and those who received licenses or training from the Ministry of Labor (i.e., human resource managers and community psychosocial workers) indicated that low standards and a lack of consistent and strict regulation currently characterize the field of counseling in China. These opinions resonate with recent scholarly findings that depict psychology in China as an ill-defined profession (Hou and Zhang 2007).

Psychology is often practiced within a medical model in China, and many psychologists work in hospitals. However, many (paraprofessional) counselors with minimal training have only a general college degree and some on-the-job experience. A national certification program for counselors exists, but most professionals are not certified, as it is not required for employment (Clay 2002). While professionally trained counselors work in hospitals and private counseling centers, social workers work in settings such as job centers, community centers, and places of employment. In Changping, social workers are often retrained party staff, paid by local governments to attend short-term training sessions in social work or counseling offered by the Ministry of Civil Affairs or the Ministry of Labor. The psychosocial workers I engaged with came from two groups: a more professional group of licensed counselors and social workers, and residents' committee members or party staff who had preliminary training in counseling or social work.[11]

In my interviews, the community psychosocial workers claimed that they were integrating their psychological or social work training into real life, making it as accessible for ordinary people as possible. Those who were once party authorities are now the ones who carry out local political and therapeutic tasks, and their popularization of psychological knowledge naturalizes the use of psychology in governance. To explain her hybrid role as a party secretary and counselor, Shao Wen, from Changping, refers to the character of Lao Liu from the 1999 award-winning movie *Xizao* (Shower). The movie describes China's socioeconomic transformation through depiction of the demolition of a public bathhouse in Beijing. In the movie, Lao Liu runs the traditional bathhouse during the 1980s and 1990s, when it provides a number of peripheral services, including haircuts, massage, shaving, fire cupping, and old-style pedicures for men. Lao Liu is the facility's all-in-one manager, staff, mediator of squabbles, and marriage counselor. He forms close bonds with his clients. One of his patrons who often sings "O Sole Mio" in the shower loses his nerve when he sings it at a public karaoke event until Lao Liu's son provides him with a shower from a hose. This connects the singer to his familiar self and environment, enabling him to perform in public. Shao uses this example to illustrate her methods of counseling; she helps workers reconnect with their real or familiar selves so they can actualize their full potential and survive in the new market economy. Lao Liu cures another patron who becomes sexually impotent after learning that his wife has run naked after a thief who stole her necklace when she was taking a shower. He arranges a late-night tryst for this man with his wife at the bathhouse. The film points to the positive healing functions of organic urban communities that mediate and relieve anxiety, stress, and trauma for residents. The depiction of the shock caused by the possible demolition of Lao Liu's bathhouse can be seen as a critique of the crippling effects of unfolding socioeconomic dislocation. Shao described her experience of this film:

> When I first watched the movie, I enjoyed it but didn't think too much. But after I was trained in counseling, I realized that the movie has psychological value. Lao Liu offers an example of behavior therapy [focusing on how the environment impacts one's specific, learned behaviors], but in a Chinese way. This is what I want to employ in my work.

Shao indicated that she aimed to provide her clients (most of whom were laid-off workers, housewives, retirees, and disabled people in the community) with the means to return to the selves they were comfortable with in the past in order to help them move on with life in the wake of the sea change caused by privatization. By paying particular attention to the social and cultural dimensions of counseling, Shao shifted from a purely psychological approach to a combination of both psychotherapy and socio-cultural therapy, or a community-based approach to healing that draws on existing sociocultural norms and spiritual belief systems in Changping. In fact, she was critical of interpretations of social or psychological disorders as problems that can be solved only through positive psychology.

However, Shao also wore a second hat: she was a party representative. In her description of *Shower*, she emphasized the connection between Lao Liu's methods and behavior therapy, of which she has acquired an understanding through her government-sponsored retraining. She implied that she must perform her duties in such a way that people could recognize this new knowledge and her psychotherapeutic skills. In other words, her expertise, mediated by psychology, added a scientific veneer and new authority to her community work. However, Shao did not adopt psychology in isolation; instead, she integrated it with social and cultural therapy. Her emphasis on community cultural resources as aids to people who need to heal from social "wounds" likely strengthened public perceptions of party staff such as herself as appropriate therapeutic authorities. She was able to place the new psychology in the context of community dynamics. Shao also consciously linked her counseling to the larger goals of the harmonious society; she viewed the two as operating in tandem.

Ostensibly, psychosocial work is focused on the needs of the people (particularly vulnerable individuals) rather than on the needs of psychosocial workers or of the government. However, as Shao indicated, in reality, the opposite was often the case. She gave an example. One day, district leaders were scheduled to inspect a local community center at 9:00 a.m. The community residents' committee members used bottles of soft drink to "bribe" retirees to be at the center playing chess, poker, or other games so they would showcase the committee's good work and create a welcoming atmosphere to impress the delegation. Many retirees came at 8:30 a.m. to get ready, but the delegation was delayed until 10:30. By then the retirees were already tired and some of them had cooking duties to attend to at home. However, they were asked not to leave until the inspection was over. In this case and others, the interests of the government take precedence over the needs of the very groups the social services are intended to assist. Shao said,

> It is awkward: on the one hand, we have been paid to get trained in social work; we understand the ethics. On the other hand, our superiors are party authorities and bureaucrats who don't know about social work. As a social worker at the community level, you have to walk a fine line between your professional training and local politics, and mostly end up sacrificing professional ethics for political needs.

This paradoxical feature of psychosocial work in China can also apply to the counseling of professionally trained counselors who often work in hospitals and do not necessarily fulfill explicit political purposes through their counseling. However, they too have a hybrid subjectivity. Even though they do not need to take part in the practices of sustaining stability and encouraging workers to rely on themselves for reemployment, these counselors cannot escape the implications of a society and culture that values *guanxi* (social connections) and practices of *renqing* (human feelings, or commiseration) (Yang 1988; Yan 1996; Kipnis 1997) but where social hierarchy has been intensified with market competition in China. For example, a counselor I interviewed in August 2011 at one of the two mental hospitals in Changping complained that her superiors had asked her to counsel their friends and relatives. To retain her job in the hospital, she succumbed to such practices, which she claimed to be unethical.

> They [clients] didn't pay you but offer you gifts, meals, or other favors. Also, you are already prejudiced because the clients are introduced to you by your boss. I was sometimes asked to orient them to do certain things. It is not objective; it is a kind of ideological orientation. It is important to establish a professional setting, a pure counselor and client relationship without much emotional or ideological involvement. A good counselor allows the client to rediscover him or her self and find his or her own solutions. The process should be paid so that the client values the counseling service and is motivated to put effort into his or her own healing.

While clients give inexpensive gifts to counselors in contexts outside China, their meanings are always complex—they can signify straightforward gratitude, represent an attempt to equalize power, or even be an attempt to manipulate the therapist (Willingham and Boyle 2011, 172). In China, expensive gifts are often sent to therapists in lieu of cash. Such exchanges are seen by counselors as a way of nurturing personal connections or friendship between therapist and client, rendering counseling unethical and unprofessional. When this happens, the traditional practices of *guanxi* and *renqing* engulf psychology. The deployment of psychological knowledge becomes naturalized into existing social and cultural practices.

Performing Psychotherapy: Irony and Criticism

The tensions I have described so far in the role of psychosocial workers and counselors in promoting psychology have provoked a host of reactions within the target population, including the people in Changping. One popular reaction has been the use of irony, as we saw with Fang Li. It is worth considering how clients (and even counselors) use irony to reject, resist, or even integrate psychologization in Changping.

One laid-off worker in the watch factory community attended a job counseling session offered by a reemployment service center director turned job counselor in the summer of 2009. In a later interview, the man ridiculed the counselor's promotion of positive psychology:

> He [the counselor] didn't know what exactly he was talking about. He tried to give an example of how optimism can benefit people, but he didn't even have an example from China. He told a story about Johnny, an American beggar. He said Johnny begged at a grocery store. After hearing a life counselor preach the power of optimism and of encouragement, Johnny began searching for encouraging phrases in books and typing them on small pieces of paper. When he begged outside a grocery store, he would place a piece of paper with uplifting words into his potential beneficiary's shopping bag. To the surprise of the grocery store owner, the checkout line where Johnny situated himself was always full of customers; people would wait longer to check out in order to get Johnny's nice saying. Johnny's optimism benefited other people too. Then after finishing the story, the director asked the participants rhetorically, "Johnny is a beggar, but we are only temporarily laid off. Johnny is in a capitalist society but we are in a socialist country. Is there any reason that we shouldn't be optimistic?" One participant interrupted, "I want to beg here but no grocery store would allow me in. I want to go to America."

The worker who was telling me this story appreciated the witty commentary. It made it possible for participants (mostly unemployed workers in the community) to laugh at their own predicament. Indeed, in triggering an explosion of laughter, this irony-inflected reaction may have helped ease the frustrations and pain of those assembled, helped them come to grips with the challenge of being marginalized, and helped them articulate their visions of a better world.

Another informant described a similar experience with a job counselor who encouraged workers to see the loss of their jobs as a blessing in disguise. He drove home his point by invoking a well-known ancient Chinese fable, *saiwong shi ma, yan zhi huo fu* (literally, an old man living in the border areas loses his horse but knows not whether it is a curse or a blessing in disguise).[12]

> The counselor said, "What I'm saying is who knows whether unemployment might not be a blessing in disguise; *saiwong shi ma, yan zhi huo fu.*'" One of the participants asked, "How about you telling us what's blessed in unemployment." The job counselor replied, "Unemployment at least gives you an opportunity for a new beginning, which can mean entrepreneurship." "What kind of entrepreneurship? An entrepreneur who drinks wind from the Northwest?" [The participant used the term *he xibeifeng*, a local term referring to having nothing to eat but wind from Siberia, meaning cold and hungry.]

The bite of this irony could be felt in my informant's retelling. As Hutcheon (1995) observes, irony is not just disbelief or creating distance between what one says and what one means. Irony has a political, ethical, and emotive force. It conveys an attitude or a feeling and has an emotional tenor—an emphatic expression of anger, indignation, and contempt.

Some scholars suggest that irony is a depoliticized mode of intellectual detachment that engages the intellect rather than the emotions (Walker 1990, 24). However, Gutwirth (1993) argues that irony has an edge, a "sting." Similarly, Hutcheon (1995) contends that any discussion of the politics of irony should include an examination of irony's cutting edge, which can be the wide and complex range of affective possibilities it opens up. Irony's affective "charge" includes a range of emotional responses (from anger to delight) and the various degrees of motivation and proximity entailed. Indeed, unlike many other discursive strategies, irony explicitly sets up a relationship between the ironist, the audience, and the targets of the irony. For example, while provoking laughter, irony can invoke notions of hierarchy and subordination, judgment, and even moral superiority (Chamberlain 1989).

According to Chambers (1990), the critical edge of irony offers a possible mode of oppositionality for those who are part of a system they find oppressive. Irony can function constructively to articulate a new oppositional position or it can work in a more negative way. In the Changping community, the irony laid-off workers express is largely negative and target the social system. These ironists stand outside the system, placing themselves in a position of power that masks their vulnerability.

By contrast, the irony expressed by psychiatrists, psychologists, and social workers targets the system from the perspective of insiders, especially the infusion of psychology in governance. They target the system of which they are a part and make their own adjustments to locate strategies that work for their clients, for example, by avoiding the more extreme (political) use of positive psychology (to sustain sociopolitical stability). This position reflects the hybrid and contradictory roles these counselors play. For example, one of my informants, Wang, a counselor at a mental hospital in Huilongguan who had been invited to the community to counsel residents, told me that she was once criticized by her party secretary for failing to implement the ideology of social harmony in her work. One of her long-term clients who had been laid off from a state enterprise had experienced improvements in her mental health and had become more aware of the unfairness of the reduced welfare package her former employer was offering. The patient became critical and challenged her former director for unfairly distributing welfare to laid-off workers. The director of the state enterprise called the head of the mental health hospital, Wang's boss, to complain about the situation and criticized him for not doing his job properly (that is, for releasing the mentally ill into society without completely "curing" them) and for not promoting the ideology of "social harmony." Wang criticized her boss for his lack of knowledge counseling.

> He thought that what I am doing is thought work, that I could impose on the clients party decisions, policies, or something like that. What I do and probably all the counselors would do is simply listen to clients and help

them sort out their emotions, gaining new perspectives. We are supposed to relieve people's pain and help them heal, not manipulate them politically. But now, to keep this job, I try to combine both. I don't see myself as a professional counselor; I am simply a worker, a psychological worker. You see, I had been systematically trained as a physician specializing in internal diseases. But to find a job in Beijing, I had to shift my specialization to psychiatry because there were not many people specializing in psychiatry. I learned psychiatry from scratch. Later on, when the leaders of the hospital asked me to study counseling, I shifted again and started to get trained in counseling. To survive in this system, you have to prioritize the party's needs, not your own interests or professional ethics.

Like others, Wang does not completely buy into the efficacy of Western psychotherapy for solving social problems in China. She was forced to change her career path to suit the party's shifting interests and needs. After her training in counseling, she walks a fine line between abiding by her professional and ethical education and conforming to the political project of constructing a harmonious society.

In this process, counselors ended up adopting the logic of psychologization—translating socioeconomic issues through therapeutic apparatuses into individual emotions and psychology. However, at the ideological level, psychology is represented through the lens of scientific socialism, which pays lip service to socialism. This also constitutes a process of depsychologization. These competing ideologies create a tension between caring for people and meeting the changing needs of the party. In Wang's case, there was also an emotional dimension at play—a sense of injured pride that derived from the fact that the director of the state enterprise who called Wang's boss associated her work with outdated thought work. This incident intensified her sense of contempt and ambivalence and led to her calculated commitment to counseling.

Psychologizing Social Problems

In the wake of mass unemployment, urban workers have begun to long for the kind of connections with the party that were formed through the thought work that took place in China from Mao's era until the 1990s. Many workers now tend to downplay the fact that thought work was a form of surveillance and scrutiny of the rank and file. They are nostalgic about the time when they could go to the party committee of their former work units even when they were dealing with personal problems. As mentioned, these "close" relationships between the party and the people were reflected in the longtime slogan "Come to the party committee whenever you have a problem." This slogan was dropped even before the privatization of state-owned enterprises began and privatized companies dissolved party organizations.

In the face of this nostalgia, party staff turned psychosocial workers have to play a dual role in their interactions with residents, as both thought workers and social workers. When the watch factory was privatized in late 2004, the deputy party secretary and the trade union leader were reassigned to the factory's residents' committee to manage the unemployed, the retired, and the disabled, in part by maintaining their *dang'an* (personal dossiers) (see Yang 2011b) and in part by conducting both thought work and counseling. Their work style became a hodgepodge of psychotherapy and thought work. Both of these individuals were subsequently trained in social work. The trade union leader was also a licensed counselor in addition to his social work training. Although neither believed that their training had dramatically transformed their thought work in their official roles, both indicated that they strategically apply what they have been trained to do in counseling or social work in their interactions with residents. For example, in one case, Liu Ji, the deputy party secretary of the residents' committee, counseled Li Jiuxi, a woman who had been laid off. Liu encouraged Li to look inward and recreate herself as a different kind of woman. Liu did this as a way of nurturing Li's happiness so she could actualize her full potential but also to steer her away from her violent past.

Li first came to the party secretary to seek help in finding local employment and to conduct thought work with her husband, who is nine years her junior. This is an unusual situation in this community, where the norm is for men to marry younger women. After she was laid off from the watch factory in 2002, Li did a series of manual jobs, including domestic jobs. At some point during her constant absence from home as a live-in nanny, or *yuesao* (a maternal matron who helps new mothers take care of their newborns), Li discovered that her entrepreneur husband had had a series of affairs with younger women. He threatened to file for divorce. Li asked the party secretary to help her find another job that would allow her to sleep at home at night and to do thought work with her husband so he would stay with her.

Instead of seeing this marriage issue as having been caused, at least in part, by the widening income gap between the husband, who is getting richer, and the wife, who is getting poorer, Liu, the party secretary, presumed that the problems began with Li. Liu subtly implied that Li's past homosexual experience had contributed to the conflict with her husband. This experience occurred when Li was in her early twenties. She was said to have been forced into a homosexual relationship with a lesbian who fell in love with her and prevented her from establishing heterosexual relationships. With the help of her family, Li murdered the woman, and she was sent to jail. Then the factory party committee mobilized Li's co-workers and friends to launch a signature campaign to pressure the court for Li's early release,[13] and after just two years in prison, Li was let go. Based on her training in counseling, Liu considered Li's homosexual experience to be relevant to her current problems. The kind of training that most social workers receive in Beijing today is still steeped in traditional notions of gender and presumes that same-sex desire is a transgression that can cause problems in people's lives even though China no longer designated homosexuality as mental illness after 2001. This training also claims that individuals who feel same-sex desire can resolve their feelings through working on themselves. In her interview with me, Liu reflected on Li's case.

> She not only married a younger husband but also has a disabled son. Years ago, we showed sympathy to her, you know, her being forced into a homosexual relationship. But now putting all these together, she might really have a homosexual orientation or have related psychological problems. Of course, I didn't tell her directly, but how come all these came together? Yes, I said, I can talk to your husband but it is you who have to grab his heart. If his heart is not with you, marriage means nothing; divorce is probably better. I tried to cheer her up and encouraged her to be confident and independent. She was constantly putting herself down. She thought she was too old for her husband. Yes. She is nine years older than her man. I said, "Start with your heart attitude (*xintai*), your language, talking to the mirror saying how beautiful you are every day." I said, "If you are not happy about yourself, you cannot make other people happy." Women need to have some backbone. I told her men are cheap—like my husband, if you are submissive, he would walk over you.

To demonstrate her new aura of scientific authority after her training in social work, the party secretary invented symptoms that she thought could be ameliorated through counseling. She connected Li's marriage to a younger husband with her having a disabled son and with a past homosexual relationship. Buttressed by her recent training in counseling ethics, Liu also believed that marriage problems are entirely private issues; the spouses can be counseled, but the party should not interfere directly anymore. Li Jiuxi's past and her relationship with the party organization were reimagined and recast through a lens informed by the party secretary's psychological knowledge. This new way of seeing Li's problems assigned all the responsibility to the individual for fixing problems that were in part caused by state policies.

Liu's framework resonates with the shift of the notion of sexuality from a moral category to a psychological one. According to Foucault ([1997] 2008), before the nineteenth century, sexual behavior was largely a matter of ethical choices that indexed a person's relationship to him or herself, to a moral community, or to God. However, within the framework of modern psychology, the discourse of sexuality became "a positivity" (Davidson 1987, 23), repudiating the older moral framework of good and evil. Davidson points out that as a nineteenth-century invention, the concept of sexuality presupposes "a psychiatric style of reasoning" that perceives sexuality in impulses, tastes, attitudes, and psychological traits. This change in thinking engendered forms of psychopathology (Lee H. 2007, 188).

According to Liu, the meeting with Li Jiuxi was dialogic and intimate because they touched on very private issues, such as sexuality and personal history, but she saw Li's past as a harmful determinant of the present situation. Liu also invoked aspects of positive psychology as a way of encouraging Li to regulate her own emotions and behaviors, reinvent her own self-perception, and come up with her own formula for coping with her difficulties and psychological distress. Instead of offering therapy to both husband and wife, Liu counseled only the wife and focused on her "homosexual psychology." Liu was trying to stave off negative potential in Li by preempting any future violence toward the husband that might develop. She reduced the complex personal, social, and economic relations of their marriage to a primary psychological cause that might be addressed if Li could adopt an appropriate heart attitude (*xintai*). In this way Liu was asking Li to channel her complex situation into a "correct" attitude toward life based on a past event that was independent of the unfolding economic restructuring that had specifically touched her life in recent years. This type of psychologization, which appears to be essential for maintaining the dialectical tension between the psychological and the social, falsifies the effects of structural forces as psychological ills. This echoes what Liu Yuli (2008) argues, a *xintai* of being grateful and positive is necessary for a happy and productive life and for building a harmonious society.

Liu Ji also indicated that workers such as Li Jiuxi often invoke the tradition of thought work to compel counselors to be consistent with socialist commitments. As she put it:

> It is a kind of control. At the beginning of the counseling, Li Juixi told me about her contributions to the factory and her gratitude toward the party committee, particularly the way that she was set free from the prison. She was grateful to the party. But her gratitude toward the party and her praise are a kind of pressure or control over me, prompting me to continue to live up to her expectations.

Critically analyzing her interactions with Li Jiuxi, Liu viewed Li as using her previous experience with the party committee as a way to convince Liu to help her again. It is important to recognize how clients of today's psychosocial workers are active agents who help shape therapeutic interventions. They attempt to optimize such therapeutic mechanisms to suit their own interests and purposes, but they are not always successful, as the cases of Li Jiuxi and Fang Li show.

Counseling as *Huyou*

While counselors criticize the limits of thought work as a way of distinguishing it from counseling, ordinary people perceive counseling as irrelevant to the present. A worker at Changping compared counseling with thought work:

> In thought work, even being criticized, at least you felt you were recognized; you belonged somewhere. What counseling offers—happiness and positive thinking—is irrelevant. When we struggle every day to put food on

the table, other lofty things are unrealistic. When everything is so negative, it's hard to feel positive. The so-called people's interest is the highest [*renmin liyi zui gao*], but we, as members of the people, must feel it in tangible ways. Or if we are not of the people, who are the people?

Workers now appreciate the party's close scrutiny of and interference in individuals' private lives that dominated their experiences in the past as attention that was paid to the working class from above. The once-probing questions from party staff are now seen as having been relevant to ordinary people, especially compared to the "unrealistic" language of positive psychology. For workers, the key to survival is putting food on the table. The source of happiness is a job, not the kind of happiness or self-realization positive psychology offers. Workers' conflicting ideas about thought work point to their ambivalent feelings about the state. On the one hand, they are critical of the deterioration in living conditions caused by privatization, even though they often blame the immediate leadership (factory directors or workshop leaders) who fired them rather than greater state powers. On the other hand, workers long for the protection, support, and "intimate" relationship they once had with the paternal state, as illustrated in Li Jiuxi's desire for her husband to be subjected to thought work. For Li, counseling was too superficial. She longed for the kind of thought work that could solve her problems. In a separate interview I conducted with Li, she described her encounter with Liu as extremely disappointing:

> I felt so vulnerable at the moment. I wished someone from the party committee would talk with my husband and engage him in thought work to persuade him to stay. I cannot imagine how to cope with life if he leaves me. But Liu Ji was simply a *huyou* [trick] and took it so easily—of course, she still has her husband. She has a decent job and makes good money. She was also showing off her happiness, telling me about how she handled her husband. That was irrelevant to her job, not professional. I never saw any counselors on TV who showed off their personal lives or emotions. I lost my job and cannot afford to lose my husband. I need some powerful intervention and support from above, the kind of support that got me out of prison two decades ago.

Note that Li Jiuxi contrasted Liu Ji's work with that of professional counselors. Because psychosocial workers are rooted in the local community, many indicated that it is difficult to embody the kind of professional aura, that is attributed to professional counselors, especially those who perform on the *Psychology Talk Show* on CCTV 12. Yet workers who watched those CCTV counseling programs assume at times that a more professional approach would better address their problems.

What Li Jiuxi had really hoped for was the supportive intervention of the party relative to her problems with her livelihood and her marriage. When Li Jiuxi said that Liu "has a decent job and makes good money," she implied that Liu was condescending or speaking to her from a middle-class position, which made Liu's preaching of happiness and positive psychology irrelevant or ineffectual in light of Li's priority of survival. When people face the reality of tremendous deficiency, it is hard for them to believe in the promise of psychology. Li Jiuxi's case illustrates how previously unproblematic issues (i.e., being "victimized" by a homosexual relationship) are now rendered problematic through the new lens of psychology. Underprivileged individuals who are now subjected to psychologization think of counseling as *huyou* (a trick or hoodwinking), and in this formulation, they contest the trend and their position as recipients of a psychology that aims to orient them to be self-reliant cogs in the new market economy.

In fact, in Changping, counseling that promotes happiness and psychology is often perceived as a form of *huyou* that is used to numb and fool marginalized people. As mentioned in Chapter 1, *huyou* makes the target feel appreciated and cared for so that he or she is unaware of falling into a trap set for emotional or financial exploitation. Li Jiuxi indicated that she felt that she had been criticized in her meeting with Liu, though not condemned in the way party staff condemned workers in the old days. In fact, she said that she had trouble articulating what sort of condemnation she was subject to now, because the language Liu Ji used was so subtle and inviting. This subtle change is probably a consequence of the shifting speaking role psychosocial workers adopt. Li described Liu's speech as follows:

> She lured you to articulate what she herself wants to say. Then you don't know how you fell into her trap and spoke the way that she wanted you to. That way she escapes easily, not taking responsibility for anything articulated during the conversation. I was confused by her subtlety, her gaze. It's like you were cheated but instead of resistance, you still praise her kindness. She spoke in a way that appeared to care for you but not really.

Indeed, the traditional forms of Communist condemnation (in terms of good or bad, friend or enemy) (Mao 1968) have been transformed into a language of therapeutic sensitivity and therapeutic rationales for reconceptualizing behaviors that were formerly seen as "bad" or "immoral" (like homosexuality) as sickness or deviance that requires psychotherapeutic intervention. Another informant, a laid-off worker in Changping, articulated a similar impression of the psychology-oriented party staff:

> They [the party staff] now speak nice words; they serve you with a smile to remind you of your duties and responsibilities with warmth and sweetness, and to implement the law with gentle feelings. It's like slamming you and beating you up, and then they give you a date to eat to sweeten your mouth. It is hard to complain, but they don't help you solve any problems, a typical *huyou*.

Conclusion

Recently, particularly since the year of well-being in 2011, positive psychology has become part of a governing strategy that is intended to make a new world dominated by market ideology meaningful to citizens. Social and political thought in China stems increasingly from positive psychology, or constructive power from the heart, rather than from the traditional exercise of criticism or coercive measures. The use of psychology in China is designed to offer people meaning and structure for novel conditions and paths to ultimate happiness and well-being. However, by casting people's problems in terms of psychological disorders while workers seek solutions to practical ills, retrained party staff, the vanguards of psychologization, marginalize people even further, demanding that they harmonize within themselves the effects of economic restructuring and consequent social antagonism between classes. In China, psychotherapy offers a venue for resolving social and political disorder and for preempting people's potential for violence and unrest while creating new subjects based on psychology and self-reliance. In its invocation of precepts of positive psychology, the party attempts to offer something new, but it does so with the goal of maintaining its power. However, this allegedly scientific approach to people's problems paradoxically ends up bypassing most people's current social, economic, and cultural reality.

In this chapter, I explored the hybrid, contradictory role of psychosocial workers to expose the paradoxical features of post-Mao governance and the turn to psychology in China. Psychotherapy, a new rhetoric for caring for the marginalized, actually exacerbates workers' frustration and vulnerability. Events and activities, difficulties and distress can be problematized and shaped into phenomena that are deemed to require expert intervention. Actions that were previously understood as abnormal, irresponsible, imprudent, immoral, or even evil have come to be understood as symptoms (such as homosexuality or unemployment) of underlying diseases that ought to be treated or cured. State-owned enterprises and residents' committees have become involved in treating these newly perceived ills. In doing so, they in effect assert a new justification for their own political legitimacy. Mentality and psychology have become not only new sites of regulation and subject formation but also sites for developing positive potential for expanding the market, particularly the psychotherapy industry. This therapeutic mode of power shows how ideologies of "expert" and "expertise" shape politics and add professionalism and scientism to the authority of the party. However, the chapter also illustrates the cynicism among workers as they contest such psychotherapeutic interventions using irony and criticism. This dynamic of top-down intentions and bottom-up skepticism and resistance can be reflected in recent governance shift from top-down government (*zhengfu*) to bottom-up governance (*zhili*) (Yu 2002; Sigley 2006).

3

Sending "Warmth" and Therapy

Give me something to eat at the table and heat for the winter, then I will talk to you about psychological problems.

—A laid-off male worker in Changping, 2003

Dignified labor is an empty slogan to us laboring at private factories—then offering us psychological assistance? My trade union grandpa, you work more than ten hours per day and eat poorly, and I will offer you psychological assistance.

—An anonymous Internet user, 2012

In the summer of 2008 the director of the Beibiao factory told me a story about the relationship between urban poverty and social stability. A sixth grader was kidnapped in a southeastern Chinese city. The two kidnappers were so poor and inexperienced that one of them had to borrow money to buy food while they were waiting for the ransom. In the process the police identified the pair and arrested them. The released pupil told the police, "They were just too poor."

In telling me this story, the director emphasized the importance of poverty relief in maintaining social stability. For him, being poor increased the potential that someone might act in a way that would cause social unrest. State-run media share this view of impoverished groups, including the "new" classes of urban poor that have been created since the mid-1990s by China's massive privatization and economic restructuring. This negative potential, or *yinhuan*, has been a buzzword in Chinese propaganda on social stabilization. In particular, urban workers whose lives have been marked by unemployment (or precarious employment), impoverishment, and downward mobility during the transition to a market economy have been perceived by the government as potentially dangerous (Zhao 2008; Yang 2010), an ironic turn, given that these same workers were once the proud ideological representatives of Mao's socialism. Economic restructuring has transformed at least twelve to fifteen million people into the "new urban poor" (Kernan and Rocca 2000); the number would be larger if it included elderly and disabled urbanites.

Unlike the broadly distributed "egalitarian" poverty of Mao's era, this recent poverty is relative poverty; income disparities are significant, the result of yawning gaps in income and wealth between workers and the expanding middle class.[1] The situation has led to widespread social unrest (Hurst and O'Brian 2002; Hurst 2004; C. K. Lee 2007). In evaluating the seriousness of working-class threats to governance in China, Marc Blecher (2004, 194) points out that "when such a massive, geographically concentrated class with a definite history of radicalism suffers so precipitous an absolute and relative decline in its material conditions, social status, and political and ideological position, the state has a governance problem." Blecher argues that unemployed workers pose a particular structural challenge to governance because having lost their affiliations with state enterprises, they have more free time and private space to think about and organize protests. However, Blecher's analysis depicts only one kind of poverty: the poverty of laid-off workers—the "new" urban poor. It does not include the poverty of rural migrants or those who never entered the work-unit system. Understanding why only former members of work units have been chosen as the objects of reemployment and psychotherapeutic interventions requires us to trace their unique experience in the Chinese economy. Most lost their jobs not only because of new technologies or innovative management strategies for increasing profit but also because of the shedding of so-called *fuyu renyuan* (redundant people) from "overstaffed" state-owned enterprises. However, when state workers at the watch factory in Changping witnessed the gradual recruitment of about 200 young migrant workers through informal channels during the period when they were being laid off, they understood that as representatives of the former socialist ideology, they had been targeted.

In response to this potential threat, China has prioritized the management of instability resulting from worker layoffs. This includes implementing ad hoc measures to create jobs and relieve poverty such as the establishment of a minimum guaranteed income even for those who have been laid off,[2] a donation-based poverty-relief program to ease the plight of the poor across the country,[3] and the poverty-relief program called *song wennuan*. The state-led All-China Federation of Trade Unions (ACFTU) instituted *song wennuan* in 1997 (Wu and Huang 2007). By the end of that year, funds, branch offices, and communication systems for the program had been established all over the country, including 27 provincial-level, 576 city-level, 2,800 district- and county-level, and 17,000 grassroots-level branch offices and funds that amounted to 2 billion RMB. Over 180,000 ACFTU cadres had established communications with 35,000 enterprises. Within that first year, more than 4 million households reportedly received support (*People's Daily*, December 17, 1997, 2), including both cash and daily necessities. For example, in Changping, each household received 200–300 RMB, a bottle of cooking oil, and a bag of rice or flour. State representatives deliver these "gifts" to "households in particular difficulty" (*tekunhu*), typically before important Chinese festivals. *Song wennuan*, which literally sends the warmth of the party to the unemployed, nevertheless emphasizes workers' personal responsibility for poverty while obscuring structural forces that cause poverty.

Although poverty-relief measures as a form of charity are nothing new in Chinese history (Smith 2009), in this chapter, I argue that *song wennuan* represents a new political and ideological agenda in China. On the heels of the dismantling of socialist job security and public welfare and the breakdown of the socialist work-unit system as the institutional basis for political control (Lü and Perry 1997), *song wennuan* reinserts the state into the life of impoverished workers. The party's action of sending "gifts" to the urban poor shows *renqing* (human feelings), "compassion," and "benevolence" to the very people its economic policies have impoverished. Compassion and "counseling" constitute the party's therapeutic strategies, which attempt to make suffering more tolerable. Through *song wennuan*, Beibiao management and community residents' committee members use gift-giving and "counseling" to selectively harness positive human potential and reduce possibilities for social disturbances. This gift-giving is done in a more strategic than a humanistic way. To some extent, *song wennuan* has contributed to the relative calm of the past two decades even in the face of the growing unemployment and underemployment urban workers have experienced (Hu et al. 2002).

Although the feelings expressed as *renqing* appear to bridge inequality, emotions shown toward a person in distress by one who is free from distress create a social relation between spectator and sufferer that may be subject to corruption (Berlant 2004, 67). Such compassion may reinforce the very patterns of economic and political subordination that are responsible for the suffering it purports to alleviate. Presenting "gifts" as a form of *renqing* is intended to elicit gratitude from the impoverished and absorb their criticism and discontent. In addition, *song wennuan* entails conversations with beneficiaries involving multiple discourses that are intended to reorient recipients of aid away from collective action toward self-reliance and hope for the future. In this way, *song wennuan* prepares the disadvantaged to become assets in the market economy, for example, by filling low-wage service sector jobs. In light of the perceived threat to stability the vast new ranks of the poor pose, *song wennuan* is an exercise of social control presented under the guise of affection and therapy.

However, unlike the Western notion of the therapeutic state in which government aid is intended to normalize marginalized individuals and minimize state responsibility for them (Chriss 1999; Fraser 1987; Furedi 2004; Miller and Rose 1991, 1994; Polsky1991),[4] *song wennuan* highlights the affective involvement of the party in the well-being of the poor and nurtures "victims" in order to redress the state-society relationship eroded by privatization. In marking this distinction in a "socialist" setting, my analysis contributes to literature on the anthropology of welfare (Clarke 2004; Kingfisher 2002; Kingfisher and Goldsmith 2001; Russell and Edgar 1998; Schneider 2001).

I begin this chapter by describing worker unrest since the mid-1990s and outlining the discourse of instability that singles out laid-off men as *yinhuan*, individuals who embody negative potential. Because of this, they are the main recipients of *song wennuan*. I then consider the relationship between affect and the therapeutic state and situate the party's engagement with the unemployed within class politics in contemporary China. I go on to demonstrate how *song wennuan* acts as a new political nexus that uses affective and therapeutic devices (through gifting and counseling) in an attempt to absorb workers' criticism and disarm potential resistance and show how this program acts as a site of contestation through the politics of *kuqiong* (crying poverty), an exaggerated discourse of disadvantage and difficulty impoverished subjects perform in front of state representatives. The final section of the chapter suggests that *song wennuan* is a stratifying mechanism that inhibits the poor from organizing together to articulate their common interests vis-à-vis the state.

Labor Unrest and the Discourse of Instability

China's emphasis on benevolence in governance resonates with its political project of constructing "a harmonious society." In the first press conference after his election, Premier Wen Jiabao (2003) credited economic achievements with stabilizing society and emphasized the importance of relying on the people to maintain stability. This rhetoric cuts both ways, however. The implication is that if economic growth equals stability and people are responsible for doing their part to maintain that stability, then people who fail economically are part of the problem and are a source of instability. Yet the project of economic growth the party-state has undertaken since the 1990s has made millions of Chinese workers redundant and cast them off from the state sector. As a result, the political strategies of benevolence and stability are enmeshed; the government's benevolence targets those whose economic "failures" could threaten stability. It is in this context that the ACFTU implemented *song wennuan*. The program melded together the party, the government, and the people in pacifying measures that have become a Band-Aid that covers the "wounds" in the social fabric caused by socioeconomic dislocation.

At Beibiao, two-thirds of the work force have been given "an extended holiday" (a euphemism for being laid off) since 1997.[5] In the absence of a well-financed welfare system or efficient reemployment programs, most of these unemployed workers have had to reemploy themselves as pedicab drivers, taxi drivers, domestic workers, *peiliao*, or "entrepreneurs" who operate fruit or food stands. Frustrated by their inability to make a living through precarious employment, male workers have often returned to the factory to "*naoshi*" (make a fuss). Violence against management increased significantly in the late 1990s and early 2000s. In February 2002, a factory warehouse was broken into and raw materials worth 200,000

RMB were stolen, even though four gate guards were on duty at the time. The police were certain that this involved insider assistance. In another instance, an agitated laid-off worker sought revenge by reporting the "death" of the factory party secretary to the local crematory and asking for a corpse-collection van to be sent to this party secretary's home—as either a curse or a cruel joke that was intended for revenge and to garner public attention. Since 1998, several workers have committed suicide, leaving notes that blamed the loss of their jobs for their decisions to take their own lives. These suicides shocked the community in Changping and aroused popular resentment against privatization. The factory director has received numerous death threats over the phone. In response, he spread the word that he would place a rubber effigy of himself at the factory gate along with a stick so that workers could beat it to vent their anger. This tactic was a diversionary strategy intended to show his "helplessness" with regard to the ongoing privatization and his understanding of the price workers had paid.

3.1. Male workers reemployed as small business owners spent most of their time playing chess or table tennis.

In general, however, benevolence, in the form of *song wennuan*, has become the chosen method of relieving tension between management and male workers in this context of growing labor unrest. The program caters to men because since the mid-1990s the state has identified unemployed males as the embodiment of social instability in China (Yang 2010). These men were associated in the past with full-time employment, and their job losses are often perceived by the men themselves, by their communities, and by the government as an erosion of their manhood. The media also represent matters in this light. Thus, implicit in the principle of maintaining stability, which China's leaders have regularly invoked, is a strategy designed to govern men and masculinity (Yang 2010). Poverty relief (or reemployment) policies and practices are thus directed toward pacifying men and bolstering their sense of masculinity instead of addressing broader needs (i.e., challenges in the economy or gender equality). *Song wennuan* thus positions men and women differently as subjects and provides gendered incentives and services. For example, although women often receive home visit teams through *song wennuan*, it is the men in their households—their sons or husbands—who legitimize the household's eligibility for assistance. In other words, a laid-off man whom management perceives to be disgruntled and harbor *yinhuan* is the trigger that opens the door to the benevolence of *song wennuan*. From the perspective of the party, poverty relief offers the family the prospect of participating in building a harmonious society as long as that masculine negative potential (for physical violence, alcoholism, social unrest) is harnessed and redirected toward the market. Thus, benevolence, stability, and market participation are all tied together through a focus on dismantling masculine negative potential.

Renqing and the Affective State

Song wennuan entails the expression of feelings, or *renqing*, in a practice that resembles everyday uses of compassion and commiseration in Chinese village life and yet differs from this norm. In everyday life, *renqing*, or the sharing of human feelings, is the practice of mutual support and commiseration in the face of hardship. For example, the concept was often used in the 1980s to describe home visits to the sick by neighbors and family members in rural North China, a practice that was perceived to contribute to curing the sick (Kipnis 1997). Through home visits, *song wennuan* performs a similar therapeutic function, ostensibly the "healing" of the poor. But within this therapeutic framework, party staff problematize the urban poor and identify hardships as issues to be modified or cured. That is, the party organization intervenes in workers' social experiences of unemployment and poverty through the affective and therapeutic measures of *song wennuan*.

The government's default rhetoric of *song wennuan* is "we understand your suffering, but at least you still have the party to take care of you." *Song wennuan* thus transforms impoverished unemployed people from subjects with rights into objects of care. Its central practices of gifting and *renqing* obligate the poor to the state, promoting feelings and attitudes of gratitude that supposedly engender attitudes of nonresistance. Care and therapy are thus encompassed in the exercise of power. In fact, both the media and factory directors in Changping emphasized the affection and warmth of the party as a key feature of Chinese socialism. These socialist ethics putatively distinguish the management of unemployment in China from that undertaken in capitalist countries. However, the affective features of *renqing* actually render the party's authoritarian rule hegemonic as such state instances of compassion invoke everyday practices of *renqing* among ordinary people. *Renqing* serves to warm the hearts of laid-off workers and aims to make them more open to the ideological orientation of the government. Indeed, as Mayfair Yang (1988, 412) suggests, in contemporary China, the exercise of power is often achieved by providing for the needs and welfare of the population rather than by force or repression, because the satisfaction of needs is suffused with normative and political contents that ultimately reinforce the state. While the performance of *renqing* among ordinary people in everyday life strengthens social bonds by constructing a sense that individuals are not experiencing the world alone and that their condition can be shared (Kipnis 1997),[6] *song wennuan* enabled the state to insert its continued presence in people's lives even in the context of privatization and the market economy.

Song wennuan's evoking of *renqing* as a benevolent and sympathetic response to the hardship of laid-off workers also obscures the instrumentalization of gifting or *renqing*. The particular distribution of *renqing* through the program also validates male workers' senses of loss when they are laid off and reinscribes the legitimacy of male entitlement to material and emotional support from state-owned enterprises. The sense that males are entitled to such "gifts" and to various other goods and services from the government is still a basic principle of current local governance. *Song wennuan* thus constructs and reinforces the normative masculinity of workers as an affective and therapeutic technique for maintaining social and political stability.

Renqing performed by the party staff or manifested through *song wennuan* gifts does not amount to the expression of real personal feelings, but it conveys feelings from the party to the impoverished and affects members of disadvantaged households in ways that may lead them to identify with the party's interests. This conveyance of feelings resembles the working of affect.[7] Recent literature on the topic of affect often defines *emotion* as a subjective feeling that can be captured by narration and *affect* as the power to act, as intensity, or as a felt space for possibility or potentiality that cannot be narrated (Grossberg 1992, 81; Massumi 2002, 28). The compassion that emanates from the stabilizing strategies of the Chinese government, or *renqing* in *song wennuan*, works as a kind of transduction—the transmission of potential from one domain to another that can be felt. In this process, ideologies or social forces tap into personal feelings with the possible consequence that those ideologies or forces convict or interpellate subjects effectively (see Tie 2004). Here I see the difference between affect and emotion as a matter of degree. This resonates with Sianne Ngai's discussion of the intertwined relationship between affect and emotion:

> Affects are less formed and structured than emotions, but not lacking form or structure altogether; less "sociolinguistically fixed," but by no means code-free or meaningless; less "organized in response to our interpretations of situations," but by no means entirely devoid of organization or diagnostic powers (Ngai 2005, 27).

Like affect which entails both cognition and bodily sensation, the performance of *renqing* potentially allows the party to open the hearts of the poor and "move" them to feel the party's care and warmth. Although workers I interacted with as part of my research in Changping understood *song wennuan* as part of the political game—a disguised form of thought work or counseling—many of my informants also considered the practice of *renqing* or home visits to be a good gesture by the party, one they saw as at least recognizing the pain and suffering caused by state policies. In this sense, *renqing* is affective, affecting the hearts of the poor; it thus performs a healing function that partially soaks up the anger and frustration of the poor because of privatization.

The affective interactions between the party and impoverished workers in *song wennuan* are also shaped by changing dynamics of class and status in the post-Mao era. Although members of the founding class of the Chinese communist party once constituted a prestigious status group (Kraus 1977; Walder 1984), in the post-Mao era, they have been marginalized in a new class structure based on the market. Entrepreneurs and members of the managerial class are now the privileged groups. According to Weber (1978), status is social stratification based on prestige and social honor, while class is economic stratification based on market relations. Given this clash in the bases of hierarchy, the groups that were most respected under Maoist socialism are often perceived in post-Mao society as likely to hinder market development. This perception can render the working class stagnant, unfit for the market economy, and "rightfully" marginalized in the post-Mao era—at least from the perspective of the party. Yet the state also wishes to take advantage, somehow, of the human potential of laid-off workers by redirecting them toward the market. Such tensions shape both affective and coercive interactions between management and workers. Management treats workers not only in formal political terms but also through state-supported compassion and *renqing*. Workers react not merely in the form of rational association and organized protest but also through the affective-emotional continuum and what I call internal bargaining.

Performing Compassion and *Renqing*

Before the 2003 Chinese New Year, I joined a *song wennuan* home visit team composed of the deputy party secretary, Liu Ji, the chairman of the trade union, and the director of the residents' committee, a mixed-gender group. The team was visiting two families that were suffering because of unemployment and serious health issues. One family consisted of an elderly female retiree with diabetes and her youngest son, San'er, who was disgruntled because of an unresolved labor dispute with management. The other family included a laid-off worker and his wife, who had twice been diagnosed with breast cancer. These families were well known in the community for both their poverty and their confrontational behavior. Although both *song wennuan* home visits unfolded around the women, the men in both households were what motivated the interactions with the team, one a disgruntled son and the other a confrontational husband.

On each occasion, the director of the Beibiao community residents' committee accompanied the team. The director, who was traveling by tricycle, brought a gift set for each household that included a bottle of cooking oil, a bag of flour, and a bag of rice. On the way to the two households, he provided the others with information, not unlike the briefing a politician would receive before a public appearance. The more the leaders knew about each household, the more they could diagnose the situation in which the residents had become mired and show compassion. Similar to welfare programs in industrialized countries in which the family is a key site for the implementation of neoliberal welfare policies (Kingfisher 2002) and a source of social support for the poor (Schneider 2001) (though the notion of family in developed Western societies is different from the typical Chinese family, which also includes extended family members), family issues are major topics during these home visits. However, in these visits, party organizations encourage families to take care of themselves while simultaneously reminding them that the party is their ultimate provider.

Indeed, *song wennuan* practices familialize beneficiaries; membership in the family is what really matters and what qualifies for *song wennuan* (see Clarke 2004 on familialization in Western welfare states). Also, bringing the performance of *song wennuan* into people's homes, often just as they return from whatever work they may have been able to create, ensures that the party's compassion is made as visible, sensational, and emotionally poignant as possible. *Song wennuan* visits are timed to take place when the team is likely to encounter as many workers as possible.

As mentioned, both the deputy party secretary and the trade union chairman received basic training in counseling or social work as part of the large-scale movement called "Psychology Enters Communities." According to the trade union leader of the team I accompanied, the self-image individuals hold in their heart is the core of the self. Counseling, he argues, helps construct a self-reflective, self-cultivating, and self-striving subject (see Chapter 1). Discovering one's true self-image requires the "right" mirror, and self-reflexivity is believed to be key to establishing the "right" self-image. This self-reflexivity is therapeutic in the sense that it is designed to bring them the relief needed to get through life more easily. But self-reflexivity also orients people away from sociopolitical structures. In one of the *song wennuan* home visits in January 2003, the trade union leader encouraged a laid-off male worker who was despairing over his lack of money to reflect constructively on his situation. The "correct" mirror is one's own past—comparing what one ate and where one lived thirty years ago with their current living conditions instead of comparing one's current position to the rest of society. This reformulation of what is relevant to know about oneself has a distinct therapeutic bent in that it prescribes normative feelings about the present (gratefulness) and infers hope and optimism about the future. The rhetoric of looking back at oneself rehabilitates the subject by transitioning him or her from a place of despair into a terrain of hope and possibility. Workers who compare themselves with the new rich become discontented. To limit such critical comparisons and minimize discontent, party secretaries encourage workers to engage in autobiographical reflection.

During home visits, party staff also make other historical comparisons to demonstrate the party's continuity of care. When we visited San'er and his mother, as the mother walked us to the door, Liu Ji said to her:

> If you have any problem, just tell us. Even though the factory is not good, the economic situation [in general] is much better than before. In the past, you had something to eat; now, we won't let you go hungry. We still have the rent [income from renting factory facilities to the university].

These words reflect the party secretary's belief that socialist ethics can coexist with so-called capitalist rationality. Indeed, while highlighting *renqing* (official commiseration) as one of the advantages of socialism, Liu did not deny the role of market reform in improving the quality of life (i.e., renting out the factory space for profit) and seemed to embrace the contradictory logic of China's national narrative, which remains nominally socialist but is increasingly dominated by market ideology. To further pacify this particular poor and elderly woman, the party secretary adopted a discourse of inclusion (i.e., the use of "we"), connecting the present personal communication with a collective ideology of state benevolence and "shar-ing in the wealth." In addition, although this example focuses on an old woman (San'er's mother) as the receiver of *song wennuan*, the hidden mes-sage of the state comfort is directed at her disgruntled son with the inten-tion of staving off his negative potential for unrest.

Given that years of communist propaganda demonized capitalism as cold, rational, and inhuman, workers (and even some party members) in-voke the putative absence of *renqing* in capitalism to challenge state policies that prioritize profit-seeking market practices over social development. The deputy party secretary insisted that one purpose of *song wennuan* was to revive *renqing* in relations between the state and workers. However, since the mid-1990s, the privatization of state-owned enterprises has grad-ually diminished the role of the party in ideological orientation, result-ing in redirection toward psychotherapy. Party secretaries are ambivalent about privatization because they deduce that in a joint venture, such as the one where a Swiss company purchased some of the operation and assets of Beibiao, they might be marginalized or lose their jobs because the new hybrid of socialism and capitalism would be driven by a desire for profit rather than by ideological work or *renqing* practices. On the way back from our home visit to the woman with breast cancer, Liu Ji said:

> As with her situation, when we are involved in a joint venture, who has time to care for someone like her? Those capitalists only know how to make money. Who fusses about these *popo mama de shi* [old womanish things]? Are they concerned about *renqing*? But emotional investment is work too. Not everyone can do it well.

Party secretaries generally see themselves as experts who combine the practice of *renqing* with their ideological orientations and balance affective practices with rational decisions. At the time of my field work at least, Liu believed that she was good at performing *renqing* because she knew how to empathize and sympathize in her ideological work.

The gifting that is part of *song wennuan* inverts the normative Chinese practice of upward gift-giving, but it also draws on the traditional under-standing that receiving rather than giving is a symbol of prestige (Yang 1988; Yan 1996). In the local ethics of *renqing*, a gift from higher-ups indi-cates that the givers acknowledge that they are in the wrong and need to make amends (Anagnost 1997, 143). Gifting acts to restore any preexisting imbalance or injustice between the giver and the receiver. In contrast to normative gift-giving practices that minimize the value of gifts, *song wennuan* highlights the value of the gift, promoting it on an ideological level as a token of the regard of the party. The healing function of *song wennuan*, which emphasizes the care of the party, is complemented by the reassertion of material hierarchy already implicit in the notion of therapy itself: just as the therapist is in the position to offer expertise, the party is in the position to give. In both contexts, in-kind reciprocity is impossible and the appropriate response for those positioned to receive is to provide gratitude.

However, gratitude involves more than feelings of appreciation, warmth, and a desire to return the favor; it also involves the structured position of indebtedness (Hochschild 2003, 104–118). Because of the devastation created by privatization, "gratitude" is easily solicited from low-income families and poor pensioners who receive *song wennuan*. The indebtedness of these families is a starting point for the stabilization that is a goal of the party. Moreover, it positions the male members of the household as perhaps grateful enough to accept even the most precarious labor if it serves the new market economy. *Song wennuan* thus prepares unemployed men to become human resources for a new time and serves as a party mechanism for using the human potential or human capital of impoverished families. The gratitude of the woman—San'er's mother Liu Ji addressed was fleeting, and it ended immediately after the above-quoted segment with a discourse of *kuqiong* (crying poverty, see below).

The Politics of "Crying Poverty"

At Beibiao, *kuqiong*, or "crying poverty," is a strategy workers use to exaggerate the disadvantages and difficulties that characterize their lives. The intent is to elicit sympathy and obtain resources that cannot normally be accessed. Recently, *kuqiong* has gained popularity as the widening income gap has polarized this formerly "egalitarian" working-class community (in which at least gender-based inequality existed).[8] Take as an example San'er's mother, a retired woman who suffered from diabetes. After giving her gifts, the chairman of the trade union said, "This is a token of the regard of the party committee, and we wish you a happy Spring Festival."

The woman bowed several times to show her gratitude. She then said with tears in her eyes, "Thank you. Thank you. We have no single penny left, nothing to eat at home." This is typical *kuqiong*. By exaggerating her poverty and crying in gratitude, San'er's mother highlights the value of the gift sent by the party, implicitly asking for more support.

To demonstrate the party's warmth, the visiting party secretary usually finds topics to chat about with the beneficiary. This informal, everyday genre of chat appears to operate outside the structures of power, a symbolic expression of temporary class solidarity. But these conversations, which encompass details of people's everyday existence, are the very sites where power is exercised in the post-Mao era (Yang 1988; Dai 1996; Rofel 1999). Chats usually focus on private and family issues to show the depth of the party's care. The following dialogue between party secretary Liu Ji and San'er's mother exemplifies this discursive strategy. When Liu asked about the mother's illness, her medication, and the filial piety of her children, San'er's mother responded with *kuqiong*, representing herself as the most unfortunate mother in the world. None of her three sons were filial: the two married sons did not come to see her and the youngest son could not marry because of a work-related injury and his unemployment status and therefore could not end his mother's anxiety.[9]

> *San'er's mother:*   They [her elder sons] did not give me money for several months. I didn't see them. They should come to see me, if not giving me money. I said to San'er, "San'er, you go to see what happened to your two brothers."
>
> *Liu Ji:*   [In an authoritative tone] **They** did not come; **we** come. I'll talk to them. What's wrong with them? No matter how busy they are, they should come to see the elderly. I understand your feelings; last month when I was busy and didn't go to see my mother, she was lonely. Seeing me, she even cried.

Liu Ji had notable communication skills and was known to be able to "talk the dead into life." Here Liu used two discourses to respond to the woman's complaints about her difficulties and to end her *kuqiong*: one of empathy, the other of authority. Using her own mother as an example, Liu showed that the phenomenon of which San'er's mother complained was common. Henderson identifies three basic meanings associated with empathy: feeling the emotion of another, understanding the experience of another, and feeling sympathy or compassion for another. The last of these can lead to action to alleviate the pain of the other. Empathy constructs intersubjectivity, which is not the same as being absorbed by the other. Rather, it is about the relationship between self and other (Henderson 1987, 1582, 1584). In this instance, Liu's empathy not only demonstrates cultural or social solidarity (i.e., sharing adherence to common norms of treatment of elderly parents and common challenges in fulfilling those norms), it also symbolically and temporarily restores the eroded relationship between the party-state and workers.

Compassion, empathy, or sympathy can nevertheless be a form of othering when they reinforce superiority or authority and justify interventions into others' lives via welfare or humanitarian acts (McElhinny 2010). Such othering is evident in Liu's discourse condemning the two sons and anticipating a possible future interrogation of them about their moral liability. Although there is an apparent erosion of filial piety associated with the commodification of life in the market economy in this community, it is still a norm for married children to go back to their parents' home regularly to visit and offer pocket money. When Liu said, "They did not come; we come," she affirmed that in contrast to the "neglectful" sons, the party was fulfilling its responsibility (and perhaps even going beyond what is morally required) to take care of the poor and the old. In this way, subjects are (or will be) incited to "step up" to their rightful duties to take care of themselves and their families. This is an instance where even after crying poverty has occurred, the pressure is still on the family to feel "grateful" to the state in such a way that the exchange redirects the energies of the poor. By condemning the two sons and promising a future interrogation, Liu positioned the primary site of responsibility for elder care with the family. Indeed, breaches of filial responsibility warrant interrogation in this community. She thus legitimized and enforced the priority of filial piety and family responsibility over *song wennuan* for taking care of the old.[10] Meanwhile, she also reinforced the notion that the government had the authority to make sure that family members accept these responsibilities. Furthermore, the intertwined discourses of empathy and authority construct an image of the party as a folkloric *fumu guan* (parent official) acting in the interests of the masses. In this sense the party emulates the role of an enlightened parent (or therapeutic expert) in guiding and supervising its child (or client) who is striving to gain the skills to navigate the world on his or her own. By defusing the discursive practice of *kuqiong*, the party pacified newly marginalized individuals and mitigated agitated workers' potential threats to governance.

During the home visit, Liu Ji inquired about San'er mother's health, which reminded the woman of her medical expenses. At that point the discourse shifted from *kuqiong* to bargaining for assistance. The grounds for bargaining include workers' sense of entitlement that derives from the fact that they supposedly had employment for life that was cut short by state-led privatization.

Liu immediately switched to a formal tone and invoked the party's principle of *minzhu jizhong zhi* (democratic centralism), a notorious bureaucratic delaying tactic: "We'll discuss your case and make a collective decision at a meeting with all the party committee present."[11] By appealing to this practice, Liu not only postponed the need for an immediate decision but also left the question open for further manipulation. Then, to justify the reduction of social provisions for workers, she practiced her own form of *kuqiong*:

> As you know, our watch movements don't make money. All the income is from the rent. But for the sake of stability, the factory can't close. I'm not *kuqiong*. This is the reality. If I present your request to management [at an inopportune moment], it may irritate them.

Such strategic *kuqiong*, including the denial that it is even being invoked, is often performed by management to handle "unreasonable" requests from retirees or laid-off workers who face loss of status and access to the traditional public welfare structure that has been compromised during the years of privatization and the growing market economy.

The Politics of *Song Wennuan*: Who Are the Deserving Citizens?

Because *song wennuan* gives special attention to male laid-off workers, impoverishment is not the only criterion for being chosen to receive assistance. No matter how needy they might be, women and rural migrants are unlikely to be prioritized in *song wennuan* because management sees them as less threatening to social and political stability. *Song wennuan* is primarily about stabilizing society and steering the impoverished toward employment in the market.

Rural migrants constitute the majority of the factory workforce. They are hired to do the heaviest work but receive the lowest salaries. They are excluded from the social security system, from subsidized factory housing, and from poverty-relief programs. To obtain any basic rights, migrants must make desperate attempts to confront management. Consider the following illustration. In 2002, a migrant worker who had worked for the factory for almost ten years was assigned a separate room in which he could live with his wife. But in 2003, he was evicted from the room so the factory could rent it out. Unsuccessful in his initial negotiations to be allowed to stay, the migrant worker broke into the board room where management was working with representatives of the Swiss company on the potential joint venture. He accused the members of management who were present of violating his basic human rights, saying, "Peasant workers are human beings too." Perhaps he understood how sensitive the issue of human rights was in Western criticisms of China and thus invoked this framework in front of foreigners. In the end, he did succeed in securing his room. He later explained his success this way: "A bare-footed person is not afraid of those who wear shoes." As a subaltern, he could be fearless because he had nothing to lose: this is the power of the powerless. Note, however, that in this case, while the migrant worker was rewarded for his destabilizing tactics, even after this outburst he was not given counseling or provided with benevolence in the form of debt-inducing gifts. Were the migrant worker an urban male (state worker), the management's response would have been *song wennuan* and *renqing*. However, as a marginalized rural worker he was ignored until he made such a fuss that his immediate needs were attended to. But there was no attempt to draw him into the relations of gratitude for state benevolence that comes with *song wennuan*.

Another group whose poverty management is often downplayed is women. In general, women are more economically disadvantaged than men because they suffer unemployment to a greater extent due to gender bias in layoffs (Wang 2003) and because they are more likely to have sole custody of dependent children. There is also a tendency to naturalize women's poverty in this community. Yet with priority given to laid-off men, *song wennuan* reinforces, or even creates anew inequalities and possibly tensions among the urban poor.

For example, when I was conducting interviews in a residential yard at Beibiao, a woman mistook me for a journalist, asking me whether I knew of any free legal aid services for the poor. She told me that her husband had been killed in a traffic accident while running a small business. Because the police judged that her husband was conducting his business at an "illegitimate" location, she was only symbolically compensated by the other party to the accident. As an early retiree, she had to support her son on her own with a meager pension. When I asked her whether she received any assistance from the factory, she said:

> He died in December [2002], just the time for *song wennuan*, but no one [from management] even stopped by to ask whether I was all right.... Who cares for me? ... If I'm that kind of person fussing around, they will definitely pay attention.

In the context of the government's emphasis on stability, *song wennuan*, putatively a benevolent redistributive remedy is biased toward benefiting and pacifying potentially destabilizing males of urban backgrounds. This gendered and classed redistribution in *song wennuan* resonates with what Nancy Fraser observes about struggle against injustice in Western capitalist societies. She suggests that virtually every such struggle implies demands for both redistribution and recognition; socioeconomic and cultural injustices are rooted in processes and practices that systematically disadvantage some groups vis-à-vis others (Fraser 1995, 72).

A crucial element of politics is the struggle to define social reality and interpret people's needs (Yang 1988; Fraser 1994). In my interview with Liu Ji, she indicated that she knew the widow who had asked me about legal aid. Liu said she believed that the woman *had* received financial compensation from the accident; therefore she was not on the residents' committee's recommendation list for *song wennuan*. On another occasion, Liu implied that the factory had to distance itself from this kind of woman (single mothers), as there was a risk that they would develop dependence on the factory. This comment revealed a gendered subtext to the notion of dependence. By refusing to acknowledge this woman's needs and the vulnerability of others in similar situations, *song wennuan* implicitly constructs settled, able-bodied, male subjects as most able to achieve independence in a market economy—that is, to be valuable human capital—and therefore as most deserving of state support.

Liu's response belied the putative aim of *song wennuan* as that of sending the warmth of the party to the poor. Even though the widow had been financially compensated, being left alone and struggling with single motherhood had been devastating for her. This woman's exclusion from party care exemplifies the view that women have nothing of value to give back in exchange for state care. Their subservience is presumed. Poor women's "dependent tendencies" are thus effectively construed as a permanent defect that is immune to socioeconomic restructuring. While in general marginalized women are perceived to harbor boundless *qianli* and are in an optimal position for retraining and reemployment, *qianli* is an elusive notion that is not attached to all women. The government perceives some women (like the one I met) to be not self-reliant and self-striving, as individuals who may develop the habit of depending on the government for their livelihood.

Conclusion: Redistribution or Restratification?

A 2003 news report titled "Local Government Sent Chinese New Year's Gifts: Jobs" describes how the Yantai municipal government of Shandong Province gave jobs or low-rent housing to the unemployed through *song wennuan*:

> Party Chief Yan Longzhu said, "Every year, we send those in financial difficulty one bag of flour and 200 *yuan* as New Year's gifts, and then follow this by a crowd of journalists [who report on the good deeds]. I feel so ashamed! Can we send those in need jobs rather than performing those rituals?" Then the government echoed this call and started to prepare "New Year's gifts" by readjusting posts and arranging low-rent housing. On Jan. 3, 2003, a laid-off worker, Wang Zhifang, received a special New Year's gift—a job as a member of the cleaning staff at the Labor and Employment Office in Yantai. Another unemployed worker, Wang Shengyang, received a key to a low-rent apartment. A warm Spring Festival was waiting for his family. In total, 127 keys to low-rent housing and more than 600 jobs were sent to unemployed workers in Yantai [this year]. (Xu 2003)

The editorial summed up by saying "one bag of flour and 200 *yuan*" can only temporarily solve workers' problems, but jobs are *heng wen* (lasting warmth). *Song wennuan*, when applied in this manner, resembles the welfare-to-work programs in the United States that provide assistance for the impoverished and move the unemployed into the paid labor force (Schneider 2001, 705). But unlike those programs, which attempt to re-integrate the poor into mainstream society, *song wennuan* highlights jobs as novel gifts, a new way to promote stability (Blecher 2004). These jobs are often temporary, unstable, low-paying, and dead-end service positions created just for *song wennuan*. Nonetheless, the rhetoric surrounding their inclusion in the program is intended to highlight the compassion of the party, which however serves as an affective and therapeutic mode of control. These jobs involve reciprocity—requiring the impoverished to repay the mercy of the government through nonresistance. The poor must acquiesce to the terms suggested by the ruling party. For many workers, these jobs are deemed patronizing and disempowering, positions that create a new form of unfreedom.

The current policies of the Chinese government increasingly reveal a free-market ideology that supports unfettered privatization. This stance has cost millions of workers their jobs in the state sector and their access to public welfare, medical care, and pension rights. Ostensibly a program of redistribution, *song wennuan* purports to reduce poverty and inequality and "heal" those who have been victimized by systemic change. By upholding the values of everyday traditions of *renqing* and reviving the practice of *kuqiong* to recognize workers' grievances, *song wennuan* highlights the party's continued commitment to socialist ethics and its obligation to ameliorate urban poverty, thus (symbolically at least) extending the life of the socialist system.

However, as a state-orchestrated ritual, *song wennuan* is a key arena for identity and power struggles. By defining who benefits and who is excluded, *song wennuan* creates new forms of inequity among the impoverished and intensifies social stratification. The program is deeply plagued by its policy of placating unemployed male workers in an effort to stabilize society instead of taking care of all of those in need, including women and rural migrants. The program uses *renqing* as a therapeutic resource in the form of gifts to dampen the hostility of the poor and maintain stability. But the gift-giving in *song wennuan* is a method of surveillance to bring home to the poor that their official well-wishers are keeping track of them and their mindset. Chinese politicians have increasingly found that the rhetoric of therapy incorporated in the practices of *song wennuan* not only increases party popularity but also provides a powerful legitimate entrée into peoples' lives, enhancing the state's power and control over the population. At the same time, gift-giving puts recipients in the position of debtors to the state. In addition, in exchange for small tokens, they are asked to redirect their gaze inward and find hope for the future. In so doing, *song wennuan* repositions beneficiaries, especially if they are men, to return to work in a new marketplace and prepares them for a role as human capital that fulfills its positive potential in the market economy.

By combining propaganda and charity and by weaving together narratives of suffering, *renqing*, and a broader discourse of stability and benevolence, *song wennuan* serves a political purpose that supports the new market economy. It exemplifies China's transitional politics, cloaking capitalism in socialist forms. The Chinese version of neoliberalism does not so much appeal to Western liberal doctrines as tinkers with preexisting social, cultural, and discursive categories in promoting market development, exemplifying the dialectics of *biantong*. The resulting new class relations based on neoliberal market logic and the rising political and legal status of the new rich intensify an already sharp social polarization to a degree that is unprecedented in China's socialist history. No matter how rapidly China's economy develops, it will be difficult to narrow income gaps and solve the problems caused by the new forms of poverty. In the next chapter, I will focus on the dynamics of combining counseling and thought work in governing the "new" urban poor at the Beibiao residents' community.

4

Thought Work and Talk Therapy

Social workers allow clients to speak, to tell their stories, and offer them
enough information so that they have their own freedom of choice; we don't
choose for them, judge them, or criticize them.

—Zhang Mo, professor of social work, 2011

Kai zhan tanxin huodong, zhege fangfa hen hao [Developing the activity of
tanxin is a good method (of political work)].

—Mao Zedong, People's Daily, June 29, 1967

In June 2010, a party secretary turned community counselor surnamed
Luo, whom I met at a social work training session in Beijing, indicated
that instead of using the term *xinli zixun* (psychological counseling), she
used *tanxin* to refer to her new synergized counseling or talk therapy.

What I deal with every day is normal, healthy people, not like psychiatrists,
doctors who treat real mentally ill patients like schizophrenics. My work is
to help them connect to a self that they are familiar with, let them accept the
social reality and move on with their lives. Using the language of Western
counseling is too far-out in my work. You have to localize it [counseling]
and come up with your own terms and counseling methods that ordinary
people can understand.

Indeed, people can grasp new information only if they can interpret it,
casting it in terms of their own knowledge. Luo invoked the form of a

familiar type of mitigated thought work—*tanxin* to do "counseling." This is not just a process of translating a Western psychotherapeutic method into a Chinese way of counseling; it also involves a form of *biantong*. Counseling is thus a new incarnation of *tanxin*; the ruling party has appropriated *tanxin* (literally translated as "talking heart" or "heart-to-heart talk"), which was originally a genre of private discourse and then an ideological ritual (Anagnost 1997; Yang 2007). In 1967, Mao Zedong stated that *tanxin* was a good method for political work. Indeed, *tanxin* or *cuxi tanxin* (a heart-to-heart exchange in which each interlocutor has their knees facing the other's) was a more friendly, open, and in-depth process of ideological orientation than typical thought work, which focused on criticism and self-criticism. Unlike typical thought work, which many in Changping perceived as twisting one's views and erasing one's individuality, talk therapy is intended to nurture creativity and individuality and actualize potential. At the Beibiao community, *tanxin* can refer to a face-to-face everyday conversation between colleagues, an interaction between a superior and subordinate(s) that is designed to achieve consensus and nurture solidarity, or a placatory ritual developed for management to "tame" unemployed men who presumably harbor *yinhuan* and who have returned to their community center to display their grievances and anger and to bargain with the residents' committee for reemployment or other benefits. These male workers have a sense of entitlement as the ideological representatives of Maoist socialism and as pillars of the former socialist planned economy.

Tanxin now also refers to other practices, including psychological counseling and soliciting public opinion through dialogues between the state and the masses. As an example of the latter, the 1996 best-selling Chinese book titled in translation *Having a Heart-to-Heart Talk with the General Secretary of the Party* is an explication of former president Jiang Zemin's policy of soliciting "public opinion" (Fewsmith 2001, 198) and recreating the relationship between the state and society that has been eroded by economic restructuring. *Tanxin* is also a popular name for psychological health centers and psychology hotlines in China. For example, *Dr. Xu's Psychology Hotline*, a weekly radio talk show on Beijing Education Radio, is referred to as *tanxin*. The founder, Dr. Xu Haoyuan, stresses that the goal of the program is to promote public awareness of mental health issues in the present context of the poor mental health of Chinese people. However, mental illness in China is highly stigmatized; people typically share information about mental illness with close friends or family members instead of seeking professional advice (Ou 2003, 10).

Using *tanxin* to promote mental health is similar to how Luo described her practice of localizing psychological counseling. As O'Hanlon and Wilk (1987) suggest, talk therapy is differentiated from other types of social interaction more by its goals than by its overt content or structure:

> "A fly on the wall" who did not know we were doing psychotherapy would not necessarily suspect that that was what we were doing: he would see and hear only an ordinary conversation. What defines the conversation as psychotherapy is simply our goal in conducting the conversation. (177)

The quotation captures similarities in two types of interactions that are, however, distinctly directed. For Luo, *tanxin* represents the intersection between thought work and talk therapy. It is a way of making use of the skills of veteran ideological workers in helping people adapt to the new circumstances of a market economy.

In this chapter I examine psychosocial workers' creative and synergistic use of both Chinese and Western therapeutic methods to facilitate the implementation of ideologies and practices promoted by state-led programs, including those on reemployment, counseling, and poverty relief. These therapeutic strategies include narrative or story therapy (White 1995; Dwivedi 1997; Lieblich et al. 2004), rational emotive behavior therapy (Ellis 1971), and client-centered therapy (Rogers 1995).[1] These forms of psychotherapy share an emphasis on telling and retelling stories about one's life (Lieblich et al. 2004, 4). Psychosocial workers in Changping allow clients to tell their stories, and they themselves also use stories infused with directives about love, power, and healing to let clients see parallels with their own struggles and find hope for recovery, healing, or growth. Through story therapy and the dialogic nature of the therapeutic process, these community psychosocial workers view their work as a social process as much as they see it as a psychological process.

Psychosocial workers in Beijing believe the key difference between rational emotive behavior therapy and client-centered therapy is the role of counselors in the client's therapeutic process. Through rational emotive behavior therapy, counselors help clients identify and overcome "unrealistic" and "irrational" feelings and actions or "irrational" beliefs about themselves and the world in order to alter illogical premises and negative thinking patterns that create mental distress (Ellis 1991b, 1993). Many counselors in Beijing feel that rational emotive behavior therapy resembles the method of thought work.[2] While rational emotive behavior therapy presumes that the individual is a vulnerable subject in need of expert help, client-centered counselors in Beijing most often assume the individual has the resources and inner strength to develop the cure for his or her mental disorder or emotional distress.

The work of community counselors in Changping, following Carl Rogers, tends to use client-centered therapy, allotting minimal agency to the counselor while emphasizing the self of the client and his or her speaking agency. Counselors serve as animators (those who voice the words of others; Goffman 1979) in order to give a client full speaking agency and help them realize their "true" selves. Counselors attempt to depersonalize themselves for the purposes of therapy and to become "the client's other self." That is, as therapeutic techniques have developed in Changping, the speech of the counselor becomes part of the client's own voice. Counselors thus help clients highlight how they think, feel, and speak in ways that make them feel accepted and unique. Developing feelings of acceptance and uniqueness is believed to be key in deep caring and in forming attitudes that are essential for actualizing positive potential. Both professional counselors and community psychosocial workers I interviewed in Beijing call this process *ziwo zhiliao* (self-therapy). The primary tenet of this therapy is the principle of *jiena* (acceptance), or full acceptance of the client as a human being with his or her individuality, not just acceptance of what he or she says and does. This orientation differs from thought work, which often denied individuality.

In Changping, psychosocial workers strategically choose elements and precepts of these therapeutic methods and synergize them in their counseling in order to maximize therapeutic and ideological effects. Gender plays a significant role in counseling. For example, although psychosocial workers who adopt Carl Rogers's client-centered, nondirective approach presume that the individual should tap into their inner authority and resources for solutions to their own problems, they (particularly female counselors) also strategically offer moralizing direction and intervention to women. A more exclusively nondirective approach is mainly used with male workers (particularly by female counselors). These distinctions are partly attributable to a gendered notion of potentiality—laid-off men presumably embody negativity and resistance so psychosocial workers give them space to develop themselves in a way that supports their feelings of mastery and independence. Women, however, are perceived as more willing to take direction, and therefore female counselors offer more advice when working with them.

In general, the nondirective approach to men's problems and the lack of emotional and institutional support for the unemployed of both genders renders former state workers vulnerable to intensified exploitation and market competition. The nondirective approach resonates with the government's current promotion of self-care and self-reliance in the wake of economic restructuring. However, clients have challenged this mode of assistance by explicitly requesting direction and quick-fix solutions to their problems. This is a manifestation of workers' continued feelings of entitlement and dependence on the guidance of the state or other authorities (Qian et al. 2002; Zhang 2014). To capture the changes in workers' experiences, in this chapter, I focus on fluid aspects of subjectivity that are acted upon, are modified, and can be improved through counseling. I examine how the behavior and the inner workings of individuals have become sites for well-defined therapeutic and political projects (e.g., reemployment and counseling; see Eghigian et al. 2007, 2) aimed at redressing social and economic deficiencies. I further investigate how the processes of self-formation shape subjects, both clients and their psychosocial counselors.

In this chapter I examine the paradoxical features of thought work and its recent incarnation in psychological counseling in order to interrogate the recent integration of techniques and precepts of positive psychology and psychotherapy in the governing of the unemployed in China. I suggest that psychosocial workers in Changping, while distinguishing their efforts from typical thought work that subdues individuality, have adopted the ritual of *tanxin* to conduct talk therapy as a way of nurturing creativity and helping workers actualize their potential in the market economy. I describe local theories of personality and psychological dysfunction that are used to justify therapeutic techniques and analyze whether therapeutic methods based on these theories are efficacious in managing unemployed workers. I address different ideologies of speaking subjectivities, including gender differences that emerge in counseling and thought work, in order to examine new technologies of the self and of governing.

Ideologies of Speaking Subjectivity in Counseling and Thought Work

Although both counseling and thought work are ideological apparatuses that structure or mediate people's interactions and render them legible according to dominant signifying schemes (Massumi 2002), community residents' committee members in Changping who have been informally trained in counseling or social work often distinguish their counseling as "depoliticized," "humane," and "scientific." In thought work, party staff often had full speakerhood, through which they transmitted and imposed policies and official ideologies to the rank and file. Now residents' committee members and psychosocial workers claim to have minimum speakerhood in order to give clients space for expressing themselves and help them actualize their potential. This transformation in speaking subjectivity and therapeutic methods puts responsibility on the individual for their problems and for their "cure" in a process that parallels the decline in public support for workers who have lost jobs as a result of privatization. Counselors, following Rogers's nondirective approach, enable individuals to speak for themselves, rely on themselves, and solve their own problems. They do this resonating with political motives to shield the party from its responsibility for the destruction created by economic restructuring but also, in part, for more complex political and humanitarian motives: to enable the individual to construct a responsible and self-reliant self fit for the market economy.

Since psychosocial workers are often (former) party staff, their talk therapy engages epistemological practices shaped by ideological commitment. Ideologies are not arbitrary beliefs; they reproduce relations of power legitimized by social and cultural institutions or by community discourse (Madigan 2011). Both thought work and counseling are discursive practices and "rituals" in which people are assigned different roles for acting and speaking. Foucault sees discourse (religious, juridical, therapeutic, and political) as associated with the functioning of ritual in designating roles to participants or speakers:

> Ritual defines the qualifications required of the speaker (of who in dialogue, interrogation or recitation should occupy which position and formulate which type of utterance); it lays down gestures to be made, behaviour,

circumstances and the whole range of signs that must accompany discourse; finally, it lays down the supposed, or imposed significance of the words used, their effect upon those to whom they are addressed, the limitations of their constraining validity (Foucault 1972, 225).

To consider different roles of speaking in both counseling and thought work, I engage Goffman's (1979) conceptualization of speakerhood. Goffman (1979) breaks down the notion of the speaker into three functional nodes in a communication system: the animator, the author, and the principal. The animator is the talking machine, a body engaged in the delivery and performance of speaking. The author is someone who makes the speech and sets the sentiments that are being expressed. The principal is not merely the speaker of words but also the one whose position is established and identified by the words—the one who commits to what he or she says.

In typical thought work in work units, party staff usually combined the three roles; they were the animator, the author, and the principal of what they delivered. Although workers were established as the recipients of ideology or policies, party staff had full speakerhood and were committed to what they spoke. Their full speakerhood was reinforced by the all-encompassing work-unit system, the institutional basis that enabled party staff to deliver what they promised to workers.[3] That is, thought work did not stop at talk.[4] Party authorities could take pragmatic, institutional measures to implement what had been imposed or promised during the talk. For example, at Beibiao, a woman worker surnamed Wu told me that in March 1992 her workshop party secretary invited her to *tanxin* and persuaded her to donate blood in order to achieve a certain quota assigned in a political mission by the local government. Wu was thinking of getting pregnant at that time and did not want to donate blood. But the party secretary did thought work with her by promising that donating blood would immediately qualify her for party membership. Wu finally succumbed to this persuasion. As a result, her application to join the party, which she had submitted one year earlier, was approved (see the section in Chapter 1 on Self-Reflexivity and the Regime of the Self for a version of this story told from the perspective of a former party secretary). Wu told me in 2007, "Nowadays, who cares about political missions? No one can talk you into donating blood or other things if you don't want to. Who cares about the party nowadays? And the residents' committee has no power [administrative or legal] to force people to do so now."

In developing an alternative to thought work, psychosocial workers in Changping today emphasize *tanxin*, a putative nondirective approach, with residents. This approach emphasizes talk because counselors have little institutional power or obligation to reach out to their clients and satisfy their pragmatic needs. However, psychosocial workers do not implement measures of "Western" counseling imbued with a professional aura (e.g., like those on the *Psychology Talk Show*). Because they are deeply embedded in the community, the psychosocial workers of today tend to adopt a synthesized and holistic approach. In addition to strategic listening, psychosocial workers also adopt affective or *renqing*-based approaches (based on human feelings) that are rooted in people's sociocultural contexts.

Shao Wen is a party secretary on a neighboring residents' committee who retired from the factory. As she indicates below, on the one hand, she showed therapeutic sensitivity by giving people full speaking subjectivity; on the other hand, she emphasizes that such voice-giving practices should not be experienced as a distancing mechanism by the client.

> Now I mainly listen, giving those who come to talk with me a full opportunity to express themselves. [I] allow them to tell their full stories. In the past, we talked and interpreted, then imposed on people what we believed was true without letting people speak on their own. I myself experienced such suffocating situations when my superior talked to me without giving me an opportunity to explain myself. The party was then the supreme authority. . . . Indeed, my own voice is not supposed to dominate, and I simply channel the client's voice. But you cannot do that in a manner that is overly professional, as that sounds too cold, too aloof, because most of my clients are also my or my husband's former co-workers or neighbors.

While highlighting her new professional aura in counseling, Shao also used this account to emphasize her social and cultural therapy, the unique notion of the self (in a network), self-reliance, and self-governance in the Chinese context. In contemporary China the self is considered to be an interdependent unit defined in relation to others, as was the case in the past. The individual has to begin with himself or herself, but he or she can only construct that self in the context of a network (Worm 2010, 224). In other words, one becomes an individual through network relations.[5] This is why the current trend toward individualization promoted in counseling in Changping does not necessarily translate into more agency for the individual.

This chapter engages studies that focus on the self in a network in the Confucian tradition (see Kipnis 2012). Appropriate analytical categories in this tradition would be persons-in-relations and intersubjective relationships (Ho and Chiu 1998). Indeed, the Chinese concept of personhood is inherently social (Hsu 1985). Andrew Kipnis (2012) calls on us to see individualism as a myth, a structure of feeling, or a problematic. Kipnis considers the "rise" of individualism to be more of a psychological problematic than an absolute social fact. He argues that "the individual psyche has never been governed solely by socially isolated individuals. It is the site of conflicts between numerous contradictory discourses, emotions, and urges, a site where the social contradictions of Chinese modernity manifest themselves as particular structures of feeling, and a target of the governing actions of a wide range of social actors" (7–8).

As Markus and Kitayama (2003, 10) observe, in Eastern cultures agency is formed through socially important others and institutions in which individuals experience themselves as interdependent, as members of families, communities, and social groups. They argue that this relational selfhood is characterized by conjoint agency. In such agency, being-in-action is carried out by agents who do not experience themselves as "free" from others. "Actions thus require the consideration and anticipation of the perspective of others and are a consequence of the fulfilment of the reciprocal obligations or expectations."[6] Most social workers in Changping are sensitive to this culturally specific notion of agency, yet the collapse of work units has reduced this type of interdependence.

The emerging individualism in China can be experienced positively or negatively (see Castells 1997). Release from traditional social ties (i.e., work units) can be positive, increasing an individual's autonomy in the management of his or her own life if he or she still maintains strong, interdependent links in other networks that provide security and solidarity. However, a person may also experience negative individualism. For example, when support is withdrawn but there is still a responsibility for self-governance, an individual must adapt within a new framework in which he or she has no connections that would support that success or make it possible. In such instances, individualism becomes political isolation (exclusion from social relations of interdependence) and social vulnerability (Crespo and Serrano 2010). This is the case for most laid-off workers at Beibiao, who have been excluded from decision making during the privatization process and cast off from the state-owned enterprise to the market. Even though community psychosocial workers like Shao Wen claimed to adopt a holistic therapeutic approach (both psychological and sociocultual therapy) to workers' problems, workers still felt helpless, betrayed, and vulnerable in the tumultuous period of transformation from work units to the private sector.

Tanxin, Subjectification, and Rational Emotive Behavior Therapy

Thought work played a key role in regulating urban workers in work units up to the mid-1990s (see Rofel 1999; Brady 2008). As mentioned, although many workers despised thought work as coercive and manipulative, they are now nostalgic about certain elements of the practice, for example, the attention to pragmatic problem-solving and the "intimate" relationship established in thought work between the party and workers.

Thought work and talk therapy make different assumptions about human nature and the world, although both try to change the subjective reality of the client. Thought work is predominantly founded on Marxism, Leninism, and Mao Zedong's thought and on local cultural resources. It is a political form of attention to state subjects. Talk therapy, by contrast, is based on Western psychology. Counselors in Beijing sometimes view *tanxin* as a mitigated form of thought work that is loosely identified with Albert Ellis's rational emotive behavior therapy. Rational emotive behavior therapy is action-oriented and is designed to cure by helping clients manage their emotions, cognitions, and behaviors. Based on the assumption that the way people feel is largely influenced by how they think, rational emotive behavior therapy is used to detect and treat "irrational" and "unrealistic" beliefs and actions or incomplete ethics.[7] However, while counselors often feel that their efforts are depoliticized, in general, talk therapy engages epistemological practices shaped by ideological commitments. Indeed, definitions of irrational, illogical, or problematic beliefs, actions, and emotions are political.

In talk therapy, the counselor confronts the "irrational" beliefs of the client and the client defends them. In this process, if it is productive, the client realizes that the beliefs at issue underlie their current problems and thus achieve a new subjective reality. This new understanding opens up the possibility for healing. However, it is important to examine which beliefs are designated "irrational" or "unrealistic" and which are "rational" or "healthy" (Ellis 1967). This method helps clients reflect on past experiences and feelings and leads to insight and the release of emotion (Rogers and Wood 1974). Opening up one aspect of a client's life to the counselor establishes one subjective reality or, more precisely, an intersubjective reality between client and counselor. The intersubjective reality changes when the process of conversation shifts from an expectation of direction on the part of the client to a process in which the client's (inter)subjective reality can be negotiated.

Unlike thought work, current counseling highlights the potential in human self-actualization. It putatively liberates and actualizes the growth potential of individuals. Indeed, governing through the psychological imaginary often means governing through the freedom and aspirations of subjects (Rose 1996). But a paradox emerges when subjects have to surrender themselves to external expertise in order to be free and happy. A therapeutic strategy such as rational emotive behavior therapy enjoins subjects to actively participate in their own subjectification while experts guarantee the framing of that process within the superior wisdom of psychological professionals and self-help gurus. This resonates with Foucault's notion of subjectification, or the ways human beings turn themselves into subjects. This involves processes of self-formation in which the person actively participates. Through certain techniques people initiate their own active self-formation in an action of self-control (Foucault 1982). That is, people monitor and conduct themselves according to their interpretations of cultural norms and meanwhile they seek out external authority figures such as psychotherapists for guidance. Foucault wrote:

> As both participants and subjects of this power through knowledge, we are judged, condemned, classified, determined in our undertaking, destined to a certain mode of living or dying, as a function of the true discourses which are the bearers of the specific effects of power. (Foucault 1982, 94)

Foucault's conception shows the inseparability of power and knowledge in self-formation. In Changping, self-formation has been depicted and experienced in disparate ways over time. Heelas and Lock (1981) term the idea of different ways of experiencing self-formation and the associated practices "indigenous psychologies" that make sense of human thought, feeling, and behavior. Indigenous psychologies allow people to cope with changing labels of normal or abnormal, sane or insane. They are the frameworks in which bodies, minds, or "hearts" in the Chinese context are represented in local knowledge and in the media.

Anthropologists of China have recently investigated various aspects of personhood, including people's "desire" (Rofel 2007), "self-enterprise" (Zhang and Ong 2008), and "moral" lives (Kleinman et al. 2011). Gaps, inconsistencies, and contestations in state-led psychotherapeutic intervention have attempted to construct the unemployed as psychologically obsessive and politically passive, market-oriented entrepreneurial citizens. This echoes with the notion of the divided self. Kleinman et al. (2011) discuss a particular form of the divided self in which sufferings and opinions that are too politically sensitive must be repressed in order to allow the entrepreneurial self to succeed. They use the image of an owl with one eye open and one eye shut as a metaphor for this divided self. The open eye takes in all that is necessary to get ahead in everyday life while the closed eye protects the privacy of an inner self that feels things that cannot be expressed in a particular political environment.

Workers in Changping have been presented with conflicting, psychologized modes of novel subject formation. The latest political culture in China is based on economic entrepreneurship of the self and a new psychological culture founded on the process of making individuals autonomous. The interdependence of these two trends often constitutes a process of producing selfhood for the middle class. However, working-class men and women, like those I analyze here, are not fully integrated into this new paradigm.

Members of the working class straddle Mao's self-formation, in which one experienced him or herself as interdependent and linked to socially important others or to work units and the current call for people to assert their individuality based on self-reliance. For example, a Reemployment Assistance Pamphlet (published by the Beijing Reemployment Guide Office in 2002) recommends that laid-off workers change their concept of employment. Instead of sticking to *luosiding jingshen*, or the "spirit of screws," which required people to obey whatever order came down from above in

Mao's era, they should now be flexible, autonomous, and mobile. Rather than *deng, kao, yao,* or "waiting, depending upon, or begging for" jobs from the state, they are to be active and take initiative in looking for jobs. Some initially resisted this rhetoric because they felt entitled to full-time employment assigned by the government. Yet with training and with the prospect of new employment, many accepted it, at least on the surface. Some have even taken up temporary or psychologized positions, such as taxi drivers-cum-counselors or housemaid *peiliao* (companions for chatting), hybrid identities that remain difficult to reconcile with once-heroic and prestigious worker identities. For others in Changping, there was no way to make the switch to a new kind of self within the current socioeconomic circumstances, and they committed suicide after they were laid off.

While both thought work and talk therapy aim to reconstruct the subjective reality of the client, thought work reframes the subjective reality of the individual and totalizes them within the ideological framework of the party, correcting, transforming, or even twisting individuals' thought processes and emotional states to suit ideological priorities. In contrast, talk therapy is intended to relieve pain and leads to the cure of certain psychological or mental problems. Postmodernists recognize that people live in the realm of language just as fish live in water, even though humans may not realize the existence and significance of language for their lives. When a kept fish gets ill, it receives medication dropped into the water. Likewise, people receive emotional support through the language that creates their "reality" (White 1995). In counseling, recreating a client's sense of reality regarding his or her situation or problem is intended to be therapeutic (White and Epston 1990).[8] The popularity of Rogers's client-centered approach in China, which relies on the listening therapist and the talking client, resonates with the emphasis on the self and personal responsibility that is currently being promoted for the new political economy.

In thought work, party staff interpreted problematic individuals through an ideological lens and determined their character and ideological status—or who they were—through what those individuals said. By contrast, psychosocial workers claim that current talk therapy engages a practice of *jiena* (acceptance) through which individuals and their individuality and rights are emphasized and celebrated by separating the person from their problems. In other words, while thought work was mainly undertaken to correct, reframe, and even twist the individual to suit a social and political platform, talk therapy is intended to accept and validate the person, a process that is now believed to lead to healing. Psychosocial workers claim to allow clients to interpret their problems; the counselor's task is to help clients bring out unsaid or unconscious thoughts so they can rewrite their narratives and reconstruct their relational and emotional contexts. According to Zhang Mo, a professor of social work at Beijing University of Labor Relations, *jiena* means accepting and respecting the person as unique—not necessarily his or her values or opinions, but the very existence of the person. It means seeing someone as a person with unique needs that are not assessed against standard measures or services.[9]

For Shao Wen, *jiena* means taking a genuine interest in other people's lives and experiences. Symbolic recognition of another takes place in the first stage of intersubjectivity, which assigns a position to people and results in a relational structure. Then this structure acquires meaning. In this regard, Liu Ji, the deputy party secretary of the Beibiao residents' committee and a retrained social worker, explained to me in August of 2010 what talk therapy is and how it differs from thought work:

> I try to acknowledge people and empathize with them, letting clients know that I understand what they are going through. So I usually acknowledge whatever they say. I may offer them new perspectives, but not like the traditional thought work, correcting them or imposing ideas on them. Allowing people to talk is therapeutic. Acknowledging people's complaint or suffering is more therapeutic. Like the other day, when I tried to talk with my mother about my husband, without me finishing what I wanted to say, she already prepared a speech to teach me to be obedient and respectful to my husband. I don't want to talk to her any more. My sister is different. No matter what I say or complain about, she always listens to me, allowing me to cry without necessarily asking me why. She may not offer any advice, but I still want to talk to her, which is therapeutic, because she accepts me as a person no matter what I do or say. If she indeed offers advice, I will be more willing to consider or accept that.

This notion of *jiena*—unconditional acceptance—is affective, and its affectivity helps open a client's heart, making ideological orientation easier (Grossberg 1992). This interpretation of *jiena* partly exemplifies the notion of kindly power, or using kindness and warmth to open up the hearts of individuals and interpellate or convict them affectively.

The Spirit of Screws and Pancake People: Story Therapy

The opportunity to find a voice and tell a story that has been suppressed through the interplay of personal and public taboos can be beneficial and therapeutic for disempowered individuals and groups (McLeod 2004). Through this process, they identify and correct values they have introjected from their social world that motivate them to disavow or distort their emotional and physiological experiences. The assumption of those who advocate therapy through narratives is that people are social beings with a basic need to socialize and tell their stories. Suppressing a story involves a process of psychological and physiological inhibition that can have negative effects on health (Pennebaker 1997). Telling one's story promotes a sense of knowing and being known that leads to social inclusion (Epston and White 1995; McLeod 1999). When a traumatic event has occurred, storytelling enables the speaker to confront and express inhibited thoughts, feelings, and images. The teller seeks an opportunity to explore, appreciate, and appropriate his or her story so that it loses its hold and the speaker can transcend its grip.

Unlike directors at the Reemployment Service Center of Beibiao who adopted therapeutic strategies that are fundamentally psychological (often using Western psychological self-help literature), residents' committee members turned psychosocial workers were more oriented toward using social and cultural resources for therapy, for example, narrative therapy. They gave the unemployed voice and allowed them to tell their stories. Going beyond relying purely on a concept of the self to theorize the therapeutic process, they regarded those seeking help as members of a culture or a community and their difficulties were understood in terms of their relationship with that culture or community. While in general there is an emphasis on individualism and individual-centered ethics in the reform era in China, a new social interdependence is also being purposefully created through storytelling and community construction in Changping. Indeed, stories are always co-constructed, told in the presence of real or implied audiences and thus are dialogic (Bakhtin 1986). Constructing a story is a situated performance, a version of events created at a particular time and place to have a specific effect; the story emerges between people instead of existing in one person's mind (McLeod 2004, 22).

Therapy through stories in Changping resonates with postpsychological therapy (Lieblich et al. 2004), which goes beyond a pure psychological approach that focuses on the inner state and notion of the self by emphasizing the social and cultural approach to therapy and by paying particular attention to the signifiance of narrative and storytelling for therapists and clients to negotiate meaning, conflict, and identity in order to achieve healing. The person seeking help is a narrator and actively (re)authors stories that enable him or her to convey a sense of identity and make sense of problematic experiences by integrating them coherently. The concept of narrative brings with it cultural resources that support individual stories (15). These stories can help the therapeutic process immensely because they provide materials and resources for deriving meaning, understanding, and insight. They also offer a framework for transformation and cure.

> Stories can provide a resource and connecting focus for therapy. They offer a way to name our experiences without imposing a clinical language (which most often emphasizes pathology) upon people's lives. . . . Stories are a bridge across clinical and nonclinical dilemmas, because in them we recognize our shared dilemmas. Moreover, the use of stories is not embedded in a particular model; no matter what the theoretical stance of the therapist, stories can be used.
>
> A central part of therapy is helping people link and understand the relationship of their stories to their own life. . . . Exploring the kind of story-making with which they are familiar may help them to better see what resources they have or have not had available to them. Working with the story styles can open up new possibilities for making meaning out of their personal histories (Roberts 1994, 22).

While psychosocial workers in Changping claimed to avoid pathologizing langauge, they still believed that naming the problem (sometimes with pathological terms) was the first step toward a cure. This was how clients begin their conversation between themselves and their problems, creating a distance that leads to insight and solution (see also White and Epston 1990). When the client achieves this, his or her emotion also changes. In my interviews with psychosocial workers in Changping, they problematized two opposing issues that laid-off workers developed in their pursuit of reemployment: the phenomenon of *jianbing ren* ("pancake people")—those who are spread too thin, are too mobile, and are constantly changing jobs in order to find the best fit and fulfill their potential—and the Maoist *luosiding jingshen* (the "spirit of screws")—those who are too stoic and reluctant to move on, fixed in their behavior, and unable to adapt to new requests. These tropes are posited with the employment pattern at work units—the supposedly full-time employment—as a point of reference. The metaphor of screws derives from Leifeng (see Chapter 2), a soldier of the People's Liberation Army who was willing to be like a little screw and was dispatched by the party and Chairman Mao. Leifeng was well known for his selfless behavior in performing his duty and helping others. The screw symbolizes compliance. This references the state's stance that individuals should make no move that might disrupt uniformity unless the party initiated it (Zhang 2005, 7). For example, the term "screw" is used to refer to workers who have been laid off but refuse to completely sever their relationship with state-owned enterprises.

Instead of sticking to the spirit of screws, which requires people to obey whatever order comes down from the party and to beg for jobs from the state, laid-off workers are now encouraged to be autonomous and to take initiative in looking for jobs in order to actualize their full potential. This new call for individuality first occurred at the institutional level by destabilizing lifetime guarantees of work, through the critiques of paternalism in all-encompassing work units (Walder 1986), and then in 1986 through the introduction of the labor contract system at state-owned enterprises. This ended the previously guaranteed lifetime tenure in the public sector and gave new recruits employment that could be terminated.

Because they lack marketable skills, laid-off workers are often re-trained to temporarily fix certain problems. Many of the jobs designed for them, such as *jiaotong xieguan* (traffic warden) or *peiliao* (companion for chatting), parallel existing positions in the formal economy and serve to fill gaps in the work force created by the inefficient or inadequate formal institutions. Thus, the wardens fill positions created by inefficient traffic management by assisting traffic police. Companions for chatting fill the gap created by inadequate mental health services (a shortage of counselors). However, such quick fixes do not lead to long-term fulfilling employment. Temporary positions created specifically for laid-off workers cannot provide legitimate identities for people (cf. Roberman 2013).

Doing this kind of temporary work reminds people of *jianbing ren*, the Chinese pancake, one of the most celebrated snacks in the streets of north China. *Jianbing ren* refers to those who cannot stay put or concentrate on any one thing for a long time. Instead of developing ideas and creativity, they divide their attention in many directions without reaching any fruitful outcome—like the cooking of *jianbing*, where the flour spreads across a large circular pan, generating a very thin layer of pancake. Pancake people live their lives in a thin layer and cover a lot of space but never become "thick." They become Jack of all trades, master of none. *Jianbing ren* in general refers to people who are versatile on the surface while lacking depth. The fierce socioeconomic competition in Chinese cities has recently resulted in numerous new "instant solutions" for people who wish to gain an advantage in professional spheres. Advice books, workshops, and *peixun* courses (to help people acquire a useful skill so they can get a job or pass an exam) all tempt people to shorten their road to success. This way of being is also apparent in tokenistic reemployment training programs. By spreading people thin, the call for self-reliance creates new vulnerabilities for them; they are under constant pressure to find whatever reemployment they can—here, there, and everywhere.[10]

Wang Liwei, a worker in his early 50s, was viewed in this community as *bu he qun* (antisocial) and *you yexin* (ambitious). After he was laid off from the factory in 2004, he entered quite a few self-initiated entrepreneurial endeavors such as running a gift shop and operating a laundry stall. However, none of these ventures were successful. His wife described him as bad tempered and becoming crazy, especially before traditional Chinese festivals, when he declined to attend family reunions because he perceived favoritism on his mother's part for his high-achieving younger brother. One day Wang's wife bumped into residents' committee party secretary Liu Ji and asked Liu for help and intervention. Men in this community seldom initiate a search for help; borrowing money or asking for favors are often women's tasks. Liu, who was Wang's classmate in elementary school, told me that she suspected he may have developed *xinli zhang'ai* (psychological obstacles).

After Wang missed a gathering of former classmates during the Chinese New Year in 2008, Liu called him. Because Wang structured his life and behavior around the normative understandings of success in this community, he felt ashamed of himself and did not want to enter into a social context where the ability to make money is often discussed, valued, and compared. He did not expect Liu or any other of his former classmates to contact him. He was touched by Liu's phone call and invited her for tea at his house. Both Wang's wife and I were present, sitting next to them at the other end of the table. When Liu asked how he spent his New Year, a normal greeting during the festival season, Wang's eyes started to get red and he tried to hold back tears. It is rare for a man to show emotion in front of women in this community. In psychotherapy (here, in Liu's *tanxin*), remembering can sometimes produce slight shifts in emotional structures by letting in, with therapeutic help and perhaps only for a brief moment, a message from the past that disturbs current rationalizations and compels recognition (Platt with Quisbert 2007, 135). Wang lowered his head. He looked at the tea cup, then slowly picked it up and sipped from it. After a long pause, he confided to us about his situation.

> I didn't go to see my parents. This is the fourth year I didn't go back. I didn't even phone them. I had thought after I become something, I will then call them. But I tried so many things, and all failed. I feel like a loser, having no "face" to see her [his mother]. She was never proud of me, probably even ashamed of me. [Liu asked: How do you know she is not proud of you?] Well, you don't know her. She is like the kind of person. . . . I give you one example: One evening we walked back after dining at a restaurant, bumping into one of her former colleagues. She introduced my brother first, what he does . . . you could see she was enthusiastic and very proud of him, and then she mentioned me by saying "This is my elder son." That's it. I am older and she should introduce me first. This is only one example. I've experienced too many of these kinds of things. I don't think I will speak to her until I succeed. But I don't know when.

Liu told me that she seemed able to identify immediately what was going wrong with Wang's life. He grew up believing that his mother liked his brother better. He needs to be as successful as his brother in order to be accepted and loved by his mother. Liu believed that these irrational emotions of shame in the context of others' orientations toward success constitute Wang's psychological obstacles:

> He always compared himself to his younger brother. I said to him, your brother is younger than you and he had a better opportunity for education.

And also it is much easier to make money in the IT industry nowadays. His brother is a computer engineer. I said, you, including me, we are the generation who went through the Cultural Revolution and were not able to go to college, going through this "system reform" [privatization]. We are unfortunate, but this is not our fault. Again, we cannot compare with others. *Ren bi ren, bi si ren* [Compare one person with another; one of them has to die, meaning there is no point of comparison between two people]. I told him we have our advantage; we understand life better. We work hard, making clean, hard-earned money; we sleep well at night, right? See how many elite suffer depression and commit suicide, Cui Yongyuan [a TV anchor and celebrity] is one. Rich, successful, and famous, he suffers depression. The same as your brother. He is a millionaire but you don't know what he has to go through to succeed. I told Wang, sometimes a luxurious bed in a villa doesn't mean a good sleep at night. His worries, concerns, we don't know, right? I told him to see things this way: you are an ordinary worker, having the courage to try so many things, that's very courageous and admirable. Not like other workers who are afraid of trying outside; like a tortoise staying here waiting for opportunities at Beibiao [like screws].

Liu invoked both Wang's brother and Cui Yongyuan, who publicly acknowledged he suffered depression as a way of raising awareness of mental illness, to help Wang find a context for a point of identification with other people. Psychotherapy through narratives seems to be the process of tapping into the power of these stories in order to discover ways of restoring the flow of meaning between past, present, and future. In this case, Liu was not a silent listener; she offered a new framework in which Wang could position himself. She was still a counselor giving advice, but instead of authoritative direction she was shifting the frame of reference for Wang. Liu's direction also involves using these stories to access memories and imagination and to find the right voices and the right vantage points from which to hear, comprehend, create, and tell stories (see Dwivedi and Gardner 1997, 24).

Liu viewed her *tanxin* with Wang as therapeutic not only because she helped Wang identify his problems—his "irrational" notion of success and his low self-esteem as the root cause of his anxiety about his failure to secure a job, but also because she gave Wang an opportunity to tell his story in a way that led him to revisit his understanding of himself. Indeed, as Kleinman (1988) suggests, the experience of having another person become an empathetic witness to one's account of troubles is meaningful and worthwhile. The role of counselor includes being both witness to and co-editor of the stories told by the person seeking help (McLeod 2004, 23). The construction and reconstruction of narrative identity take place in a complex social and cultural context that includes a community of shared values and morality (Lieblich et al. 2004, 4).

According to McLeod (2004), a double agency is implied in the concept of storytelling. The person telling a story is engaged in purposeful social action. In addition, the opportunity to tell a story offers an individual the potential to build an account in which they are portrayed as overcoming obstacles and challenges in their interactions with other people and their participation in social events. (Of course, not all narratives are positive accounts.) The agency that is expressed in and through narrative reflects the assumptions of an everyday folk psychology, in which people are viewed as having socially informed purposes and intentions instead of being objectified by the assumptions implicit in psychological theories founded on notions of internal states (White 2001) or by psychological processes (such as object relations, schemas, and the notion of the self) (McLeod 2004, 17).

As the conversation flowed and Wang became more aware of and expressive of his feelings, Liu observed that he became more light-hearted, gradually moving from a point of fixity to a process of fluidity in his understanding of his situation. Counseling offers a space for human creativity, intelligence, and relational connections to be developed and enhanced in a life-transforming experience. Such counseling aims at nurturing creative change and courage centered in realistic hope, in seeing and pursuing the promises of new life in the here and now. Liu offered her clients a freedom to choose their life direction and shape their attitudes within the given limits and challenges of human existence. Her therapeutic approach synthesizes rational-emotive behavior therapy, affect (*renqing*, or human feelings), psychology, and common knowledge from the sociocultural background she shared with her clients. Her deep embeddedness in the community affords her opportunities to know people and adopt a synthetic or holistic rather than a pure psychological approach to people and problems in her psychosocial work.

Liu also touched on another "irrational" belief that emerged in Wang's narrative about his failure to secure long-term employment. She recounted Wang's case:

He [Wang] believes *shu nuo si, ren nuo huo* [A tree dies if it is moved too often. However, a person thrives if he moves often]. He seems to have become a pancake person, not sticking to anything for long, knowing a lot but nothing in depth. Constantly changing jobs in order to find a job that makes big money, but on the contrary, he cannot make money because if he cannot stick with one job for more than six months, he earns the income of an intern at each job. . . . He doesn't know how to quickly adapt to changes, new co-workers at new jobs. I told him to integrate himself into the social environment wherever he is instead of going against the environment.

Although in her retelling Liu gave explicit advice and direction, such direction was unusual; it was possible because of Liu's close relationship with Wang. Wang seemed to embody the character associated with the personality of "pancake people" in the market economy. Unlike other pancake people, who can produce flexible self-representations and can make autonomous adjustments to market demands, Wang has difficulty adapting to changes quickly outside the work-unit system. Without offering any pragmatic help, Liu enabled Wang to identify his beliefs as irrational and unrealistic and to see them as responsible for his failure to secure a job. The next step for Wang is to be realistic in choosing a direction for his job search and in dealing with the new work environment—that is, self-adjustment and self-striving.

Gender and Psychosocial Work in Changping

Despite the clear advice Liu gave Wang, she considered her approach in general to be nondirective. Psychosocial workers in Changping were strategic in their use of such nondirective therapy, depending on whom they counseled. When Zhang Yi, the party secretary and director of the Beibiao residents' committee, counseled a woman surnamed Li who came to him seeking help for her husband, Zhang adopted a more directive and even intrusive strategy for "counseling" this woman through a moralizing discourse.

After Li's husband, a male worker surnamed Chen, was laid off in 2003, he could not secure any lasting job because he always wanted to find employment comparable to his former job at Beibiao—a job that was close to home and would not require him to work the night shift. Eventually, in 2008, he quit trying and stayed at home, responding only to occasional calls for plumbing jobs, while his wife kept her job at Beibiao. He awaited new openings at Beibiao. Although not many people think that work at state-owned enterprises is fulfilling, because of the intensified exploitation and lack of regulation that pervades the private sector, many laid-off workers at Beibiao (even though privatized in 2004) would still prefer to continue to work there. This perception of work at Beibiao as more stable and comfortable is attributable to the fact that it continues to produce watches—a familiar territory for workers.[11]

However, since its privatization in 2004, Beibiao has prioritized hiring cheaper and supposedly more docile rural migrant women. After he was laid off, Chen began to feel anxious and insecure because normative manhood in this community is associated with full-time employment and being a breadwinner. Unemployment eroded his sense of masculinity, and his mental health declined. As Kessler and McLeod (1985) suggest, the impact of stress on mental health is buffered by emotional and social support, but not simply by membership in social networks (Aneshensel 1992, 17). However, for laid-off workers such as Chen, stress was intensified not only by the lack of emotional support they experienced but also by the fact that they still enjoyed their membership in employers' organizations, a resource that was denied to workers who had been laid off. He observed that his wife was always chatting with one of her co-workers, their male neighbor, as they returned home from work. One afternoon as his wife walked home chatting with this neighbor, Chen rushed out of his building and beat him up. His wife Li was shocked and managed to comfort the neighbor and convince him not to call the police, but she simply did not know how to handle her jealous husband. Li finally realized that her husband really needed a job. She then went to the residents' committee and talked with Zhang Yi to see whether he could find her husband something to do in the community center or at Beibiao in order to get him out of the home and mitigate his desire to find fault with her.

However, instead of seeing this marriage issue as something that could have been caused, at least in part, by the unemployment of her husband, Zhang put the problems of the marriage on Li's shoulders. Zhang encouraged her to be cautious at home, sensitive to her unemployed husband's psychological stress while he was still stuck with the spirit of screws and had to face a wife who was still employed—an uncommon situation in this community, where women are often laid off while men stay at work. In my interviews with him, Zhang recounted what he told Li. Zhang said:

> I told Li, you should be very careful to attend to your husband's face, be un-assuming at home. It's not easy for a man to stay at home while seeing his wife working outside. You know, this is a dignity issue. Did you see *gang de qin* [A piano in a factory, a 2010 movie about laid-off workers]? You see those laid-off men, their struggle, trying to survive after job loss with dignity. [One of them tried so hard to win over his daughter that he made her a piano at the factory where he had been laid off because he couldn't afford one after his wife left him for a rich man.] That is dignity, a man's dignity to provide for his daughter to be a good father. The same with your husband.

Instead of offering therapy to both husband and wife, Zhang counseled only the woman. Li and Chen both need direction and pragmatic help, but Zhang adopted a thoroughly nondirective and nonsupportive approach to the issue of Chen's reemployment, while giving concrete direction and guidance to the wife on how to behave with her husband. Women in general tend to be treated in therapy either as victims who are casualties of circumstance or as blame-worthy and responsible for their situations (see Lieblich et al. 2004, 8). Zhang embodied a therapeutic ethos that reduced complex social and economic relations to a matter of gender and wifely duty. This kind of psychologization appears to be imperative for maintaining a dialectical tension between the psychological and the social in China. In this case, that dynamic makes it possible for Zhang to ignore structural forces and empowers him to hold his client personally responsible for her husband's distress.

Zhang counseled Li to be a more observant and sensitive partner; he told her to be more attentive to her husband's heart attitude and his feelings. In Chinese psychologization, psychology is only a part of the process. It is also about the heart—the heart of the people and the "heart" of, or the projection of their hearts upon, an event. The heart is key to China's model of psychology and it is really to the heart of the matter that this therapist turned, specifically to the hearts of Li and Chen. In China's traditional ethos and in its modern psychosocial practices, the heart refers to an intersubjective relationship rooted in cognition and virtue, in emotional and moral experience mediated by social and gender norms.

Men and women typically offer different kinds of counseling in Chang-ping. Zhang, the director of the residents' committee who claimed he was a Marxist intellectual in Mao's era, is still an expert in Marx's work and Mao's dialectics of *biantong*. He has recently updated his skills through training and reading in psychology, counseling, and social work, but he has often revised or twisted what he had learned through these training sessions to serve his continued practice of thought work. Liu, by contrast, often played the role of "red face" (a popular understanding of the Beijing opera facial design associated with gentle characters). She was gentle, flex-ible, and caring, a mother figure, especially to men who came to her for help. Zhang played the "white face," a strict, sinister and cunning official and rule-abiding father figure, offering discipline, a negative message, or even rejection to those who came to the community center to make a fuss or bargain for reemployment or other benefits. However, women residents (except Li) thought highly of Zhang and often preferred to go to him when they needed something from the residents' committee. People often jok-ingly explained to me that opposites attract (or the unity of opposites).

Shunqi: The Communication of Affect

As Greenberg and Paivio (1997) suggest, emotional arousal plays the most prominent role in the interactions between clients and psychotherapists. Psychotherapy provides the client with an atmosphere in which he or she can experience emotion and the psychotherapist can validate the client's emotions and work with him or her to promote positive emotional frame-works and qualitative changes in the client's life (see Pawelczyk 2011, 156).

Emotions manifest themselves in psychotherapy in various ways. In Changping, negative emotions such as anger can cause the building up of *qi* (air, breath, vital energy, flow of the inner body) (Chen 2003) within the body, producing *qi gugu* (a bloated belly full of bad air), which is believed to disrupt the normal flow of blood. This creates tension and pressure that may lead to internal damage if it is not released. *Qi* can be a constructive or destructive force, depending on the context. Humans are both subject to the workings of *and* agents of *qi*; this is true for every person in different ways and at different times. Normally, *qi* is the reuniting of inner peace with outer body. *Chuqi* (getting out one's negative air) or *shunqi* (smoothing out one's negative air) refers to venting out or speaking out about *qi* caused by anger that manifests itself, for example, as symptoms of a bloated stomach. Psychosocial workers use various strategies to prod clients to reveal their emotional experience in order to release negative emotions or *qi*. They attempt to tap into the desires, concerns, needs, and interests of their clients so they can release buried or pent-up emotions.

One day in August 2008, as I was walking with Liu Ji to inspect the sanitation at one of the residential yards at Beibiao, we bumped into a woman surnamed Tian. While chatting with Liu Ji, Tian mentioned her recent insomnia and her feeling that life was meaningless. She was feeling hopeless and even suicidal. When Liu asked her what had happened recently in her life, Tian said that her 23-year-old daughter had met a man and eloped with him. Liu accurately pointed out that her relationship with her daughter must the issue that was keeping her awake at night. Tears immediately began streaming down her face, and Tian wept uncontrollably standing there in public. Liu pulled her to the doorkeeper's office, at which "counseling" was often carried out, and allowed her to weep. In Changping, the psychotherapy session is one of the few social settings in which clients' crying is not viewed negatively or commented on in a way that would make them promptly stop. This is because counselors understand that crying constitutes an important and healing element of the psychotherapeutic process (see also Pawelczyk 2011, 181).

After Tian stopped weeping, Liu told her that she herself was raised by a single mother and entirely understood the mutual dependence of a mother and her daughter. Tian had single-handedly brought up her daughter after her husband divorced her when the daughter was 18 months old, but the daughter had become strange to her after she met that man and eloped with him. Liu Ji felt that pointing out the very thing or event that elicited emotional outbursts from clients was the key to helping her clients release their pain through her *tanxin*-cum-talk therapy. She indicated that some clients had a low crying point (*kudian di*); these clients opened up to the therapist easily and could cry easily. In contrast, those with a high crying point (*kudian gao*) found it difficult to open themselves up to the therapist and to be aroused emotionally. However, this type of evaluation is highly subjective and context specific. Liu believes that this is the process of recognizing and accepting one's real emotions (which may be less socially acceptable) because they reflect one's real needs, concerns,

4.1. Four residents playing poker in front of a CRC door-keeper's office, where *tanxin* or counseling could take place. Photo by He Jianhua.

and interests. These are an important source of information for her as a therapist. Liu had seen numerous clients spontaneously externalize internalized emotions during talk therapy, thereby releasing emotional tension or psychological conflicts.

Greenberg and Safran (1987, 1989) recognize a correlation between the level of emotional experience during a psychotherapeutic session and the outcome of psychotherapy. They observe that the higher the level of emotional experience, the more benefits the client receives from the psychotherapeutic endeavor. Frank (1961, 1974) points out two emotionally oriented aspects of the process of psychotherapy that lead to positive effects for the client. One is the therapeutic practice of bringing the client's emotions to the surface during a session. The other is the corrective emotional experiences a client undergoes in his or her dialogue and therapeutic alliance with the psychotherapist. According to Liu, eliciting the client's emotions in her *tanxin* helps the client get over emotions or find emotional relief, arrive at a sense that he or she is understood and accepted, and gain access to hope and happiness. For Liu, it is important to establish trust and assure her clients of the safety of the therapeutic alliance they form with her because of the nature of the emotional work they do (see also Pawelczyk 2011); this is also a form of *jiena*.

After precipitating a very emotional event, what Liu called *kudian* (the crying point), she then prescribed ways to resolve the issue that causes the pain. Liu comforted Tian with a local folk saying: *nu'er shi po chuqu de shui, shou bu huilai* [Daughters are water poured out; it is hard to get them back]. That is, mothers have to let go their daughters sooner or later and cannot keep them forever. Then Liu kept a long silence and let Tian reflect on the folk saying.

Liu also uses silence to enhance therapeutic effects. Silence is an established technique in psychotherapy (Cook 1964) and an accepted and expected part of therapist-client interactions. Levitt (2001) states that what distinguishes psychotherapy from an ordinary conversation is that in a conversation sustained pauses are rare and often indicate discomfort, while in psychotherapeutic interactions shared silence is an expected aspect of client-therapist interactions. Trad (1993) presents three important purposes of using silence in psychotherapy: to share interpersonal experience, the client's use of silence to promote self-revelation, and the use of silence by both parties as a means of self-reflection. Hill et al. (2003) suggest that therapists use silence to facilitate reflection, encourage responsibility, promote expression of feelings, avoid interrupting the flow of a session, and to promote empathy. According to Sabbadini (1991), silence is a space for words that cannot be spoken; silence in the context of psychotherapy indicates that significant, intimate material of high emotional significance is about to be spoken.

In general, Greenberg (2004) conceives of emotion as a basis for the construction of the self and for self-organization. He uses a dialectal-constructivist view to explicate how people constantly make sense of emotions. The ongoing process of making sense of experience is manifested by being aware of sensations felt in the body and articulating them verbally, thus constructing new experiences. Emotional experience is also substantially shaped by a person's life experience and the culture he or she is immersed in. In this process, clients are helped to recognize, understand, channel, and modify their emotional experience (Greenberg 2004, 6). Putting emotion into words enables the clients to incorporate it into their conscious and conceptual understanding of self and the surrounding world (7; see also Pawelczyk 2011, 159). As Ledoux (1998, 7) writes,

> Emotions are notoriously difficult to verbalize. They operate in some psychic and neural space that is not readily accessed from consciousness. Psychiatrists' and psychologists' offices are kept packed for this very reason.

In the hands of a psychotherapist, language and communication are tools that help the client make sense of traumas past and present for the purpose of living a better life, and become aware of their needs and make sense of their experience (Pawelczyk 2011, 1). However, narratives or cognition cannot entirely capture emotion or affect that include bodily and sensual dimensions. It requires non-verbal communications such as silence that cannot be articulated but can be felt and sensed.

Conclusion

Psychosocial workers in China have adopted the ritual of *tanxin* in their counseling work, creating a hodgepodge of thought work and Western psychotherapy to help (unemployed) workers position themselves to actualize their potential for a productive life. Party staff and former party members deployed indigenous practices, communist ideological practices, and precepts of Western psychotherapy as strategic tools in their attempts to govern the unemployed. This combination enables psychosocial workers to combine their professional and ethical training, the party's ideological framework, and local social, cultural, and political practices in their counseling. By granting clients full speakerhood, counselors enable them to speak for themselves, rely on themselves, and solve their own problems. This is aimed at empowering workers and helping them become productive in the new economy, but this strategy also serves the purposes of the party by shifting the burden of responsibility for coping with the consequences of economic restructuring to individuals. This unique process of psychologization is part of the political self-preservation of the government. The underlying motive of counseling that is centered on clients and gives them full speakerhood resonates with the government's need for constructing responsible and self-reliant subjects for the market economy.

Instead of a purely psychological process that might identify the values clients have introjected from their social worlds, community psychosocial workers view their therapeutic encounters as dialogic storytelling events that take place within broader social and cultural processes. They perceive therapy to be a process of enabling the client to develop a narrative that brings a degree of coherence to a chaotic life, a process that is inevitably social, even if it appears to be oriented to the individual. The narrative techniques community counselors use are gendered and affect men and women differently.

I show that while attention to emotions (including cognition and bodily sensation) in counseling, appears to constitute a new political register that goes beyond the neat conceptual framework of ideology, it paradoxically facilitates further ideological investment because it creates a hegemonic space in which people open their hearts for ideological teachings. This is another example of kindly power. However, that is not to say that the client has no power or control within the counseling relationship. Shao Wen once remarked that one of her clients kept telling her how much the former party organization at Beibiao had helped her and how much she missed its help. Such "high praise" for the past assistance of the party, according to Shao Wen, constitutes a form of control through which the client pressures the counselor to offer quick-fix solutions to her problems and to not disappoint her (see also the case of Li Jiuxi in Chapter 2).

Residents at the Beibiao community employ a range of strategies to both embrace and challenge psychologization. Some residents visited the community center to use its collection of daily newspapers, books, and magazines, which included not only books in party history and propaganda but also a large variety of books and magazines in psychological self-help and bibliotherapy. These workers seem to develop their own psychological resources to cope with their situations and solve their problems. Others adopt the principle and art of *nande hutu* (it is not easy to be muddled), a philosophy that originated with Zheng Banqiao (1693–1765), a Qing Dynasty official and artist from Jiangsu Province. His philosophy has regained popularity in China since the 1990s and has given rise to a popular practice based on the concept of *hutuxue* (the art of being/pretending to be muddled). *Nande hutu* is a commonly accepted strategy for becoming successful by knowing when and when not to pretend to be muddled. It is also used for dealing with conflicts and feelings of powerlessness as a way to remain mentally healthy (Matthyssen 2012).[12]

In the following chapter, I turn to how women cope with new vulnerabilities caused by gendered reemployment programs and empower themselves through the new job of *peiliao* (companions for chatting).

Part II

GENDER AND PSYCHOLOGICAL LABOR

Peiliao and Psychological Labor

One of my informants, surnamed Ling, was employed by a rich entrepreneur as a housemaid and *peiliao* for his mother, a lady in her early 70s. The old lady has a daughter who suffers from epilepsy. Because of her daughter's illness and her failure to produce an heir for her husband, who is the only child in his family, the old lady was very concerned that after she died and had passed her house to her daughter, her son-in-law would ignore and eventually kill her daughter while she was having an epileptic seizure. Then he would have sole ownership of the house. Her daily ritual was to worry about her daughter's future and pour out her worries to Ling. Ling told me how she "counseled" the old lady,

> Why you are always worrying when current situations look fine? You worry about something that may never happen. Why not use the same energy of worrying to hope and wish for the best? Thinking of too much what you cannot control is useless, unhelpful for solving the problem. You've already sacrifice so much for your daughter; now you need to value and enjoy the rest of your life. Worry is not good for your health either.

The mother responded, "I will try my best to prevent tragic things happening to my daughter when I am still alive and able." Ling answered, "What you are doing is actually actualizing something that you fear if you project your bad opinions onto your son-in-law." The mother repeatedly asked Ling to consult lawyers about how to write a will that would guarantee that her son-in-law had to treat her daughter well regardless of the situation. Ling told me, "My days went by like this. I think she is depressed or obsessive-compulsive. Her negative outlook makes me gloomy and unhappy. But to make enough money to feed my kid, I have to endure this."

Across the street from the largest shopping mall in Changping, at an informal job fair that has held in front of an office building year-round since the mid-1990s, fifteen or twenty rural migrants and urban workers who had been laid off from state-owned enterprises were standing or sitting on the stairs, waiting for potential employers. Some of them were holding posters highlighting their skills, such as plumbing, construction, driving, and welding. Others wrote their skills in chalk on the concrete stairs where they stood or sat. A few of the unemployed even put their toolkits next to them or sat on them; they were ready to work.

One day in August 2007, three people in line were hired by a contractor on his way to a construction site. Most days, however, I saw more or less the same group of people waiting. Occasionally, people stopped by to inquire about their employability, but they left without offers. I went to this job fair with several of my informants, middle-aged women who had recently been laid off from the watch factory, but none of them were hired. Instead of continuing to wait there, I followed them to the central park located several blocks away from the shopping mall. These women interacted with people in the park, mostly retirees and seniors who were doing exercises, walking their dogs, or looking after their grandchildren. As they chatted with these seniors, my informants offered tips for healthy eating, healthy living and ways of *xiang kai* (opening one's mind to sort out things, or untying heart knots). They then asked whether those in the park needed a helping hand at home or if they knew someone in their neighborhood who might hire a housemaid or a *peiliao* to *jiemen* (resolve their depression or loneliness). When the seniors were about to leave, my informants gave them their telephone numbers. One of my informants,

Na, handed her phone number to an elderly woman with a contagious big smile and said:

> *Da ma* ["big mother," a colloquial term used to address older women in Changping], so good to talk with you today. If you like, I can chat with you at home and be your company; we can then help each other *jiemen*. My factory was closed; I have a lot of time during the day. I can help you clean, cook, run errands. If you like, you can pay me so I can buy a bus ticket or give me some pocket money for my child to buy pencils.

Instead of saying that she had been laid off, Na said that her factory had closed, because in Changping being laid off can imply a fault on the part of the employee. By mentioning a bus ticket for her and pocket money for her school-aged child, Na was telling her potential employer that she wanted to be paid for her companionship but that she did not charge much. Instead of solely relying on the community job center for reemployment, some of my informants have found work this way as housemaids or *peiliao*. Indeed, job counseling targeting unemployed women teaches them to be active (*jiji*) and to use their initiative (*zhudong*) to find work. The counseling process constructs subjects who embody the kind of happiness and positive psychology they wish to deliver in their *peiliao*, or housemaid work. Unlike professional counselors whose skills and knowledge constitute professional expertise, *peiliao* are expected to generate care and companionship through applying what mainstream Chinese society presumes—their innate, embodied knowledge of positive psychology. This knowledge is honed through training to enable them to find employment in the precarious market for household labor that operates in the informal sector without government regulation.

Since the mid-1990s, the Chinese media have created an image of workers who had been laid off from state-owned enterprises as happy, productive subjects who have transformed themselves into "reemployment stars" and "taxi stars" with the help of the government and psychotherapists (Dai 2004; Won 2004; Yang 2007). The new jobs the media showcase include nannies for foreigners (Lee 2006), housemaid counselors (CCTV New Year's Gala, 2000), and taxi counselors, or "counselors on wheels," who are busy preventing suicides (Yang 2013a, *Psychology Talk Show*, October

2009). This type of representation goes beyond normalizing marginalized men and women; it glorifies their suffering and sacrifice for the sake of state enterprise restructuring and glamorizes them as ideal, psychologically healthy, and entrepreneurial subjects. The media make clear that they have benefited from preliminary training in psychology or psychotherapy through reemployment counseling programs and can now themselves perform "counseling" for others. Indeed, the Chinese party-state has increasingly used mass media to alleviate social problems, frame public opinion, and present psychological education (Zhao 2008; Krieger 2009; Kong 2014).

In state-led reemployment efforts, women and men who have lost their employment at state-owned enterprises are exposed to different psychotherapeutic training options that offer work strategies rooted in perceptions of a person's uniquely gendered potential for caring for and nurturing others. Women are seen as embodying a nurturing disposition and are thus perceived to be especially suitable for becoming domestic care givers. Men, who are evaluated as more dangerous subjects because of their supposedly inherent negativity, can still be trained for the unusual role of taxi driver counselors who calm distressed passengers who appear determined to end their own lives. As valuable as these gendered positions may be, rendering socioeconomic problems as matters of psychology to be treated in the ways that are "naturally" available to differently gendered subjects downplays the tension associated with class stratification intensified by the recent privatization. Some scholars have suggested that seeing subjects as representative of their gender rather than as representative of their class has the potential to depoliticize social conflict (Gordo and De Vos 2010).

In the two chapters of this section, however, I emphasize that gendered psychologization in China actually constitutes a new arena for politics. As a discourse, psychologization overlooks the structural forces that produce unemployment while highlighting the psychological and moral traits of the unemployed as potential that can bring about individual growth and provide opportunities for subjects to enter the market economy, thus improving their own situations and creating value for the economy. In this chapter I address the government's recent psychotherapeutic interventions aimed at managing the unemployment and mental health of marginalized women. The government exploits the emotional and psychological labor of these women to advance the psychotherapy industry and relieve the mental health "crisis." At the same time, women struggle to seek beneficial ways to position themselves in relation to these new kinds of work.

Peiliao

The profession of *peiliao* or *peitan* (companion for chatting) emerged around the mid-1990s to solve the problem of gendered layoffs (Shi 1999; Wang 2003) and fill a market niche created by the shortage of mental health care workers in China. Through state-led reemployment programs, women who had been laid off were provided with training in techniques of basic nursing, domestic work, and counseling or psychology, and these women have subsequently been employed as housemaids, or *peiliao*.[1] Their work is generally caring for the young, the old, the sick, the dying, and the depressed wherever those individuals live (i.e., in private households or in state-sponsored housing for the underprivileged). Job counselors often told unemployed women that these new types of work without a definitive job description constitute opportunities for them to exert their imagination and actualize their potential for self-realization and self-fulfillment.

Peiliao was slow to gain recognition as a profession, due in part to the assumed link between the idea of women's companionship and sex. For example, in Shanghai, *peiliao* was not officially approved until 2010, when the director of the Shanghai Psychological Counseling Association decided that *peiliao* should be recognized as a profession and be strictly regulated. Regulations are required because *peiliao* often work in intimate spaces where they may find it challenging to maintain professional relationships with their clients.[2] However, official approval of *peiliao* as a new profession has been controversial and is not a universal policy in Chinese cities. Many consider it to rest on a shaky moral ground; they suspect that *sanpei* (sex workers in nightclubs and companions for eating, drinking, and sleeping with clients) will automatically be perceived as *peiliao* and that the reverse might also occur. Since the 2000s, illegal agencies have reportedly begun offering employment as *peiliao* as a front for recruiting sex workers in many areas of China. *Peiliao* has yet to be officially approved as a profession in Beijing.

Informally, however, the implementation of *peiliao* has occurred in the city through the training of laid-off women or rural migrant women as domestic workers. In the Beijing district of Changping, job centers increasingly look upon training as a *peiliao* or the acquisition of basic skills in counseling as minimal qualifications for almost all of the new women's "professions." These include domestic workers, *dou xiao shi* (assistants in professional photography studios who encourage young children to smile while being photographed), *daole* (personal assistants who guide women through childbirth in an informative and pleasant manner), and *yuesao* (live-in nannies who help mothers care for newborns). In Changping, those who undertake these new professions are predominantly laid-off women. Approximately 80 to 85 percent of laid-off women have been employed as domestic workers, as *peiliao*, or as workers in other care-related jobs.

Instead of focusing on creating jobs or regulating the labor market, recent job training programs for the unemployed in Beijing have emphasized the moral or psychological qualifications of those who seek re-employment. In the training domestic workers or *peiliao* receive, laid-off women workers are encouraged to treat certain moral traits that were nurtured and valued in work units such as *laoshi* (honesty, obedience), as psychological attributes to be highlighted and strategized as they compete with rural migrants and younger urban women in the domestic work market. In general, in post-Mao China, women are perceived to be the ideal caring subjects who embody feminine morals and the therapeutic ethos. Trainers consider the psychological care work these women do to be an inherent virtue of their gender identity rather than a relational skill that is developed through education and practice (Noddings 2000; Kitanaka 2012). For this reason, the efforts of the women who undergo psychological training to establish, maintain, or enhance caring relations do not bring them increased moral, social, and economic standing or value. Instead, their efforts engender new forms of vulnerability such as devalued labor and discrimination.

Also, unlike other psychological caregivers who empathize or sympathize by imagining the situation of another who suffers, laid-off women are encouraged to tap into what they have directly experienced themselves during their loss of employment to help those in their care. They are to share their own embodied knowledge of how they coped with the distress and impoverishment caused by job loss with clients who have gone through similar difficulties and losses. To many women, this is a process that reinscribes their past pain. A housemaid and *peiliao* put it this way:

> We suffered a lot during the layoffs, but we have to relive those difficult mo- ments again in our work—to make a living, you have to work with those who are going through tough times and similar difficulties like you.

Underpayment and low status may accompany the modes of "expertise" *peiliao* offer. They have no formal professional training, and in their in- formal job training, their job counselors or social workers encourage them to embody the kind of care and positive psychology they deliver to their clients. They are seen as performing a naturally gendered form of "know- ing how" rather than "knowing that" (Ryle [1949] 1981). The former is the knowledge of a skill: it is dependent on a situation and performative. "Knowing that" is theoretical or factual knowledge that conveys meaning based on rules or laws. In addition, it is not dependent on context. "Know- ing that" is identified with professional counselors who perform psycho- therapy in private counseling or on psychological counseling programs on CCTV 12. In reality, both modes of knowledge production are merged in these reemployed women's informal counseling work. Both are activities that convey meaning (M. Harris 2007, 3) and both are evidenced in the practices of both professional counselors and *peiliao*. That is, the training *peiliaos* receive entails both cognitive and embodied knowledge. However, the emotive, sensory, and embodied modes of knowledge production of *peiliaos* render them more vulnerable to exploitation and inequality in the new job market.

Alison Jaggar (1989) points out that in the West, emotion is often associ- ated with women and subordinate groups while rationality and knowledge production are associated with dominant groups. However, she argues that emotion also constitutes a mode of knowledge production. In China, despite the fact that emotions play such an important role in social connec- tions and the political economy (Yang 1988; Yan 1996; Kipnis 1997; Lee H. 2007; Yang 2014), the cognitive dimension of counseling is perceived to be produced by professional counselors (who are predominantly male) while informal *peiliaos* perform low-level embodied psychological labor that is closely related to their putative feminine virtue of caring. How- ever, the training *peiliaos* receive and the therapeutic practices they provide are more complex than the state and the public are willing to admit, and *peiliaos* are poorly remunerated for their work. The naturalization of these women's care labor is attributed to their economic disadvantage and the social injustice they suffer.

In this chapter, I explore the psychological and moral processes through which laid-off women's putative dependence on their former employers and the state is pathologized. Their perceived moral virtues—caring and *laoshi*, for example—are treated as core components of gendered psychology and are conjoined with the notion of self-reliance in order to advance the psychotherapy industry. This psychological and moral approach to the training of *peiliaos* shifts responsibility for unemployment and reemployment from the state to the individual, constructing a particular subjectivity based on moral self-control and on a new form of individual self-reliance that is emerging in China. These processes downplay the structural forces that intensify gendered exploitation. I draw on ethnographic data to illustrate both the training practices and the struggles of women to utilize the new tools of psychologization for their own survival. I suggest that instead of seeing care or psychological labor as an intersubjective relationship that requires efforts to sustain, psychosocial workers who train laid-off women for *peiliao* treat such psychological care as a feminine virtue, an ideology that legitimates low payment for the services and low social status for the women who provide them.

Gendered and Psychologized Reemployment

The new profession of *peiliao* emerged, in part, from mass layoffs of women (Wang 2003) during the downscaling and privatization of the state sector in China. Middle-aged women workers were laid off in disproportionate numbers during this process. This fact and women's subsequent difficulties in finding new jobs in a competitive market have been two of the most controversial consequences of economic reforms in China (Zhao 2002). Since the reemployment service centers at state-owned enterprises closed in 2003, grassroots organizations such as street agencies, residents' committees, trade unions, and women's organizations have worked to help the unemployed find new jobs. However, the jobs the government creates for laid-off workers often shadow existing professional jobs and

provide only temporary relief for problems such as inefficient traffic regulations (i.e., traffic wardens parallel traffic police) or inadequate mental
health care (i.e., *peiliaos* parallel professional counselors or social workers).
These transitional jobs have no formal or institutional recognition and do
not generate long-term employment or "legitimate" identities; they are irregular, flexible, temporary, or on-call jobs. An example of this rocky road
of temporary appointment is the reemployment some of my informants
found during the 2008 Summer Olympic Games in Beijing. They com-
muted three hours every day between Changping and downtown Beijing
to work as traffic wardens who helped traffic police maintain order. They
worked for only three months, and their daily wage was only 80 yuan
(about US$13).

Instead of being sensitive to the trauma many state workers experience
during mass unemployment, the government has adopted a psychosocial
approach that focuses on modeling workers' behavior, attitudes, and motivation in the direction of self-reliance or self-governance. Reemployment
programs are infused with ideologies and practices that encourage people,
particularly women, to rely on themselves and focus on their gendered
psychological advantages (see Shi 1999). To this end, counselors and psychologists have been integrated into reemployment programs since the
mid-1990s.

These professionals pathologize the unemployed and their anxious reactions to unemployment. The intent of the programs is ostensibly to help
the unemployed redirect their emotions and energies toward the market
and discover within themselves the value structures that make for positive
self-esteem and self-sufficiency (Blecher 2002). These qualities purportedly
include the ability to project confidence and put on a mantle of happiness
even though they do not feel it. The individual-focused psychologizing
framework omits the importance of interdependence as an inherent factor
in workers' agency. As Durkheim (1982) pointed out, in industrial societies, the more interdependent individuals are with others, the more autonomous they become. In other words, the recognition of interdependence
is essential for authentic personal autonomy. Yet in China, the kinds of
autonomy and self-reliance promoted in the official reemployment frameworks ignore the key place of connections, particularly the importance of
close-knit communities of workers, and tend to reduce individual potential and agency while creating social isolation and vulnerability.

Within these reemployment frameworks, job counselors emphasize the importance of being active. They often described jobless people as "depressed" and "inactive." Being active and initiative became a new moral imperative for the unemployed. One of my informants, Yuan, described the form of activity that was suggested to her after she lost her job.

> When I was just laid off, the director of the reemployment service center once told me to be active and to take the initiative in seeking reemployment. He gave an example: "When you wake up in the morning, you see it snowed last night. Then you should go out and knock on the doors of restaurants or offices to ask whether they need someone to shovel snow in front of their buildings." Now to get a job that pays five yuan per hour, you have to use such initiative or be that active; does this sound too extreme? Something that pays you five yuan is still called a job [*gongzuo*].

As Yuan explains, according to the director, her failure to knock on doors was the reason she remained unemployed. This emphasis on personal initiative in reemployment functions to shift the focus from state or corporate job creation to individuals' self-promotion and to their moral or psychological qualifications for employment.

It is no accident that psychology has become important in official Chinese responses to unemployment. As mentioned in the introduction, China has recently been gripped by a mental health "crisis" that is perceived to be most serious among the unemployed (Shi 1999). Yet the crisis has not garnered much public support for increased mental health care. One solution has been to create more informal "counselors." In part, the profession of *peiliao* emerged as a means to address this crisis.

But even before the mental health crisis was perceived as a crisis, the field of psychology and its experts had begun to play a significant role in shaping labor politics in China, including justifying gendered layoffs (Wang 2003). In the mid-1980s and early 1990s, economists and reformers claimed that internal psychological obstacles made it difficult for women to survive in the market economy. They argued that women had low self-esteem and a desire to sacrifice themselves for their families, which made them less competitive in the job market (Rosen 1994). Yet as the Chinese economy has not developed fast enough to absorb unemployed workers, the government now encourages the unemployed to rely on themselves for reemployment (Blecher 2002). This policy has turned the claim that women cannot compete in the market on its head. Women are encouraged to tap into their domestic femininity as entrepreneurial capital. Indeed, in state-led reemployment programs, the character traits that used to be labeled psychological "obstacles" now constitute the very traits that state-trained counselors insist are essential for workers in the new market economy.

Unemployed women, in particular, are trained for reemployment as psychological care workers, housemaid counselors, hotline talk therapists, or ghostwriters for psychological self-help magazines (Tamara Jacka, professor of anthropology, the Australian National University, personal communication, August 2010; Wan Li, a job counselor at the Changping Labor Market Service Center, personal communication, July 2010). At state-led reorientation programs, training workshops sponsored by nongovernmental organizations, and job centers run by residents' committees, retrained women are called upon to capitalize on their own experiences with unemployment as they counsel others who are going through similar hardship and despair. The training of laid-off women to promote "psychotherapy" thus not only addresses the market's demand for more psychological care workers in China but also advances the development of the new psychotherapy industry.

Gender, Class, and Therapeutic Governmentality

The logic of psychologization renders unemployment a matter of psychology and views social and economic problems as issues to be addressed with therapeutic methods (cf. Miller 1986; McLaughlin 2010; Gordo and De Vos 2010; De Vos 2011). In China, this psychologization occurs as a process through which psychology (particularly positive psychology) makes it feasible to reform those on the margins of society and shape their employment trajectories toward political and economic ends that benefit the state, a process that resonates, to some extent, with the notion of the therapeutic state Thomas Szasz (2001) proposed in the 1970s and 1980s.

Yet psychologization in China is more than the injection of the language of psychology into everyday life; it also uses "psychological" modes of thinking to make sense of change and everyday life in the wake of widespread socioeconomic dislocation. Today, there is practically no social space in China that does not include a psychologist, particularly in large cities: psychologists are present in parenting courses, in schools, at work, on TV, at sports events, and at disaster sites.

In this context, the Chinese government normalizes the role of women as domestic workers or *peiliaos*. It supports the notion that it is "natural" for a caring woman to take a job like *peiliao*, and in so doing she serves both families and the state. In Shanghai, for example, the approval of *peiliao* as an official profession acknowledges the role *peiliaos* can play in contributing to the well-being of individuals, to social stability, and to the local economy.

More important, the mobilization of laid-off women in the emerging therapeutic strategies of the ruling party occurs in the context of post-Mao politics of class and gender. Unlike Mao's gender ideologies, which erased biological differences between men and women in order to maximize the use of women's productive and reproductive labor, in the post-Mao era, biological and sexual differences between men and women are emphasized. This was first done to justify the disproportionate number of women who were laid off from the state sector (Rosen 1994; Wang 2003). The rise of biologized and essentialized understandings of gender (Yang 1999; Brownell and Wasserstrom 2002) also facilitates the mobilization of marginalized women to embody the feminine ideal and act as caring subjects, as, for example, as *peiliao*. According to Joan Scott (1988), gender used in this way reframes and legitimates class inequalities that can be hidden by the new focus on gendered differences. Pun Ngai and Chris Chan (2008) suggest that class in China is doubly displaced, first by the Chinese party-state as a hegemonic political strategy to hide the class positions and social privileges of the new rich, and second by the market to clear the way for a neoliberal economic discourse that emphasizes individualism, professionalism, and the open market.[3] In China, class as an analytical and political concept is often replaced by gender and race (Dirlik 2007). The emphasis in China on the vanguard role of marginalized women in promoting psychotherapy and on their particularly feminine qualities ignores the role of class in their unemployment experiences, even though their very marginalization demonstrates the country's intensified class stratification.

Arlie Hochschild (1983) examines the alienating effects of psychological and emotional labor on workers' psyches and their sense of themselves. She points out that in contemporary societies, emotional and psychological labor is increasingly demanded of workers. Examples include being forced to sell one's smile for free or being required to empathize with an angry or rude customer. Junko Kitanaka (2012, 195–196) points out how Japanese cultural discourse justifies and naturalizes psychological labor as a woman's virtue. Scholars of emotional labor argue that care work is often an extremely gendered practice, because "the image of the ideal emotional labourer is female, as the work is assumed to require attributes and capabilities which are stereotypically defined as feminine and believed to be 'naturally' possessed by women" (Lewis 2008, 131). Care labor is still considered "women's work," and in the eyes of dominant males, such work deserves neither good wages nor respect.

Laoshi and the Politics of Care

Scholars suggest that unemployment and reemployment policies in China are based on a combination of socialist ethics and new market rationalities. The goal of these policies is to transform laid-off workers from individuals who depend on work units and the state for job security into self-reliant, market-oriented people (Won 2004, 72). To some extent, this stance resembles the new European Union employment discourse on fluxicurity (flexibility + security) as a strategy for managing employment and social security. These employment frameworks emphasize independence, autonomy, and individual responsibility (Crespo and Serrano 2010, 51). Resources that were traditionally associated with the socialist work-unit system, including skills, social relations, and work ethics, have been appropriated strategically as resources for developing the new market economy.

In the training of *peiliao*, one of these characteristics is the moral quality of *laoshi*, which is presumably derived from the socialist work-unit system that nurtured workers' dependence on their superiors and the state (Walder 1986; Lü and Perry 1997). *Laoshi* has a cluster of meanings, such as honesty, naïveté, reliability, flexibility, or adaptability (Yan Y. 2003, 2011). In Changping, when referring to women workers, *laoshi* also means being obedient, genuine, and caring. Noddings (2000, 36–39) suggests that there are two concepts of caring: caring as a virtue and caring as a relationship between the carer and the person who is cared for. Caring perceived only as a virtue does not necessarily translate into the moral and social worth women's care labor deserves. Noddings proposes that caring be understood as a relation in which women's caring is accepted and appreciated; this imbues it with moral, social, and monetary value. However, in Changping, *laoshi* casts caring as a moral virtue rather than a relationship between the carer and the person being cared for. Women workers in Changping have tended to see themselves as too *laoshi* (as less disruptive than male workers) and have blamed this disposition for their layoffs from state-owned enterprises, but job centers have touted *laoshi* as the quality that can get those women reemployed, especially as domestic workers or *peiliao*, because employers appreciate obedient and reliable people when hiring workers for their households (see also Yan H. 2003a).[4] Yet many reemployed women still believe that the general perception that they are *laoshi* (in this case, the idea that they have insufficient knowledge about market competition) is the reason they are often exploited and abused in the new domestic work market.

The work of the informal counselors including *peiliao* is complex—both history informed and future oriented—new forms of psychological knowledge are linked to the older, community forms in a process that promotes acceptance of the new knowledge—an application of the dialectics of *biantong*. For the newly trained ranks of community job counselors, it is as important to encourage those they counsel to forget the past, as it is for them to ensure that their language and practices can be understood within the lingering memories of lives in work units extant not so long ago.

One element of psychosocial work at Beibiao is done at a job center offering jobs that pay by the hour. At this center, residents' committee members are paid by the state to train laid-off workers and help them find work. The government also offers free job training and counseling like the event Zhang Yi organized in the ethnographic vignette that opens this book. Women are presumed to be easier to recruit to such events than men, who have to be invited. The job center was initially set up in 2009 by Li Ying, a former workshop party secretary. After Li retired from the Beibiao factory in 2002, she worked on the Beibiao residents' committee. The center trains residents, especially laid-off women, then finds them jobs, typically as paid-by-the-hour housemaids, as *peiliaos*, or in other new types of care-related jobs. The job center charges a service fee of 80–120 yuan for training workers and helping them find jobs. This fee amounted to a day's wage for some women workers in 2007, when a housemaid's hourly wage in Changping ranged from 15 to 25 yuan. Li serves as the center's all-in-one manager, staff person, treasurer, and trainer. In 2011, the center began to be jointly operated with two neighboring residents' committees. Since 2006, Li has taken preliminary training in counseling and social work, which was paid for by the local government. While both her subject positions and methods of training have been labile, Li's background as a party secretary has influenced the job counseling she offers, which combines typical forms of thought work (i.e., orienting women to take certain jobs in order to fulfill political requirements of the district government, for example, sending enough people to work as traffic wardens during the 2008 Summer Olympic Games) with techniques of social work and counseling.

For former party secretaries such as Li Ying, elements of the socialist past are a constant point of reference for conveying their authority and facilitating their current jobs. In her training sessions, Li Ying either advocated *laoshi* as a virtue that was unique to laid-off women because of the commune-like lifestyle at work units (although *laoshi* is not necessarily

5.1. Within the CRC office, a specific table and personnel were set up to help workers get (re)employed with a sign on the table "Employment Service Station."

a gendered trait) or spoke of *laoshi* as a psychological trait that could be manipulated to impress clients or employers. She encouraged trainees to psychologize the public's perception of their *laoshi* and maximize their advantages so they could survive in the domestic work market:

> We workers have a reputation of being *laoshi* [honest] and *shizai* [down to earth], so bank on this; you can easily gain trust from employers. Of course, how to perform *laoshi* requires skills. You cannot perform yourself in a way that you are too *laoshi* or gullible; you'll become an easy target for abuse or exploitation. You have to be flexible, know how to do it appropriately.

According to Yan Yunxiang (2011), until the early 1980s, *laoshi* meant being honest, trustworthy and was highly regarded in village society. However, as Yan observes, in the postreform era, some of the qualities of *laoshi* has gradually become a negative trait, one that engenders scorn. It can even be a fatal shortcoming outside the local community, as it invites aggression and cheating in a market economy (Yan Y. 2003, 77–78). And yet in efforts to find new jobs, *laoshi* is seen as a possible employment advantage. Li Ying acknowledged *laoshi* as a virtue of women workers, although she felt that being too *laoshi* was problematic. For laid-off women workers, being *laoshi* is associated with their long-standing presence in the community; people know them and their family background. They are therefore more likely to be reliable and trustworthy than migrant workers. Employers highly value these qualities in a domestic worker or *peiliao*. Li Ying thus highlighted *laoshi* as a selling point for women's reemployment. I was permitted to overhear a phone conversation with a potential employer (also a family friend, as she later revealed to me) in which Li Ying emphasized the virtue of *laoshi*:

> They are laid off, *laoshi*; some of them are *xiao xing* [filial piety stars] and care for people. They make perfect housemaids and *peiliaos*. They can do whatever you ask them to do. They won't complain about the money. But for the sake of me saving face, you cannot pay them too low. Have some conscience. These women are middle-aged and have senior parents to support and young children to raise [*shang you lao, xia you xiao*].[5]

In this conversation, Li emphasized women's caring as a kind of moral virtue and portrayed *peiliaos* as complacent workers who would not complain about having to enact that virtue in order to survive in a competitive job market. In the training she offered, Li Ying encouraged trainees to emphasize *laoshi* in order to impress employers. Here is what she told several women in a training session in the summer of 2010:

> *Laoshi* was a virtue at the work unit and is still a virtue in the market, but we have to go beyond the traditional notion of *laoshi*. Yes, we are trustworthy people, but we have to be flexible and adjust ourselves to the job market. In the past, we chatted with people freely. But now we charge money when we talk to clients. The moment we walk into their houses, we charge money. That's why we need to do it professionally, talk something out of our clients: their worries, concerns, depression, or negativity. How? Very easy. Your experience, your experience with layoff and its consequences. No one could be lower than us workers, the way we were treated in layoffs. We workers were laid off because we were believed to be too *laoshi*. How we overcame that despair and stand up for ourselves will be inspiring, so mobilize that to cheer people up. But when you talk, you have to be humble, not bragging about how great you are in overcoming the difficulties. Highlight your weakness to amplify their [the clients'] greatness and strength. We need to understand their psychology and to show sympathy to their difficulties and also gain sympathy from the clients so they will treat us well and pay us.

In this training session, Li Ying used the first-person plural even though she had not been laid off. This rhetorical strategy allowed her to identify with laid-off women and showed solidarity with them. She used the logic that they had been laid off from state enterprises because they were perceived as *laoshi*. She was aware that this reasoning was widespread and popular among workers: those who made a fuss and cause disruptions ("violent" male workers) or were likely to do so would not be laid off until it was necessary for the enterprise to avoid bankruptcy. Li's identification with the unemployed women is a method of healing them of the trauma of their layoffs, yet it is oriented toward opening the hearts of these women and encouraging them to accept her moral and psychological preaching. Li's strategic invocation of workers' virtues and experiences in former work units echoes what Arif Dirlik writes about the intertwining between the past and the present. The past should be viewed as a store of past struggles, which reappear and are experienced anew in the present, shifting or undermining, however slightly, the sedimented effects of history (Dirlik

1997). The training session was a dual process in which trainees were rendered as objects of psychological care while they were being prepared for their future performance of psychotherapy for others as housemaids or *peiliaos*. The plasticity of the self promoted in this job counseling is required for and legitimates the informal, irregular, and temporary employment patterns that are available to laid-off workers in Changping.

The job counseling and training available to women workers attempted to harness the full potential of the knowledge that is incorporated in the bodies of workers. The job training offered to *peiliaos* was embodied; counselors putatively equipped them with *xinjian* (heartware) or *gong xin shu* (the art of "bombing," touching, or moving the heart) to enable them to offer services that touch and warm the hearts of their clients. This is congruent with the Chinese understanding that psychology is "the study of the heart's reasoning," the seat of cognition, virtue, and bodily sensation (Ots 1994; Worm 2010).

Li's teaching also illustrates that feelings (i.e., compassion, sympathy) can be developed through psychology; helping women become morally virtuous requires psychological work. In the job training for *peiliaos*, the *laoshi* that developed in work units was joined with the notion of self-reliance in a market economy. An imaginative reenactment of past actions, thoughts, and virtues in work units, with an immediacy and faithfulness that can bring them directly into present minds, would not appear alien or incomprehensible to these women. However, isolating *laoshi* from its original context cannot generate genuine moral agency. Li's use of psychology erodes moral virtue and character and confuses social control with psychological education, trivilizing both the genuine hearts of her clients and the equally genuine problems (structural forces) that create the difficulties unemployed women encounter in their efforts to find new jobs. The way Li manipulated ideas and emotions highlights the individualizing and psychologizing tendency in reemployment: it emphasizes making laid-off women employable instead of focusing on creating jobs for them.

Li instructed the women to expose their own vulnerability in their approaches to their clients. She believed that performing vulnerability would ensure appreciation and empathy and would lead to higher or more reliable pay. Also, the status of *peiliaos* remains somewhat illegitimate in the public eye, and this makes it difficult for them to establish formal caring relations with those they care for. In this context, the psychotherapeutic strategy that asks marginalized women to perform their vulnerability in the name of care and healing can exacerbate and prolong their original suffering.

Peiliao and Companionable "Counseling"

At a job center in Beijing, one counselor I observed in summer 2010 instructed a woman to use her whole presence (i.e., her smile, her energy, her warmth, and her body language) as a message in itself, one that could lift up whatever household she might work in.[6] Yet many workers I spoke to had nagging questions, including why they were the ones who had to perform happiness when they were really unhappy, and making a living in the new job market caused so much anxiety and stress (see Yang 2007 on their unemployment experiences).

The distress associated with being a laid-off woman is exacerbated in the rituals of seeking market-generated labor. As mentioned, several of my informants sought clients in public places such as the parks that seniors especially visit. One of the women who got trained at a domestic work center in Beijing as a *peiliao* said,

> It appears easy to strike up a conversation. But when you offer to work for them as a housemaid or *peiliao*, people sometimes see you as someone like a prostitute. Even though counseling is performed by high-profile people on TV, in reality, you have to be affiliated with a formal institute and do it in a formal setting so people can trust you. But we are not affiliated with any institution. There is no institute supporting us; the job center did not care about us after our first employment.

Comments like this show that psychological empowerment cannot override real life and the power of stereotypes about women. "Normal" women in this working-class community of Changping are not supposed to be so forthcoming in social interactions, especially with strangers. People often perceive those who strike up conversations with strangers as abnormal and possibly as prostitutes. At the park, another woman said, "One needs to be very subtle to even start the conversation on *peiliao*. Many people still believe that only those with mental problems need counseling, and they don't realize how psychology can help even healthy people." As performers of a new category of work without legal regulation, institutional protection, or even consistent descriptions of the work entailed, those who practice *peiliao* often experience intensified discrimination and exploitation. A woman who worked as one of the first housemaids and *peiliaos* in this community said,

> People seldom think of a chat as worth any money if there is no formal setting to establish a professional therapist and client relationship. That's why employers dare not pay you or want to do something else—touching you, exposing himself to you, or harassing you.

The absence of respected boundaries and the public's lack of awareness of what psychological support can offer lead to discrimination and exploitation. Because *peiliao* appears to be a fake profession, the clearer lines that exist in a professional counseling setting are not established, leaving these women vulnerable both physically and mentally.

Some of the *peiliaos* have been treated like *sanpei* (a companion to eat, drink, and sleep with). Feng Yi was laid off from a fabric factory in 1999, after which she undertook a series of domestic jobs. Having completed her preliminary job training as a housemaid at a domestic work center in Changping, Feng was reemployed as a paid-by-the-hour housemaid and *peiliao* for a retired man. Feng's job at her client's household included cleaning; cooking two meals; boiling herbal medicine; massaging the man's left leg, which had been disabled by a stroke; and chatting with him. Feng said that she endured temper tantrums, verbal and sexual abuse, and other forms of mistreatment by her client. She ran away in the midst of an argument with him, taking his house keys so she would be able to claim her salary later. Feng explained her experience this way:

> They thought of me as *laoshi*, an easy target for abuse, but I am not that *laoshi*; I took away their keys, more than ten keys. If they don't pay me, I could go back to their house and get something that is at least worth my salary.

Feng wondered when she would get paid and where she would find her next job. Such stories illustrate how gender exploitation is intensified in the new psychotherapeutic work women were trained to do. Feng also reinforced the idea that paying for care from a housemaid *peiliao* has not been entirely accepted, especially by the older generation.

> The old man did not like to have a care worker at home; it is not him but his three sons who hired me. He sometimes used me as a target to vent his frustration with his sons. He complained [that] none of them assumed filial responsibility to take care of him.

Indeed, in traditional Chinese families, it is unusual to hire a stranger to take care of the old; many still believe that family members should take care of their elderly. Feng's encounter with this tradition speaks to the shift in the role of family in elder care in China in the wake of the commodification of domestic labor in the market economy. Indeed, the trend in Beijing is to replace family caregivers, especially daughters or daughters-in-law, with *peiliaos* or housemaids. In the context of lingering resentment over rapid changes in care work, Feng's care was rejected, no matter how hard she tried. Her labor was also devalued or rejected. That is, the woman charged with care work and the old man who needed care were unable to form care relations because the man did not think a *peiliao* should be the source of his care. Maintaining the care relation depends on contributions from both parties (Noddings 2000).

Many women workers I interviewed had doubts and uncertainty about the efficacy and sincerity of the state's psychotherapeutic strategy. For example, Wang Yu, a laid-off woman worker turned taxi driver from Changping, has been designated a taxi star in Beijing, partially because of her achievements in preventing suicide attempts in 2007 and 2008. (Typically those who attempted suicide or their families called or wrote to taxi companies to praise those drivers who saved their lives.) However, Wang wondered why so much attention has been given to suicide and mental illness in recent years and why at this moment taxi drivers have been mobilized to prevent it. For her, suicide has always existed and taxi drivers have long been voluntarily engaging in suicide prevention because they are aware of certain locations where people attempt suicide in Beijing. Wang did not explicitly articulate but implied that mental illness has been politicized. Instead of attributing her suicide prevention work to her preliminary training in counseling, she emphasized humanity and being attentive to clients' needs.

> It's difficult to compete with men, so I try to be more attentive to clients' needs, offering them shopping tips, chatting with those passengers who looked depressed in order to attract more clients. They spread the word, especially for women who prefer a female driver if they have to travel alone at night. And also it's human to talk with someone like a weeping girl who gets into your taxi alone at night, telling you to go to some strange, remote area. You cannot help talking with them and asking whether they are doing okay, then find a way to remind them that it is not easy for your parents to bring you up, we should value life. Such simple words from a stranger sometimes help change their hearts and prevent them from attempting suicide.

Wang Yu seemed to care less about the title of taxi star than about being a good person and attracting more clients in order to survive in a male-dominated job market. Yet counseling skills can offer an advantage for the women taxi drivers competing with men in the job market (about 5 percent of taxi drivers in Beijing are female). Some of my informants had gone to training sessions on psychology or suicide prevention because they understood that such training would improve their chances in the competition for passengers. These women used their own agency to take advantage of programs offered and then used the new tools they acquired for their own benefit. Preliminary knowledge of counseling and suicide prevention has recently been integrated into job training for taxi drivers in Beijing because they are perceived to sometimes be the last person with an opportunity to save someone. Women such as Wang Yu exemplify the tensions in the politics of the psychologization trend: on the one hand, they are suspicious of the politicization of mental illness and the commodification of women's "virtues" for market purposes; on the other hand, they are ready to be trained for work they need and for their own benefits.

Conclusion

Since the mid-1990s, psychology and psychotherapy have provided a language for the people to interpret the sea change caused by widespread socioeconomic dislocation and constituted a mechanism that is used to resolve social, economic, and mental disorders in China. This trend of psychologization is a politically charged process that creates new subjects and promotes certain emotions and outlooks, including happiness and self-reliance. It constructs those who have been displaced and impoverished by recent economic restructuring as both objects of psychological care and self-reliant subjects who can contribute to the market economy. This therapeutic mode of governance gives marginalized people, particularly women, the minimum skills they need to embody the therapeutic ethos and therapeutic strategies of the ruling party. Reemploying laid-off workers to fill the market niche created by the shortage of counselors in China demonstrates that the people, the characteristics and work ethics associated with state enterprises (and with Maoism generally) have been appropriated as resources for entrepreneurial capital. Laid-off workers are now expected to achieve the state's sociopolitical objectives in the new millennium through the dialectics of *biantong*.

The practices of informal psychosocial work in Changping provide employment for laid-off workers. The unique experiences of dispossessed working-class women as they navigate recent state-led psychotherapeutic interventions shed light on a paradoxical feature of the development of psychotherapy in China: the state emerges as both cause and cure of social and mental disorders. Psychologization goes hand in hand with the repoliticization of subjectivity. By mobilizing, optimizing, and governing the agency and potentialities of the people, the therapeutic strategy reveals both the flexibility and power of the Chinese state. The state clearly associates itself with the rhetoric of caring for people's happiness and psychology, presenting itself as a benevolent government. However, the benevolence through state-led psychotherapeutic intervention has inevitably intensified gendered and class-based exploitation.

The explicit focus on gender over class in China and the push for marginalized women to embody the feminine ideal in the context of the emerging therapeutic ethos help explain the abuse suffered by *peiliaos* (apart from their obvious structural lack of power). They are positioned as both "counselors" (of prestigious status) and "female company" (caring, sexualized, low-status women). Both subject positions are united in *peiliaos*, which has a paradoxical effect on these women's identities and produces new vulnerabilities to gendered exploitation in the job market. For laid-off women workers whose livelihood and psychological well-being were destroyed by economic restructuring, participating as *peiliao* is a complex experience that can reinscribe their often traumatic experiences with unemployment and trap them in a low-status, vulnerable position that nevertheless provides a means of survival. The embodied learning of *peiliaos* is more complex than psychosocial workers or the government perceive. Both gender and psychology have become sites for accessing resources in a market economy and for articulating or downplaying intensified class politics.

In the next chapter, I will strengthen this thread of my argument by focusing on the training of laid-off men turned taxi drivers and their experiences with intensified class-based exploitation.

6

JOB BURNOUT OR SUPPRESSED ANGER?

Every morning when I open my eyes, I already owe the company 200 yuan.
No matter what happens that day, you have to work and make that amount,
hoping to have leftover money for food.

—TAXI DRIVER LI DA, CHANGPING, 2008

We make about 500 yuan a day and pay the taxi company 200 yuan and
200 yuan for gas. Then a part of the remainder goes to pay for the vehicle's
maintenance. We earn really nothing and live on pocket money.

—TAXI DRIVER WANG XIAOLAI, CHANGPING, 2007

The party always claims to represent the interests of the working class. But
once there are problems, workers are the ones to be blamed and reformed
while higher-ups remain unchanged. Trade unions of course are
always correct.

—A LAID-OFF MALE WORKER IN CHANGPING, 2010

One day in July 2008, a male worker surnamed Hui greeted me in the corridor of the main production building of the Beibiao factory. "Doc, see," he said, pointing to watch parts he was carrying, "I finally return to *shengchan di yi xian* [the production line]!" The pride of being a worker on the production line was written all over his smiling face. His countenance was a stark contrast with the downcast gaze and disgruntled attitude he had displayed when he was driving a pedicab in 2002 and 2003, after he was laid off. His wife later told me that her uncle had undertaken crucial political maneuvers after he was promoted to head of the local taxi bureau and it was thanks to these efforts that Hui had been able to return to Beibiao—by then a very competitive environment, given the fact that many laid-off workers wanted to return to the factory. Even though Hui did not make more money at Beibiao than he did riding a pedicab, his wife indicated that Hui was much happier and felt more "fulfilled" to be back at the factory. Being affiliated with a *danwei* (work unit) gave him a sense of belonging and identity that he never had while driving a pedicab or taxi.

Taxi driving has become one of the most common ways for workers laid off from state-owned enterprises to make a living in Changping and in China at large (see Chang 2001). However, given rising gas prices and the hefty franchise fees taxi companies charge, the popularity of the work has created excessive competition that is made worse by the large number of licenses taxi companies hand out. In addition, because of an inadequate roadway system in Beijing, drivers are often forced to endure congested conditions that reduce already meager incomes. In this context many taxi drivers suffer job burnout and seek reemployment in the state sector.

The Chinese term for those who suffer job burnout is *xiangpi ren* ("eraser" or "Plasticine" people). In this chapter, I show how this term is a window into a set of social phenomena that converge in the behavior and treatment of reemployed cabdrivers. I argue that attempts to control the percolating anger of these cabdrivers through forms of psychotherapy and gendered discourse mask dramatic class conflict that has resulted from privatization and massive layoffs in China.

Xiangpi ren refers to the numbness, hopelessness, and loss of passion for life people experience with burnout. The term comes from a 1986 novel written by the famous Chinese writer, Wang Shuo, about a lost generation of urban youth.[1] As described in an article posted on the Web site of the Guangzhou Heart-Light Counseling Center, *xiangpi ren* are amenable even though they are kneaded this way and that, much like Plasticine modeling clay, which is elastic and resilient. And, like modeling clay, which does not conduct electricity and is waterproof, *xiangpi ren* are numb, senseless, inefficient, and irresponsible. They can get their own way and refuse to accept new things and suggestions.[2] They are represented in novels and in Chinese media in general as having lost their ability to think critically; they have no sense of either honor or disgrace.

These representations in media may be exaggerated, but it is clear that the notion of *xiangpi ren* points to real material conditions. A survey carried out last year by *Beijing News* and the Sino Web portal that canvassed 1,700 people across China found that 70 percent displayed signs of job burnout. Almost 60 percent of the companies polled said that the incidence of burnout among their employees had increased. *Xiangpi ren* are mainly white-collar workers. The only blue-collar workers who have been reportedly suffering from symptoms of *xiangpi ren* are taxi drivers. Typically, they work alone for more than 60 hours a week. They feel as if they exhaust all their energy and receive as recompense only a sense of emptiness.

Yet the emergence of *xiangpi ren* is more than a media story or the depressive symptoms of individuals. It is also an example of how macroeconomic processes cause individual stress (see Catalano and Dooley 1983). Broader economic change produces individually experienced life changes, life events produce symptoms of psychological disorder, and symptoms create a demand for services. For example, economic restructuring generates layoffs and a cheap labor pool that is expected to fill undesirable jobs. This, in turn, increases illness and injury and the use of mental health services (Dooley and Catalano 1984). Thus, unemployment is an essential link between macroeconomic change and individual stress. It exerts negative effects on emotional functioning and physical health. The psychological impact of involuntary job loss is exacerbated when social and emotional support are absent or networks are thin. So while psychologists treat the emergence of *xiangpi ren* as a symptom of depression or psychological disorder, workers consider their burnout to be the result of structural violations of the economic order in China.[3]

Xiangpi ren is many things: a media construct, a symptom cluster, a cultural idiom of distress and the result of structural change. I want to suggest that *xiangpi ren* is something else still: a form of suppressed anger. This anger, which accumulates among workers who spent years in work units, was triggered by the mass layoffs and dislocation workers experienced during the privatization process since the mid-1990s. Chinese revolutionary pedagogy described repressed anger as "swallowed bitterness" (*chi ku*), a silenced memory of injustice that can be reconnected to anger only by "speaking bitterness" (*su ku*) (Hinton 1966). Similarly, *majie* (cursing in the street), a public display of socially induced anger that sometimes escalates into uncontrollable rage, makes it possible for individuals to become conscious of and articulate suppressed anger or previously unfelt or unconscious emotional responses to injustice (Lyman 1981, 2004).

As a discursive construct and an ambivalent concept, *xiangpi ren* can be framed as a medium for maintaining social order that reinforces dominant power relationships. I also propose that alongside their promotion of happiness as a means of domesticating the anger of vulnerable groups, psychosocial workers in Changping use the notion of *xiangpi ren* to depoliticize workers' suppressed social anger and recast it as a form of depression or a psychological disorder. Simultaneously, workers use *xiangpi ren* as a subversive and protective strategy to help them resist further marginalization. In this sense, the phenomenon of *xiangpi ren* among laid-off workers turned taxi drivers constitutes a new arena of political contestation. The source of workers' anger is not so much the interpersonal relationships they have with passengers as it is their perception that their status has been injured. They have experienced significant downward mobility, from prestigious ideological representatives of Maoist socialism to workers who do not even earn a living wage.

Taxi drivers in Beijing claim that they have become *xiangpi ren* not only because of overwork but also because the restructuring of state enterprises has ended their lifelong employment and replaced their once-egalitarian experiences in work units with a highly stratified and classed experience in the market economy. In Changping, where the majority of taxi drivers are laid-off workers, the challenges and frustrations of their new jobs have intensified their hatred of privatization. Drivers see the managers of the state-owned enterprises where they used to work, the individuals who laid them off, as symbols of the mandate to privatize. Most taxi drivers still live in the residential compounds of their former employers, and their interactions with these former employers and community residents' committee members constitute opportunities for them to vent their anger.

In many cases, they have resorted to airing their intense emotions through cursing sessions at their former workplaces or before their local residents' committees. This speech practice, called *majie*, traditionally associated with feminine behavior, has been appropriated in recent years by unemployed men who seek to regain their status, vent their extreme frustration, and find some kind of recompense for their loss of jobs and status. While these taxi drivers themselves are often mobilized by the government to identify passengers whose behaviors suggest that they are potential risks to social harmony, they are now often perceived by residents' committees as harboring *yinhuan*. Particularly in Beibiao, after a major taxi strike in 2003, residents' committees targeted laid-off men turned taxi drivers as latent (if not actual) troublemakers.

In what follows, I first demonstrate how the difficulties taxi drivers have experienced in the treacherous taxi industry in Beijing make them resentful of the privatization that has displaced and impoverished them. I then examine how the phenomenon of *xiangpi ren* among reemployed taxi drivers is a form of suppressed anger and how psychosocial workers and residents' committee members at Beibiao view this anger as a form of unrest that threatens social harmony. These psychosocial workers and residents' committee members have taken on the task of domesticating the anger of these workers. I also explore the disempowering potential of the move to govern the unemployed through psychology and the domestication of workers' anger through the notion of *xiangpi ren*.

Echoing the work of Chapter 5, I illustrate how the emphasis on gender and psychotherapy that trickles down from government leaders to residents' committees can downplay class antagonisms by expressing them in gendered terms or through psychotherapeutic apparatuses. This process recasts the social consequences of privatization or management issues in the taxi industry as individual stress and personal dilemmas.

Reemployment as Taxi Drivers

Waves of protests among taxi drivers have occurred in Changping and in China at large. In May 2003, over 300 taxis in Changping lined up to block traffic in front of the district government for several days in an attempt to pressure the local government to regulate the taxi-driving industry and create more jobs. At Beibiao, many laid-off men perform *majie*, expressing anger as a form of political speech (Lyman 2004). These emotional rituals, based on otherwise typically female speech practices, express both masculine prowess and vulnerability in an effort to force community residents' committees to respond to cost-of-living demands and obtain other benefits. These anger displays are also rituals of class tension, highlighting the social polarization that has been intensified by economic restructuring and the plagued taxi industry in Beijing.

In 2013, there were 252 taxi companies, 660,000 taxis, and 100,000 drivers in Beijing.[4] On any given day, 59,200 taxis operate there, which means 33.7 taxis for every 10,000 people, more than enough transportation for the capital. Service is undermined, however, by the low efficiency of the taxi system due to the crowded roads and high *fenzi qian* (franchise fees) taxi companies demand. One of the most common complaints from members of the public in recent years has been the refusal of drivers to take passengers during rush hour. This is because drivers are afraid of getting stuck in traffic as they will lose money. Hundreds of taxis flee to parking lots to dodge passengers during rush hours.[5] Drivers almost uniformly feel that the franchise fees they must pay are too high. Private taxi drivers (who own the taxies) pay about 1,042 yuan per month to maintain a taxi, but commissioned taxi drivers (who rent the taxies) pay much more, 5,175 yuan per month, to their taxi companies. As one taxi driver of five years described the situation:

> Every day I spent 10 hours working for the rental fee and after the 10 hours, I can make money for myself. Because of the rising price of gas, to make enough money, you have to prolong your work hours. Every month, I make 3,000 yuan. This is the ideal situation. It will get worse if you have a traffic accident or fines from traffic police. Taxi companies are inhuman; no matter how sick you are that day, you have to pay the money for that day.

Beijing taxi drivers were well known for their sense of humor, garrulousness, and knowledge of domestic and international affairs. In transit, many people (including myself) took joy in hearing unsolicited lectures about the possible composition of the party's Political Bureau or updates on celebrity scandals. Yet recently passengers have begun to find that Beijing taxi drivers are more often silent and are not always honest. I have heard informants complain about being overcharged by cab drivers at the airport. And taxi drivers have started complaining to passengers. One driver in Changping told me how he vented his annoyance with passengers who traveled only short distances. "I speed on the freeway at 140 km, overtaking every car in sight, changing lanes swiftly as if no one were in my way. Then sometimes the passengers succumb to my annoyance and beg me to slow down. They sometimes pay more." Without proper channels to voice their opinions, drivers resort to "unethical" means, such as the speeding just described. Another driver of fifteen years told me:

> The early 1990s was the good old days when a taxi driver's income was well above the average made by urban residents. Taxi driving was a decent job then. However, nowadays no one wants to be in the trade any more. It is very hard to make a living. Each day I wake up, I owe 200 yuan to my company [the fixed monthly franchise fee he has to pay]. In addition to rising costs and long workdays, this high fee has made the job unattractive and the quality of service decline. I would have quit this job a long time ago if I didn't have to pay college tuition for my kid.

Scholars have documented the grievances of Chinese workers who have been laid off from state-owned enterprises—particularly those that concerning subsistence issues, corruption, welfare or pension payments, back wages, state enterprise restructuring, and the effects of the political economy of a region (C. K. Lee 2000; Hurst and O'Brian 2002; Hurst 2004; Solinger 2006). Grievances related to corruption among local state officials and the malfeasance of managers seem to exist in all types of firms and across all regions (Hurst 2004, 100). This chapter explores a type of grievance that has not received much attention in the literature: an anger that is caused by both the restructuring of state enterprises and dissatisfaction with reemployment in the taxi industry. Scholars have examined how the ways grievances and collective action are framed can significantly influence the course of contention. Ching Kwan Lee (2000) pays attention to how Chinese workers in northeast China framed protests; they emphasize both nostalgia for the Maoist era and modern, almost liberal conceptions of citizenship and legal rights. At Beibiao, workers framed their protests mainly within the context of their sacrifice for and contribution to the factory and their current struggle to earn a livelihood. In this community, cab drivers are increasingly opinionated and critical. A laid-off worker turned taxi driver commented on his work:

> We are supposed to be positive and happy, at least the counselors instructed us to be so because we are in the service industry, presumably transmitting happiness to our passengers so that we become a good *chuangkou* [window] to the capital. But we are also critical *shishi pinglunyuan* [commentators on

current issues]. We see what is happening firsthand as we travel to every corner of the city and contact a lot of people. We labored like slaves for the factory and now for taxi companies. We work long hours, more than full time, but we cannot make enough money to support our family especially when I have a sick wife and a child attending college. Deng Xiaoping said, "Diligence can get one wealth" [*qinlao zhi fu*]. [Yet] we work so hard, so diligently, but we are so poor.

The problems of the taxi industry (Shank 2012) were captured by a recent report of an incident involving China's new top leader, President Xi Jinping. China's Internet was abuzz early in April 2013 over a report that President Xi, who is striving to portray himself as a humble man, hailed a cab in Beijing. Ordinary people praised Xi as a refreshingly down-to-earth leader, feeling that his incognito ride revealed a yearning to share the pain and congested streets of a frustrated public. Even though the report was later said to be false, tremendous praise for Xi has nonetheless come from Internet users and others because of the contrast between the image of a chauffeur-driven chief of the Communist Party and the image of one hailing a taxi (which in Beijing are notoriously hard to flag down). The sensationalism of this representation of China's top leader highlights the woes of the taxi industry.

To complicate a bad situation, in Changping, taxi driving has become more precarious as the number of pedicab drivers and unlicensed black market taxis have increased. The number of illegal taxis in Changping is staggering. An interview with local traffic police suggests that they are fully aware of the situation but because of the emphasis on stability, they choose to "open one eye while closing the other."

At least some of the illegal taxi drivers claim to have no alternative. One unlicensed taxi driver in Changping told me:

> My wife's cancer treatment and my child's college tuition both need money; I have no alternative to make enough money. It is risky; if I were caught by the police I would be fined thousands of yuan. I also rely on friends and friends' friends for snowballing [referrals] to transport passengers.

However, the main rivals for licensed taxi drivers are pedicab drivers, whose fares are much cheaper. Local people call pedicab drivers *xiangzi*, the name of the protagonist in an old film titled *luotuo xiangzi* [Rickshaw *xiangzi*], based on a novel written by the famous Chinese writer Lao She. The film describes the bitter life of the urban poor in Beijing *jiefang qian* (before liberation, before 1949). The comparison of the current poverty, exploitation, and intensified social stratification of the new urban poor with conditions in the old society that existed before liberation has become a theme in people's everyday discourse (see Hurst and O'Brian 2002, 259 for similar comparisons by workers).

Two rival and mutually hostile groups drive pedicabs in Changping: rural migrants and laid-off workers. The migrants predominate in the pedicab industry in Changping because they ask for lower prices than laid-off workers. One of my informants, Hui, who, as mentioned, returned to the production line at Beibiao in 2008, described his pedicab-driving days and interactions with migrants.

> Sometimes I couldn't get any passengers the whole day. They [passengers] would ask whether two yuan was ok. I would tell them I couldn't lower the starting price of 3 yuan, but *nongmingong* [peasant workers] can. They'll transport clients for any amount of money, so they get most of the business. I can't do it. Having been relegated to be a pedicab driver, feeding myself on my blood and sweat, I'm already very low. I cannot be lower. Peasant workers are different. Leaving their village and entering the city, this is upward mobility for them. . . . They have nothing to worry about, as they have a way to retreat. . . . They can always go back to their villages, where they may have a piece of land to cultivate and have a house in which to live. We workers are really propertyless. We have nothing except our labor, our bodies, over 130 *jin* of flesh. [I said, "But you have your apartment now, you bought it."] How I bought it, you don't know. The money is "saved from between the teeth" [saving on food]. I still have debts now.[6]

Rural migrants are often derogatorily labeled as *nongmingong* (peasant workers) by urban workers. They are often perceived as having grabbed away workers' *tie fanwan* (iron rice bowls) because they are seen as a labor source that is more docile and cheaper, thus eroding the employment security state workers once enjoyed. They are simultaneously competing for workers' *ni fanwan* (clay rice bowls), that is, irregular, informal reemployment such as pedicab driving. As in the worker's account above, urban workers express class consciousness in relation to migrants when they note that they are "really propertyless" (see C.K. Lee 2007). Unable to change their circumstances, drivers are exhausted, impoverished, and bitter, and they are labeled *xiangpi ren* by others and by themselves.

Although taxi companies have realized the importance of counseling in improving the quality of service, the support they offer to drivers is strategic and sparse. The psychological support that is offered is insufficient and disingenuous: it is designed to appease disgruntled drivers and enhance their work performances and efficiency. In addition to being insufficient, the care offered can be detrimental because it may put people in positions that compound their frustration.

Xiangpi Ren and Job Burnout

Unemployment is stressful and harmful to well-being, but being reemployed is not always beneficial, as exemplified in laid-off workers' reemployment in the taxi-driving industry in Beijing. Perceived occupational stress is related to various physical and psychological disorders, and chronic job pressures can increase mortality (Kitanaka 2012). While media representations have depicted taxi drivers as "taxi stars," or counselors on wheels who are busy preventing suicides, in reality many suffer job burnout or are in the process of becoming *xiangpi ren*. While Chinese psychologists suggest that taxi drivers as *xiangpi ren* suffer anxiety, depression, social withdrawal, the loss of drive, and other psychological disorders, taxi drivers contend that the sources of their stress and anger are rooted in *si-youhua* (privatization) and in the fact that as workers they are dislocated and impoverished. The process of turning nonpsychological issues into issues of individual pathology or personal dilemma, depoliticizes structural forces that cause the problems, and disguises social control (Conrad 1992). This psychologizing condemns individuals for "ills" such as impoverishment on the grounds of psychological problems, real or invented, even in the absence of factual evidence or when the facts would contradict such a diagnosis.

Economic stress plays a major role in connecting social class with psychological impairment. Yet such personal stress is created by and embedded in macrolevel economic dynamics. Reemployed workers suffer from chronic stress related to the inadequate return they receive for the effort they invest, excessive demands at work, and the fact that their role expectations (for example, breadwinner for the family) can no longer be met. Supplemental support for them is minimal because of the inefficiency and incompleteness of the social security system in China. Taxi drivers in Changping are simply coping on their own with minimal public support from government programs and residents' committees.

Studies of job burnout in the West often focus on three elements: exhaustion, cynicism, and feelings of inefficacy. Exhaustion refers to feelings of being overextended and depleted of one's emotional and physical resources. Cynicism refers to a negative, callous, or excessively detached response to various aspects of a job. Feelings of inefficacy refer to feelings of incompetence and a lack of achievement and productivity at work (Maslach et al. 2001, 399). Burnout, as Western studies demonstrate, is related to the specific situation of one's job; it is more specific than general depression (Freudenberger 1983; Warr 1987). Western literature identifies the factors that cause burnout as both individual and situational.

These three dimensions can all be applied to, but do not fully explain, the burnout of Beijing taxi drivers. Poor working conditions and intense market competition with licensed drivers and illegal "black taxi" drivers constitute the immediate context of exhaustion for taxi drivers in China. Cynicism and feelings of inefficacy emerge from the constantly but unsuccessful efforts of drivers to convince those in authority to regulate the taxi industry. A taxi driver from Changping, Wan Li, complained of the taxi-driving situation in Changping in 2007:

> There are at least 300 taxis and 100 pedicabs every day. Taxis and pedicabs outnumber passengers on streets because these are automatic jobs for laid-off workers. The starting price for pedicab is 3 yuan; if driven by a peasant, it's 2 yuan. Who will take a taxi?

The stress of these circumstances and the burnout among taxi drivers has even triggered suicides. One day in May 2003, in the middle of an argument with his wife, a reemployed taxi driver in a neighborhood next to Beibiao walked to their balcony and jumped to his death from their fourth-floor apartment. The man's mother held the wife responsible for her son's suicide because the wife often complained about the husband's inability to provide for the family, a constant badgering that destroyed the man's self-esteem. According to the mother, the taxi driver had been depressed for a long time. Even though the man worked so hard that he did not even have time to visit his mother, he still could not make enough money to provide for his family; his wife had to work as a cleaner in a student dormitory of a nearby university. It was reportedly the wife's constant complaints coupled with the man's guilt for his inability to make it possible for his wife to stay at home that caused the suicide. This death shocked the community. People inferred that ultimately the taxi industry was to blame. The suicide partially triggered the 2003 strike of 300 taxi drivers, but even this had little effect. Pressure for the government to regulate the taxi market and create more viable jobs for laid-off workers was simply not forthcoming until a series of attempts to reform the taxi industry in Beijing was initiated in early 2013.

One way to interpret this particular case is the inability of the depressed taxi driver to enact a social role. Leonard Pearlin (1983) argues that ongoing strain may result from the difficulty of satisfying the demands of conflicting roles, losing or acquiring roles, and the restructuring of continuing roles. Women, young people, and those of low socioeconomic status encounter the most severe role strain. Ongoing difficulties with enacting social roles are both a product of eventual change and a pathway through which events can damage an individual's emotional well-being (Pearlin and Lieberman 1979). For the taxi driver above, it was difficult to fulfill his role as a father, husband, and breadwinner who was supposed to make enough money that his wife would have the freedom to choose whether to work or not.

From the perspective of the party secretary turned psychosocial worker of that community, Shao Wen, the driver who committed suicide was someone who had long manifested the symptoms of *xiangpi ren*. In his diagnosis, psychological symptoms took precedence over historical events. However, a diagnosis that ignores the function of social roles and context does not go very far to explain the wider problems of laid-off workers whose burnout is caused by the loss of a job they thought they had for life, the loss of the institutional support that accompanied that job, and the absence of adequate technical, economic, and emotional support to help them find new jobs. Instead of benefiting from the prestigious, stoic characteristics they presented as the ideological representatives of Mao's socialism, these men are now being trained for the service industry, which requires them to develop new types of emotional and mental flexibility and adapt to ever-changing market demands. They are required to adopt new roles and even create new subjectivities to fit in the new market. Counselors tell them to emphasize *biantong*—flexibility or change with continuity—and focus on the good side of taxi driving (a job that purportedly transmits happiness to customers) instead of dwelling on a sense of entitlement that was associated with their glorious past, state work and socialist ethics in Mao's era.

Taxi companies and counselors have begun to pay increasing attention to the mental health of taxi drivers, especially after a series of suicide attempts in 2010 by workers at Foxconn, the world's biggest electronics contractor.[7] Since 2007, preliminary counseling techniques and suicide prevention strategies have been integrated into job training for taxi drivers in Beijing to help them cope with stress and encourage them to transmit happiness and prevent suicide. Yet these positive steps are undermined by the government's lack of attention to the challenges—including too many licenses, crowded roads, high franchise fees—to the taxi industry. Although the contradictions and uncertainties of the new market economy are clearly sources of psychological stress, the emphasis counselors place on psychological disorders distracts both workers and policy makers from the need to systematically revitalize the economy. Instead, this type of analysis lays the blame for present circumstances firmly on the shoulders of those workers.

According to Vanheule and colleagues (2003), there are two types of burnout. One type involves an imaginary tension with colleagues. The person who is dissatisfied holds someone else responsible for what goes wrong. This results in conflict escalation driven by an individual's feeling that he or she has been personally targeted and wronged by the other person. Typical reactions include feeling wronged, disappointed, envious, or aggressive (330). The person concerned is convinced that he or she is in the right, and this perception frames all emotions about problems at work. This swallows up the energy of the person; the more a worker worries about a problem, the deeper he or she sinks into it (332). In Changping, the real and imagined commission of wrongs by superiors at state-owned enterprises is one reason why unemployed individuals remain imprisoned in hypothetical vengeful scenarios and spiraling burnout and anger.

This type of job burnout often leads to overtly expressed hostility. Laid-off workers often target former employers or the particular individuals who laid them off at the state-owned enterprise where they used to work. Work units valued workers' obedience to and dependence on their superiors or the state. However, during economic restructuring, workers have realized that obedience may not be rewarded and in fact has led to "punishment" when those who are perceived as least likely to cause trouble are laid off.

The consequent disillusion has inspired working-class men to reverse their behavior patterns. Frantic violence often becomes one of the attributes of manliness instead of the deference and reticence generally associated with men who work in the formerly state-owned watch factory. In periods of unemployment and economic dislocation, when passions run high, words and rhetoric became charged with emotion and "irrationality." A worker who had been a member of the party for twenty-two years spoke with me about his emotional response to being laid off in 2003:

> At the moment I was laid off, I knew my connection with the party was over, completely over, twenty-two years of party membership was nothing, twenty-two years of hard work, being a good, obedient worker equals zero. All my hard work and achievements during those twenty-two years are meaningless. What I learned during the twenty-two years was *tinghua* [obedience], nothing else, but now they kick you out. I have no other skills, how could I make a living? I rebelled. I went to complain for the first time in my life. I don't care about duties or rules. I am like a *xiangpi ren*, just ignoring them. Now it is so easy for me to lose [my] temper, I *majie* a lot.

His loss of temper is a way of acting out accumulated suppressed anger. In this case, *xiangpi ren* also conveys the sense that one's honor or disgrace no longer matter. Performing like a *xiangpi ren* legitimates a decision to ignore rules and regulations. When anger is silenced in its native context—the state enterprise where workers got laid off—it becomes free-floating, emerging in unexpected places and forms that seem inappropriate (Lyman 2004). This is why workers' public display of anger is psychologized as *xiangpi ren*, through which, like the worker above, they say and do things without thinking, or is feminized as *majie*. Now that the market is the new driving force for social activities, a new form of masculinity associated with market prowess is valued in China. Losing a job, being relegated to less privileged or even "feminine" service work, or being unable to provide for one's family all erode male workers' masculinity. The feelings this engenders erupt as *majie* or the use of physical force when a male worker experiences this first type of burnout associated with paranoia and imagined hostilities.

The other type of burnout comes about through extreme self-effacement, a problematic strategy in which one's identity threatens to disappear into another's (Vanheule et al. 2003). From the perspectives of taxi drivers, structural forces create pressure on them to meet normative expectations of men as breadwinners. Their inability to fulfill these expectations challenges their ability to maintain the family relationships they desire. Taxi drivers in Changping who experience this form of burnout attempt to sacrifice for their families. Their efforts are more a form of self-sacrifice than self-effacement. Their sacrifice is also intended to boost their perceived masculinity within the Beibiao community. They try to meet family expectations in order to maintain their most intimate and significant relations and retain their self-esteem, but the structural conditions of the contemporary political economy foil their efforts.

One effect of this burnout is that people feel the weight of their work. They take their work so seriously that other aspects of their lives threaten to collapse under it. When things are not going as expected, they are inclined to hold themselves responsible and interpret work difficulties as signs of personal failure (Vanheule et al. 2003). For example, in June 2002, a 26-year-old laid-off worker committed suicide. One of the man's neighbors offered this explanation:

> The guy felt so ashamed of being laid off at the age of 26 while most of the unemployed were in their 40s or 50s. He just couldn't figure out why he was the one to be laid off. His wife was then six months pregnant and his father was still in the hospital at that time. He drove a pedicab and made 40 yuan per day. That is nothing these days. As the only son of the family, I bet he wouldn't choose to take his own life to avoid responsibilities if he could find a way to survive.

The pressure of supporting his family and the prospect of having a new baby weighed so heavily on him that he was not able to endure it. Both types of burnout—enacted anger and self-effacement—can be part of the burnout experience of the same person alternately.

Yinhuan, Counseling, and Domesticating Anger

Two types of counselors with different responsibilities and modes of intervening in personal or social issues are involved in the counseling and management of taxi drivers. Residents' committee members act as reemployment counselors and psychosocial workers who often witness and intervene in workers' *majie* and other activities in their home community. In addition, professional counselors hired by taxi companies help drivers adjust to their new work on an irregular basis.

I followed a counselor from Beijing Normal University, surnamed Lin, who was invited by one of the biggest taxi companies in Beijing to counsel taxi drivers on how to manage work-related stress. Lin was one of the very few professional counselors I have met in Beijing who implicitly suggested that the only way to feel happy and resolve one's own stress is to see beyond one's own problems and help others. While the means to this end is usually self-reflexivity, Lin encouraged taxi drivers to combine their work with counseling to relieve both their own pain and the pain of their passengers, even occasionally preventing suicide. Such preaching identified with the interests of both taxi companies and the government. Unlike the counseling training offered to laid-off women that enabled them to become *peiliao* and emphasized companionship above counseling, the counseling taxi drivers received was often framed in the rhetoric of empowerment; male taxi drivers were encouraged to play the role of expert counselors.

Community psychosocial workers whose training in counseling or social work is less formal or systematic than professional counselors such as Lin have intervened in situations of unrest using a mixed array of techniques learned through employee assistance programs. They invoked ethnopsychiatric labels of madness or cultural idioms of distress such as *shenjing bing* (nerve problems), *naozi you wenti* (problems or strains in one's brain), *xiangpi ren*, or masculinity crises. Based on these diagnoses, they launched therapeutic strategies aimed at addressing individual, moral, or family concerns. Compared with the "scientific," "professional," or "detached" approach to counseling for women who become *peiliao*, these community psychosocial workers tended to show more empathy and sympathy for laid-off men. This emotional support is one of the key features of counseling therapeutic interactions, which were intended to appease male workers who are perceived to harbor *yinhuan* and maintain stability. However, most drivers view such "counseling" as insufficient, useless, or even ridiculous, and drivers continued to struggle and act out through *majie*, violence, or other forms of resistance.

Because stress and anger can spur action, if psychotherapeutic interventions successfully smooth over emotionally expressed discontent, they may actually domesticate anger and disempower workers who are cobbling together efforts attacking socioeconomic reform (like the 2003 taxi driver strike in Changping). If the therapy orients them away from collective resistance, the workers lose the strength or momentum they might gain from collective action. When psychosocial workers interpret *majie* or worker unrest as symptoms of burnout or *xiangpi ren* or as part of a crisis of masculinity, they mobilize both gender and psychotherapy to defuse efforts to respond to what would more accurately be deemed class struggle (Dirlik 2007; Ngai and Chan 2008). Intensifying class struggle in Changping is linked to feelings of burnout via the dramatic life changes outlined in this chapter. Yet class struggle is often ignored when the focus is on diagnosing individual symptoms. But what about taxi-driver counselors? Can they be of help in keeping present the link between structural social change and personal burnout, even while helping others?

Counselors on Wheels

On November 24, 2008, China Central Television's *Psychology Talk Show* broadcast an episode called *chuzu che shang de xinli yisheng* (A Psychological Doctor in a Taxi). The episode revolved around an interview that the show's host, Xiao Qin, and counselor Yang Fengchi did with a taxi driver named Zhen Fengxiang. At the time of the broadcast, Zhen had been driving a taxi for fourteen years after being laid off from a factory. For eight years he had also enjoyed the title of *dishi zhixing* (taxi star).[8] Zhen had reportedly prevented over 100 suicides. The counselor asked Zhen to describe how he counseled his passengers. Zhen talked about some of his counseling sessions, particularly one involving a young woman with whom he talked for three hours, during which he managed to turn her from suicidal to happy and positive (see Yang 2013a). Counselor Yang then commented on Zhen's approach from a professional perspective with the dual aims of helping Zhen improve his counseling skills and holding him up as a role model for other taxi drivers.

In this television segment, counselors represented taxi driving as an opportunity for Zhen and others to discover their potential as "counselors." Both Xiao and Yang presented Zhen as a psychologized and psychologizing subject who is exhibiting his potential to become a worker who creates value for moral, economic, and political ends.[9] For example, at one point Counselor Yang emphasized the advantages of taxi counselors: unlike professional counselors who wait for clients to come to them, taxi counselors can be proactive in counseling those who appear downcast and suicidal. The counselors went on to weave the survival stories of this underprivileged man into a logic of psychologization: they psychologized the negative consequences of state-led economic restructuring by presenting the devastation of job loss as a personal dilemma to be healed with the professional help and moral support of experts. They praised the now-healthy Zhen for his accomplishments in suicide prevention and happiness promotion and presented these achievements as possible goals for all taxi drivers in China (Yang 2013a).

This episode was but one media representation of taxi drivers as "counselors on wheels," happy, enthusiastic, and selfless workers who transmit happiness and prevent others from being depressed or committing suicide. Such representations abound. They depict taxi drivers as "taxi stars" who know how to pursue happiness so they can release their potential to achieve their goals and help others do the same. Part of the job training taxi drivers receive is intended to help them develop the skills and attitudes for providing quality services. Taxi drivers are expected to be the "window" of the capital by highlighting the beauty, civility, safety, and hospitality of Beijing to outsiders. This is why preliminary knowledge in psychology and suicide prevention were added to job training for taxi drivers particularly before and during the 2008 Summer Olympic Games. Since taxi drivers are sometimes the last people to engage with those who want to commit suicide, they have been seen as natural helpers. They are well aware of the specific locales in Beijing that are popular sites of suicides.

Both laid-off women and laid-off men are mobilized as a target force to undertake state-initiated psychotherapeutic interventions. Unlike the glamorized media representations of laid-off women as "reemployment stars" that emphasize the significant role of state-led psychotherapeutic interventions in transforming the outlook of women from depression and frustration to happiness and triumph after reemployment (Dai 2004; Yang 2007; Chapter 1), media representations of taxi counselors instead highlight their counseling skills, the effective strategies they use to pursue happiness, and their witty and pragmatic "expertise" in dealing with difficult people and situations. Both representations note the efficacy of recent psychotherapeutic interventions in reemployment and human resource management aimed at maximizing the positive potential of people while minimizing manifestations of *yinhuan*.

Community psychosocial workers recognize the negative potential of unemployment and rampant poverty to incite conflict. Part of their daily work is to scrutinize the flow of social and political life for signs of disharmony, suspicious noises, and indications of negative developments. They watch for symptoms of "crazy" people, *xiangpi ren*, or early signs of *majie* in those who are disgruntled. An imagined potential for destabilization drives this surveillance. Violent forces and violent figures are seen as potentially present, especially at crucial moments such as the June 4th anniversary of the 1989 Tian'anmen Square students' movement. Such imaginings are prevalent and can be seen in the preemptive measures taken on important national occasions.[10]

Counselors must be attentive to the hint of negative potential that might erupt during conflict. Their work is delicate and full of impending risks. This was especially true in 1999, when Beibiao was laying off the first group of workers. The unrest that did occur, coupled with the imagined existence of underlying negativity with the potential for destabilization, made social unrest a potent form of absent presence (see Vigh 2011).

Diverting attention away from the potential for unrest and class conflict is an intentional part of state efforts to manage the negative consequences of economic restructuring. That is, the state and its arms have chosen to translate economic restructuring into personal dilemmas and to develop strategic assistance to achieve *shehui xiaoyi* (social effect) and *weiwen* (maintaining stability). In a 2002 interview, Zhang Xiaolong, deputy director of the Ministry of Labor, emphasized the importance of managing unemployment through stabilization (*Finance* editorial board, 2002). This is also a significant reason why the Beibiao factory was not allowed to completely shut down, even though it was no longer profitable. Government officials concluded that the privatized company should continue to employ at least 500 of the employees of the former state enterprise to avoid devastating too many workers in one locale. (The original number of workers in the factory's heyday of the 1980s was over 2,500.)

But no state strategy of control is perfect. In fact, the care offered to taxi drivers has at times done nothing but compounded their frustrations. In the next section, I explore the rituals of anger expression through *majie* these drivers engaged in.

Majie, Suppressed Anger, and the Crisis of Masculinity

In Changping when life gets difficult, taxi drivers perform *majie*, a ritual of anger that involve cursing in the streets on an almost daily basis. Such public displays not only channel their stress, anger, and vulnerability but also constitute a performance that highlights their male superiority and the entitlement they feel as former state workers. While there are some "burnouts" who lack enthusiasm or passion in life, and some of these have committed suicide, other taxi or pedicab drivers enact *majie*, sometimes transforming their performances into expressions of uncontrollable rage. Particularly when payments for electricity, heating, TV cable, or other utilities come due, these former state workers articulate their frustration or long-suppressed anger through *majie* or by using *naoshi* (making a fuss) to apply pressure at residents' committees to waive utility payments and other related costs of living.

Disgruntled laid-off workers also *majie* in the residential yard to complain about or curse those who laid them off and deprived them of their livelihoods. In one case, after suffering health issues as a result of years of driving taxis, two men were successfully reemployed at the privatized Beibiao factory in 2005—perhaps in an effort by management to subdue their protests. Yet such success from *majie* encourages other performances.

Majie originally referred to any argument, quarrel, curse, or name-calling that took place in the residential compounds of Beibiao, but it is performed on the factory grounds as well. As a local speech genre, *majie* has distinctive pragmatic features. The accuser uses abusive language to display his or her anger and condemn social wrongs. In one of the most popular Chinese-English dictionaries, *majie* is defined as "to shout abuses in public; to call people's names in public" (*Hanying Cidian* 1997, 654). The only example given in this dictionary is a set phrase *pofu majie* (a shrew shouting abuse in the street). Associating *majie* with a shrew draws on derogatory and negative connotations rooted in popular stereotypes about women. Indeed, similar to the linguistic genre *kros*, through which women use abusive language to display anger in a Papua New Guinean village (Kulick 1998), *majie* at Beibiao is gendered; it is perceived as "women's speech." In Changping, it is often used by people who are perceived to be of low *suzhi*, or quality (Yan H 2003a; Sun 2009), especially women or "womanish" men. Couched as an ambiguous genre of resistance, *majie* is also a subversive linguistic strategy that was once used primarily by full-time housewives, the unemployed, disabled people, retirees, the people who least embodied the ideals of the factory life and had the least to gain in work units. It is a negative form of power that makes or breaks reputations, causes conflict, and disrupts relationships. For a man to engage in such public displays of emotion is an extreme step; the man who does so risks being labeled as "womanish" or "irrational."

Majie is a site of struggle for both definitions of gender and power. In Changping, men ideally represent and embody cooperation and sociability through paid public work. Women who are *jiashu* (household dependents) and are not affiliated with any work units are more likely to be seen as divisive troublemakers whose "individualistic" actions threaten the harmony of the work unit. *Majie* is perceived as "irrational." Both men and women of "quality" avoid such verbal practices, which index "undesirable" groups. But when men find themselves in a vulnerable position vis-à-vis "the government" as embodied in factory managers and residents' committees, they appropriate this ill-regarded and "womanish" genre of *majie* as a last resort to win over "the government." Borrowing a female mode of communication to show and even exaggerate their anger and vulnerability, male workers acted out their suppressed anger, transforming *majie* into a more general mode of social (rather than personal) critique (Lyman 2004).

Majie includes two kinds of linguistic practices: one is a loud complaint or curse about specific social wrongs for the purpose of identifying the wrongdoer. For example, one woman found that some Chinese onions she had put in the sun in the residential yard had gone missing when she woke up from her afternoon nap. After dinner, she enacted *majie* in the yard to identify and accuse the thief and get her onions back. Another example involves a middle-aged woman doorkeeper for the community residents' committee. Realizing that taxi drivers were erasing or removing orders she had posted on the blackboard outside her office about issues such as where not to park their taxis or where they could blow their horns (not at the residence), she *majie*'ed them thusly: "I know we have many *xiangpi ren* (rubber eraser), but choose to erase something else, not my announcements. Those who dare to act against me will be damned. Act and see how I will 'repair' you. Come forward; if you dare to erase my words, you should dare come forward to rewrite them for me!" In a more masculine type of *majie*, the accuser curses collective entities (i.e., the government, the residents' committee, the Communist Party, or a particular group) in order to vent his or her anger and grievances. In both cases, the accuser is ready to directly confront the wrongdoer or anyone else who responds.

Two significant motivations underlie men's public practice of *majie*. Workers' sense of entitlement because of their past glorious contributions and their expectation of lifetime employment in work units has been so seriously violated that men usurp *majie* to accentuate the loss of what they perceive as their fundamental rights. In addition, the *shangfang* system (petitioning the government) that might allow them to complain and protest social wrongs has become largely inefficient.[11] The municipal government has failed to address several cases of workers' *shangfang* in this community, and repeated visits to higher levels of the government were neither well received nor further encouraged. Once legitimate channels where ordinary people can vent their grievances are blocked, discontented men return to their immediate institution—the residential community—to vent their anger and seek social justice. As one taxi driver told me:

> If passengers have any grievances, they can take down the driver's ID number and call the complaint hotline on the passenger seat dashboard. No matter what happens, they can use their receipts to make complaints, but where do we taxi drivers file complaints? The only venue is home, the residential community. We *majie* to vent our anger and frustration.

This situation has the potential to create more serious escalations of social unrest. Public displays of anger are often contagious and free-floating. This is why residents' committee members and psychosocial workers often attend men's rituals of *majie* to show that they are listening and so they could take action when possible in an attempt to maintain stability.

As subordinates, taxi drivers and other laid-off workers are angry with their superiors or the system. At a symbolic level, this anger ritual elevates the workers to an equal level to their superiors and becomes an act of insubordination. The act of expressing anger publicly suggests not only that the workers take their actions seriously but also that by doing so they take themselves and their rights seriously as judges of the systems and agents of power.

In one example, a laid-off worker turned taxi driver applied for a job at the central park in Changping in 2007, seeking employment that he felt would better replicate the status he once enjoyed as a factory worker. He was rejected, however, because he was considered to be already employed as a taxi driver. As he sat in front of the doorkeeper's office at a residential compound of the Beibiao factory, a former co-worker casually greeted him and asked how he was doing. In the presence of a group of residents, including the mother of the director of the residents' committee, this worker performed *majie*:

> Who said taxi driving is *zai jiuye* [reemployment]? It's an automatic job; anyone can do it. But it's not the kind of reemployment a worker should do. It enslaves you like a dog. But you cannot even make enough money to survive. Our dear party knows how to bully workers. Why have so many misfortunes happened to our workers? I was *laomo* [a model worker]. *Laodong mofan* [model workers], do you know? They also labored like dogs, but they were prestigious, enjoying lots of bonuses and holding their heads high. Now I am a second-class citizen, exhausted and downcast. Is there any group who is as downtrodden as us?

This *majie* went beyond complaint or ranting; it was loud, full of emotion, and expressed with the purpose of turning the audience into a target for argument or even a fight. It was expressed anger resulting from disillusionment about their present and future. Economic dislocation and mass unemployment not only deprive male workers of their salary but also reconfigure the masculine hierarchy, suppressing working-class masculinity associated with full-time employment in the state sector while celebrating hypermasculinity based on prowess in the new market in China. *Majie* presents the outward expression of personal attempts to internalize this reconfigured masculine hierarchy that has deposed the worker while celebrating his capitalist counterpart. Indeed, as Comaroff and Comaroff (2001) note, neoliberalism not only feminizes labor and disrupts gender relations, but also creates crises of masculinity.

Men's use of a stereotypically female linguistic practice for their own purposes appears at first glance to reverse gender relationships. In fact, the act of *majie* unites both genders and highlights feminized experiences of oppression suffered by male members of the working class. As men turn to *majie* to demonstrate "vulnerability" and even "irrationality," they reinforce the general association of the genre with the common conditions of the oppression of women, exposing the process through which women's voices have been suppressed by a system that largely perpetuates male dominance. As Lutz (1988, 69) elucidates, "Any discourse on emotion is also, at least implicitly, a discourse of gender." The powerful affect that emerges through the current practice of *majie* constitutes a central ethnographic problem when trying to understand transformations in the male-dominated culture of the Chinese working class today, because it has been altered in the wake of mass unemployment.

When displaced men return to the Beibiao community to demonstrate their social anger and vent their frustration, the former Beibiao managers, now residents' committee members, label their practices as *majie* and even vilify them as *naoshi* or *daoluan* (rioting or making a fuss).[12] Psychosocial workers also label *majie* as a symptom of *xiangpi ren*. These workers were perceived to be numb, and spoke without thinking. Once disruptive behavior is labeled as *majie*, it becomes feminized. This places men in the imagined subject position of women; it bisexualizes them and makes them "doubly fit to be governed" (Louie 2001). Indeed, *majie* is not only a ritual of subjectification or subject making but also one of objectification; the men who perform these rituals objectify themselves, thereby legitimating even extreme strategies of governance in the eyes of authorities. This result only compounds their decline. *Majie* results in greater justification for the authorities to further psychologize male workers, and affects the way tokenistic welfare programs, including counseling, are delivered. These programs become tailored to meet men's needs more often than women's in order to appease men and maintain stability. *Majie* also further reinforces the perception of male workers as the main source of *yinhuan* in this community.

A man whose wife committed suicide by walking on the highway kept *majie*-ing and kept telling me and other people that he would use a kitchen knife to cut management into 1,000 pieces. In my interview with the factory director, he described the wife as "emotionally immature" and *shenshen daodao* (superstitious or abnormal) and the husband as someone "who needed to go to Huilongguan soon [where two mental hospitals are located]." However, the worker saw things differently. He once complained that

> You cannot win arguments with them [Beibiao management and community residents' committee]. They have time to ponder how to argue with residents. You need to be unreasonable and talk like a scoundrel to win them. You have to use unusual ways to handle them. I cursed loudly in the corridor of the office building, kicking the walls and their doors, just like a drunkard.

One narrative strategy in male workers' *majie* is to assume an image of a "true man" whose loss of employment hobbles him in his ability to fulfill his family responsibilities, a source of great guilt and justifiable grief. Working-class men construe themselves not as powerful agents but as hapless victims who are responding to offensive action with defensive moves. Through public displays of anger and violence, these men present their situations as desperate. They perform "irrationally" and emotionally to highlight their "helplessness," their impoverished living conditions, and their anxiety stemming from their eroded sense of identity.

Men and women can draw on the same linguistic resources even though these resources may be associated primarily with the female gender. It is important to determine under what circumstances gender transgressions in language use occur and why they do so in order to examine more fully the relationships among gender, language use, and political economy (McElhinny 1995). In this context, men's use of a female mode of communication has a dramatic effect; it highlights their plight like nothing else can, even though it may simultaneously subject them to increased scrutiny and control. They are in a terrible situation and lash out with whatever means they can find in order to construct a sense of emergency, a crisis of masculinity that demands an earnest and effective response from authorities.

One afternoon in July 2008, while I was talking with a group of residents who were playing poker in one of the Beibiao residences, Wu Liang,

6.1. Unemployed/underemployed men playing chess at a Beibiao residence. Photo by He Jianhua.

a reemployed taxi driver, walked toward us after parking his taxi in the yard. One of Wu's neighbors greeted him, "Yah, Lao Wu, business must be good; you come home earlier." Wu started to *majie*.

> Yes, business is really good?! If it's good, I won't take a break. Rush hour, all traffic jams, you don't want to get stuck there and lose money. You say, why is life so hard? You see, I am not capable, end up becoming a taxi driver. My son doesn't save my face; he didn't pass the university exam this year. Now I have to pay extra money to get him into a training program to prepare for another year. Things couldn't be worse. My wife was laid off again. Damned *juweihui* [residents' committee] deceived people. They told me that the work can be renewed but my wife returned home only after one contract. The central park [which was being gentrified; many laid-off workers got reemployed in those gentrification projects] is so big with so much work. Why did they lay her off? You see, Zhang Yi [the director of the residents' committee] *buban renshi* [acted inhumanely, engaging in things that a normal and moral person is not supposed to do]. He knows the manager

so well. Just one kind word and she would get hired. I will go ask him why he did such a thing!

The neighbor comforted Wu, "Well, Zhang Yi could have done a better job. Or he might not know about this situation. But I guess he will know this very soon" [looking at Zhang's brother-in-law, who happened to be there.] At that moment, Wu himself realized this and directly confronted Zhang's brother-in-law, "Tell your brother-in-law, act like a man [act humanely]!" Zhang's brother-in-law replied, "It's not human or inhumane. He is not in charge. But I will tell him if I get a chance."

One week later, Wu's wife was called back by the central park management for another contract job. It was believed that Zhang Yi had helped negotiate this reemployment. Instead of his wife negotiating her own employment, the husband agitated for her through *majie*. By attending to this man's *majie* and satisfying his need to protect the interests of his wife, the director of the residents' committee helped redress Wu's perceived eroded masculinity, and his assistance legitimated Wu's male superior status over his wife. This is important, as it demonstrates that even when men are laid off, they still have more control over their lives and their relationships to their previous workplace than most women. Male workers are considered to be the basis of social instability, and benevolent social programs and residents' committees prioritize their concerns and needs (see Chapter 3). However, the process of using anger as a medium for social stabilization entails a compromise between the paternal state and working-class men and a way of legitimating and reinforcing male privilege and male power.

Unlike the gender politics of Mao's era that celebrated women's political bravery and ability to transcend traditional gender roles, which resulted in "masculine" potential for women, the gender ideology of the post-Mao era naturalizes and essentializes biological differences between men and women. Indeed, one of the folk gender ideologies is *yin sheng yang shuai* (the rise of the feminine and the decline of the masculine) (Sun 1983; Zhong 2000). Today women are reassuming traditional roles that recreate gender inequalities that were suppressed during Mao's era. Chinese men have correspondingly internalized gender roles that have traditionally benefited them. In his discussion of Jia Pingwo's story "Human Extremities," Kam Louie (1991) claims that the aggressive reassertion of the macho image is really "an image of the working-class man, stripped of political and economic power, trying to re-assert himself" (181). The masculinity associated with the socialist planned economy has been discredited and working-class men have had to readjust. But in order to reclaim a sense of masculinity, they must move from the periphery to the center and resituate themselves in the new economic hierarchy. This means transcending class boundaries. At present, this is unlikely under the neoliberal order in which political agency has been extended primarily to wealthy entrepreneurs and the expanding middle class.[13]

According to Henrietta Moore (1994), in the West, a particular type of hegemonic masculinity associated with global capitalism and the domination of the West in economic and political life shapes structural relationships between alternative (or marginalized) femininities and masculinities. This global hegemonic masculinity finds resonance with a number of local and indigenous masculinities in China. Thus, analysis of gender should recognize the ways local masculinities are implicated in broader processes of economic and political change that are well beyond the control of local communities. The assumptions and values of global capitalism and the new hegemonic masculinity have infiltrated individual consciousness and impacted the daily discourse and practices of individuals. These assumptions and values create anxieties and vulnerabilities that male workers often express in the form of anger and violence.

In a survey entitled *zhongguo: xin nanxing he xin shidai* (China: Neo-Men and the New Era), neo-men are defined as synonymous with urban elites and entrepreneurial men with financial security and market prowess (Liang 2002). These neo-men play a leading role in reform-era China. In contrast, men from lower social strata are perceived to be marginal in the symbolic market of masculinity. However, in a debate regarding gender distinctions launched by a program on China Central Television called *banbiantian* [Half the sky], some male participants admitted that they experienced pressures and anxieties when they tried to achieve normative expectations of masculine strength and success, particularly in the context of essentialized gender roles in the reform era. These debates opened up a discursive space that enabled men to articulate their dilemma and publicly exposed their melancholy about the manhood they are expected to perform. Individuals have experienced macrolevel social and discursive changes at the microlevel, and these changes motivate working-class men's public displays of social anger.

Male workers' public displays of anger are a ritual of both masculinity and class tension. Urban residents' committees focus on the former in order to downplay the latter. Many working-class men sometimes choose to display their vulnerability and anger in terms of personal, sexual, and familial concerns—that is, they display their anger by mobilizing their perceived inadequacies as men, husbands, fathers, and breadwinners to show their "vulnerability." To some extent this is a response to the attempt of the Beibiao residents' committee to redefine men's class-based social anger and violence as problems in the realms of gender, the family, and personal life. Class conflicts between management and workers are redefined as gendered discourses. By redefining class conflicts as gender issues, the residents' committee makes working-class men feminine and governable as pressure to stabilize the community intensifies.

As a way of lamenting their "lost" male superiority, the once-prestigious proletariats display their anger in public in order to return to their sense of being strong and potent men. They feel empowered by the process, especially as it sometimes yields a positive result, such as a job opportunity, cancellation of utility fees, or a "chat" with the party secretary of the residents' committee (Yang 2010). Although protests and social unrest derived from mass unemployment are not unusual in western capitalist countries and in developing countries, the situation of the Chinese working class deserves special attention because of its unique position in China's political economy. Both social instability and the notion of *yinhuan* are embodied in an image of a desperate unemployed man, which challenges a positive sense of masculine identity. In recognition of such challenges to desired gender identities, there is a tendency among reformers and policy makers to offer men greater opportunities for pacification or appeasement, even though women suffer unemployment to a much greater degree. This partly explains the official tolerance of male workers' riots or public displays of anger at the local level. In sum, economic hardship and eroded masculinity have made men feel besieged and restricted. Understanding this emotional desperation is the first step in accounting for the current and historically atypical gender imbalance in this new use of *majie*.

Structural Causes and Psychological Diagnoses

Community psychosocial workers see their role as enabling people to put their circumstances into perspective in order to prevent them from becoming lost in vengeful fantasy. They look for channels through which their laid-off or underemployed clients can express their anger constructively. These counselors tended to downplay their scientific authority with laid-off men more than they would with women being trained for *peiliao*; with men, they adopted the role of an amiable next-door neighbor or a concerned former co-worker.[14] Yet in their diagnosis of *xiangpi ren*, Beibiao psychosocial workers often operated by instinct, particularly in dealing with taxi or pedicab drivers. That is, diagnosis is sometimes made even in the absence of significant objective dysfunction. For example, one day in the summer of 2010, having seen a laid-off worker turned taxi driver surnamed Bi park his taxi inappropriately in the residential yard, one of the residents' committee members, Wan, asked Bi to move his vehicle. Without replying, Bi stared at Wan emotionlessly and walked away, the weight of the world clearly on his shoulders. On the spot Wan "diagnosed" Bi as someone in the process of becoming a *xiangpi ren*. Later, at the morning market near Beibiao, Wan and I ran into Bi's wife and Wan kindly reminded her to pay more attention to her husband's psychological state (*jingshen zhuangtai*), given the prevalent burnout among men in this community. Much to Wan's surprise, Bi's wife not only dismissed Wan's concerns but accused Wan's husband of laying Bi off in the first place.

Residents' committee members and psychosocial workers are not always sensitive to the way their work might stigmatize workers and sometimes fail to soften their language. Here, Wan used the term *xiangpi hua* (the process of becoming a *xiangpi ren*). The wife looked annoyed and retorted, "You mind your own business, okay? If you care, you would have asked your husband to keep my husband [at work at Beibiao] in 2004 instead of laying him off." Wan's husband was the director of the workshop where Bi was originally employed. But Wan was surprised that people were attributing their current difficulties to layoffs that occurred six years ago. Wan replied, "We are neighbors; why do you say things so bluntly? Work is work. My husband had to lay off a certain number of people—it was a [political] mandate; if he had the final say in layoffs, he would never treat his good neighbor this way. Now he himself has been laid off." As she put some fresh chives on the scale and gesturing to the peddler to weigh it, Bi's wife retorted, "That was called retirement, not layoff, okay? Even if he is laid off, he is still much better off than we are. A starving camel is bigger than a horse [*shou si de luotuo bi ma da*]." She referred to the fact that Wan's husband was running a wedding service company after his retirement from Beibiao. Wan then stopped shopping, looked at Bi, and lectured her like an eloquent and enlightened party secretary:

> You know what, I try to be a good neighbor [by reminding you to pay attention to your husband's well-being]. We really have to look forward and move beyond Beibiao and *tie fan wan* [iron rice bowls]. We have to think now [that] the iron rice bowl is not to get stuck at one place for a lifetime, but [we must shape] a life that no matter where we are, we have rice to eat and can feed ourselves and survive. We have to change our old heart attitude, moving on with life. You know, this is *biantong*—the flexibility and gentleness in living and enjoying life [regardless of one's circumstances].

Bi's wife pushed her shopping cart forward, ready to leave, and replied,

> You mean we [former workers] are not *biantong*? We don't know how to enjoy life? My husband is not as capable as your husband who can thrive everywhere? But you have to understand we come from different classes. Beibiao management had already been fattened; your life circumstances are much better in the market. We workers are not that lucky. Without a job that brings money to survive, other things are too fancy for us. We, my husband, has no luxury to enjoy life; he is too busy to feel depressed.

Reflecting back on this conversation, I believe it was complicated by the fact that I was there. Bi's wife was offended when Wan informed her of the possibility that her husband was burned out in my presence, given the stigma associated with mental illness in China. As a result, she strongly disputed Wan's claim. Meanwhile, Wan wanted to impress me with her new ideological arsenal she had acquired in her training, which is required for a diploma in social work. However, perhaps also because of my presence, the argument did not escalate into a fight. Wan's notion of *biantong* is to reinterpret an old concept of *tie fan wan* positively to urge people to rely on themselves and strive forward. Another aspect of Wan's *biantong* is gentleness and flexibility. She is well known in this community for being a model wife and "filial piety star" (*xiao xing*), famous for her conceptualization of the saying *wenrou jiu shi biantong* (feminine gentleness and flexibility is *biantong*); she patiently cares for her notoriously confrontational and temperamental mother-in-law. She brings her gentleness and dialectic *biantong* into her daily community work. However, since psychologization functions to conceal the lack of efficient governance, the psychologized subject is left without any firm ground (viable livelihood) to stand on. This psychological approach to those working in the taxi industry further exacerbates the subjective abyss of drivers, such as Bi, who have already felt alienated and displaced by privatization.

Later on, I interviewed Bi. He told me that he performed like a *xiangpi ren* so he could ignore the regulations community leaders made. "You simply ignore them; otherwise they will bully you and trodden you down further. We cannot be lower." His choice to appear completely defeated and burned out resonates among many workers; when isolated public display of anger like *majie* cannot bring positive change (and in truth, little can be done by individuals to stop or slow down the force of privatization), they choose to subdue their anger and use silence as a defense mechanism. Peter Lyman (1981) points out that anger is more than words; it is a bodily reality. Performing like a *xiangpi ren* is a form of silent resistance; it shows contempt for authority and regulation. For workers who adopt this stance, choosing to become numb is a means of survival.

Nietzsche (1968) suggests that rage may lead beyond anger speech and aggressive action to a self-destructive adaptation to subordination through the internalization of anger. He calls this silent rage ressentiment, an unconscious rage that creates a drama of revenge out of everyday life, but this revenge is acted out unconsciously as a latent motivation that hides beneath seemingly ordinary speech and action. It is a rage that is manifested in a free-floating anxiety that is ready to be mobilized around any cause that brings injury to the subject. Ressentiment contains an element of latent aggression, of inflexible righteousness, a need to impose order upon the world, and a need to find catharsis. It may manifest itself indirectly as a latent motive that silently introduces powerful and dangerous emotional currents into politics. That is, political anger may manifest itself silently, indirectly, or in self-destructive psychological symptoms (Lyman 1981).

And yet Chinese psychosocial workers did not always view silent anger as a political statement, because they seldom incorporate context into their analysis of the workers' behavior. Even though psychosocial workers are deeply embedded in the community and tend to adopt a holistic approach to social and psychological problems, they adopt the logic of psychologization in their daily interactions with restless taxi drivers in their efforts to alleviate the effects of social and economic dislocations.

Conclusion

Social stress is an inevitable consequence of the unfolding economic re-structuring in China, which has intensified social polarization and in-creased opportunities for social unrest. When once-valued workers who spent their youth acting on absolute faith in communism and Chairman Mao are victimized by steadily declining status and an increasing cost of living, they are devastated and suffer greatly. Their victimization and the price they have paid for the restructuring of state enterprises inevitably renders them *yinhuan* from the perspective of the government. The lack of formal dialogue between the people and the one-party state nurtures incipient crises and actualizes *yinhuan*. The absence of a system for effec-tively pacifying and rehabilitating the aggrieved creates an environment that sustains protest. Unable to voice their discontent through approved official channels, workers resort to alternative channels and even drastic action. This is reflected in the increasing number of labor disputes and the high rate of violence and strikes (Hurst and O'Brian 2002; Hurst 2004) and in the rise of *majie* as an expression of anger and male "vulnerability." *Majie* is the last resort. It is a public display of anger that must be humiliat-ing to these men, given the normative gender expectations in the commu-nity. In this dramatic shift in which men present themselves as vulnerable and needy and assume a female identity vis-à-vis the culpable state, the structural crisis is manifested in the form of a crisis of masculinity.

As McElhinny (2003) points out, understanding how social change takes place requires understanding of both rational and emotional responses to events. As a ritual of anger, *majie* constructs a fantasy world that is the psy-chic counterpart to the real political economy. By presenting a subversive discourse and temporarily recentering themselves in the power structure, working-class men intend to restore their eroded masculinity and reestab-lish their positions in the social order. The increase in the number of such rituals not only shows the efficacy of this masculine strategy but is also evidence of residents' committees' compromise with men to domesticate their anger and stabilize society.

To address recent unrest triggered by economic tensions, China has embarked on a "harmonious society" campaign that tacitly acknowledges a newly recognized lack of social harmony. Stability is of paramount value for the current government; maintaining stability is closely related to governing mass unemployment, according to Zhang Xiaolong, the director of the Ministry of Labor in an interview conducted by *caijing zazhi* (*Finance* editorial board 2002). At the local level, residents' committees have been increasingly charged with finding ways to pacify rioting or disgruntled male workers who are perceived to embody *yinhuan* and mobilizing them to fulfill their *qianli* for the new market economy. Worker unrest is widely interpreted as a manifestation of burnout and as central to an ongoing and widely experienced crisis of masculinity. Whereas psychologists call the emergence of *xiangpi ren* a symptom of depression or a psychological disorder, workers view the diagnosis as ignoring the socioeconomic stress that frames the present plight of millions.

To preempt largely male-driven labor unrest, residents' committee members in Changping offer both personal counseling and pragmatic solutions that seek to reorient the individual to the new economy and revitalize the role of the male as breadwinner. The emotional trauma experienced by these laid-off workers is real, but it raises the larger question of the appropriateness of psychotherapy as a strategy of governance. These practical and psychotherapeutic interventions fail to lead to productive change because they ignore the larger context of workers' discontent and anger. By recasting structurally induced worker unrest as personal concerns, they help obscure class stratifications that have been intensified by economic restructuring. This is what lies at the heart of the mass distress that presently characterizes China's once noble working class.

CONCLUSION

THERAPEUTIC POLITICS AND KINDLY POWER

This book offers a theoretical and ethnographic analysis of the use of psychotherapy for social, economic, and political purposes in China. Through my exploration of the therapeutic modes of governmental intervention that have developed through the psychologization of unemployment, I suggest that this psychologization is neither an attempt to integrate China into the globalizing sphere of psychotherapy nor a departure from authoritarian political rule. Instead, psychotherapy in China is an appendage of the government that is mobilized to reduce social and psychological disorder and expand the nation's new market economy.

Theoretically and ethnographically this volume contributes to the study of post-Mao governance. It looks at how political authorities target the private sphere, the individual, and the biological as significant domains for ideological control and political legitimacy (Dai 1996; Anagnost 1997; Rofel 1999) by governing through programs based on the hearts, the emotions, and the potential of the population (especially those who are marginalized). The "heart" and psychology are united in this trend of psychologization, which draws on historical threads from the dialectics of *biantong*, or change with continuity. Governance in this mode both appropriates current psychological apparatuses (counseling, social work, employee assistance programs) and retools older Mao-era ideas and categories including the heart, thought work, and self-reliance to embrace pragmatic counseling for the labor sector, although mostly targeting those who do not currently have work.

In addition to maximizing the actualization of *qianli*, or the positive potential of the unemployed, the therapeutic mode of control that emerges within psychologization is also preemptive and attempts to prevent marginalized individuals who putatively harbor *yinhuan*, or negative potential, from destabilizing the sociopolitical order. Local authorities, including members of urban residents' committees and community psychosocial workers, are predisposed by the anxieties of the state to imagine and identify *yinhuan* as characteristic of unemployed men. Their efforts at psychosocial counseling are designed to reverse negative attitudes and affects that might erupt and unsettle the local community and its domestic units. This preemptive tactic plays an important role in everyday interactions with, training of, and management of the unemployed, especially unemployed men.

By focusing on the emotional states and problems of individuals, this tactic seeks to prevent workers seeing their difficulties as structural and organizing for collective action. So long as workers remain divided along institutional and regional boundaries, it appears unlikely that any meaningful labor movement will arise at the national level (Hurst 2004). Ching Kwan Lee (2007) uses the notion of "decentralized legal authoritarianism" to describe the kind of decentralization that makes local government responsible for developing the local political economy and implementing labor laws promulgated by the central government to resolve labor conflicts and maintain social stability. Thus the local state rather than the central government becomes the target of worker resistance. This type of decentralization also leads to fragmentation of worker interests across localities and work units. Token welfare programs also participate in measures to preempt social unrest by prioritizing the needs of laid-off men who are most likely to cause disturbances, offering them reemployment assistance and poverty relief primarily in an attempt to appease them.

These preemptive measures partly explain the relative stability in China as the party-state has intensified its economic restructuring. Given the widespread socioeconomic dislocation and the huge number of workers laid off from state-owned enterprises since the mid-1990s, one might expect to see large-scale organized strikes, demonstrations, protests, and other violent worker actions and resistance aimed at overthrowing the government. Workers sometimes do respond violently, and protests sometimes accelerate in scale and scope. But none of the resistance in recent decades has escalated into major social unrest that threatens local or central governments. Considering its tremendous impact on Chinese society and the lack of radical social unrest, economic restructuring since the mid-1990s has often been claimed by reformists and economists as "a peaceful revolution" (Hu et al. 2002).

Hu and colleagues (2002) argue that this revolution has been so peaceful because of the gradual and experimental ways layoffs were carried out and the safety net provided by prioritizing the reemployment of the newly marginalized (see also Yang 2007). Others argue that including *renqing* (human feelings) and *guanxi* (social connections) in the help that is offered to those who have been displaced and impoverished has smoothed their pathways as they transition to new forms of employment and new ways of life (Liu 1995). While these studies tend to essentialize *renqing* and *guanxi* as key features of Chinese society, they also emphasize that the support of family, extended family, kinship and other social networks for the newly marginalized serves as a safety valve that prevents large-scale social unrest in the wake of mass unemployment (Zhang 2002).

This book challenges interpretations of the socioeconomic transition in China as peaceful. I look at this massive transformation from a more dialogic and holistic perspective, highlighting this historical development as state orchestrated, deceptively hegemonic, and highly contested. Through analysis of new political and economic dynamics, gendered and classed dimensions of reemployment programs, and the new emphasis on the personal and the psychological, I demonstrate how the Chinese government used psychologization to advance the sociopolitical transformations it desires and how this trend of psychologization was challenged especially by unemployed workers.

In what follows, I lay out the actual mechanics of what others have seen in China's socioeconomic transformation as "peaceful." I then summarize the way my research complicates this assertion by drawing on the mechanisms, modes, and technologies of governance discussed in the preceding chapters that constitute dynamics of the so-called peaceful revolution. Drawing on my ethnography, I make six interrelated arguments in this process. First, I argue that the emerging trend of psychologization is a therapeutic mode of social control that emphasizes the self and the heart over structural forces. This trend turns political ideology toward a focus on "scientific knowledge," particularly psychological knowledge in the form of self-help, counseling, and social work. Second, I argue for the use of affective governance and kindly power as primary methods in managing unemployment. Unlike Mao's governing technologies, which focused on external criticism, self-criticism, and self-denial, current governance emphasizes self-realization and the happiness of the heart, implicitly allying individual desire for happiness and fulfillment with broader social, economic, and political objectives. I call this contradictory practice, *kindly power*, because it constitutes no less a mode of governance for its emphasis on caring for the wellbeing of those who have been displaced, impoverished, and distressed by state-enterprise restructuring. The emphasis on affect and emotions such as happiness, compassion, and *renqing* enable community leaders to focus on positive, constructive, and preemptive forms of power rather than on coercion and domination, but always with a view toward appeasing the marginalized and maintaining stability.

Third, I argue that an emphasis on human potential for market advancement directs people's attention to themselves and their hidden capacities, energy, and imagination while also diverting them from a critical focus on structural forces responsible for their plight. Psychotherapy is used to open people's imaginations to future possibilities oriented to their own place in a larger project of achieving "socialist" ideals or utopian political projects such as the harmonious society and the "Chinese dream." Fourth, I demonstrate that the continuous application of the dialectical principle of *biantong* constructs an illusion of socialist continuity, which not only sustains discursive, social, and political stability but also downplays the adoption of neoliberal market imperatives. Indeed, discursive and subject forms, socialist ethics, and ideals of Mao's era have been strategically invoked, revised, and repoliticized in the reform era to serve various purposes such as remolding subjectivity, legitimizing neoliberal ideology, and advancing entrepreneurial capital. Fifth, I explore the creation of new forms of expertise entailed in the transition from Mao's ideology to a meritocracy acknowledging the power of science and knowledge. I highlight the impact of psychological expertise on the subjectivities of clients from the working class. Finally, I argue that the use of gender to express class differences and the translation of class-based experiences into individual psychology and personal emotions defuses class tensions intensified by economic restructuring. In the following I briefly summarize each of these dimensions of my project and develop their significance for the contemporary ethnography of China and the array of theoretical perspectives that converge in the framing of this work.

Psychologization and the Psycho-Political Economy

Alongside other significant ethnographic works (Martin 2007; Davis 2012; Kitanaka 2012) that examine the use of psychiatry as a political process, this book opens fresh territory for debate on psychological sciences by examining this political process in the unique context of postsocialist China, where counseling and social work are often coordinated in the training of community-based psychosocial workers. While I engage with Western scholarship on the political uses and misuses of psychology, I also reconsider the insights developed in this literature and challenge, where appropriate, implicit assumptions of universalism that sometimes emerge regarding the foundations of Western psychotherapy in order to speak to those processes as they unfold in a non-Western and "socialist" context.

Anthropologists of China including Judith Farquhar (1994) and Yanhua Zhang (2007) have written extensively on the significance of traditional Chinese medicine in addressing physical and psychological disorders. Scholars such as Arthur Kleinman (1986, 1988) and Nancy Chen (2003) have contributed significantly to the study of Chinese mental illness and psychiatry, while Robin Munro (2002) has advanced our knowledge of the political misuses of psychiatry during Mao's era. However, I address the psychological sciences as part of an emerging trend of psychologization and governance through counseling and psychological self-help, which has not yet received significant attention. I offer here an ethnographic study of how counseling, social work, and psychological self-help are engaged in China to intervene in social issues, especially among vulnerable groups.

Psychologization as it is implemented in China encourages individuals to turn inward toward the heart and the inner self for meaning and solutions. It adapts a form of positive psychology with the goal of promoting formal movement toward well-being (Yang 2013a), particularly in evidence since 2011, the year of well-being, and 2012, the year of "positive energy" in China. Central to this psychologizing process are the marginalized people and the subalterns who are embedded in this complex network of relations; they serve as subjects who can realize the desires of the party-state.

Psychotherapy not only reproduces the power and hierarchy of the status quo; it also creates new trajectories of inequality. Indeed, no knowledge is neutral or escapes the pairing of power and knowledge (Foucault 1982). When people experience fragmentation in the face of social rupture, the Chinese government often creates new narratives or renews existing narrative structures to help people make sense of their nascent experiences (see Dirlik 1989). Psychology in China has offered such a language and a strategy for interpreting and contesting socioeconomic dislocation since the mid-1990s. Despite the wide accessibility of psychological self-help in China, psychotherapy stratifies Chinese society through unequal access to psychological resources: the well-to-do middle class accesses private counseling while members of the working class are left with state-sponsored psychotherapeutic interventions. Within the working class, men and women are also treated differently based on the different potential they presumably embody. Male workers are often perceived to embody negative potential, and reemployment counseling and poverty relief programs are oriented toward appeasing them. The state-led psychotherapeutic interventions create differentiated, multiple, and sometimes contradictory effects. Given the inequality embedded within the psychologization trend, this effort itself emerges as a new site of struggle for marginalized individuals.

Psychological expertise holds the promise not only of curing pathology but also of reshaping subjectivity. At least four strategies of psychologization arise in programs that seek to govern disadvantaged groups, particularly laid-off workers. The first strategy is pathologization. Authorities identify and pathologize the "irrational" thoughts of the unemployed that are deemed unsuitable for market competition, including workers' dependence on their former employers at state-owned enterprises. Being thought of as someone who might hold such "irrational" perspectives makes one a ripe target for psychological intervention. The second strategy is normalization; psychosocial workers use psychological precepts and psychotherapeutic techniques in diagnosis and job counseling to normalize the unemployed and push them into the market or mainstream society. Third, psychotherapy is used to nurture the "wounds" of those who have been impoverished by privatization. The subjects the government finds most in need of this nurturing counsel are laid-off men who are thought to harbor *yinhuan*. Therapy is intended to pacify them and maintain stability. This emphasis on laid-off men is revealed in reemployment or poverty-relief programs that are designed to benefit men more than women, even though in Changping women suffer unemployment and impoverishment to a greater extent than men. Finally, psychotherapy is used to glorify and glamorize certain groups, for example, laid-off women, who presumably embody boundless *qianli*. This glorification highlights the ideological and psychotherapeutic efficacy of the processes that therapy implements to animate and realize positive potential and entrepreneurship, which are now believed to have been suppressed by the old planned economy.

The emerging psycho-political economy relies on the subjectivities and agencies of those on the margins of the state. It is a hodgepodge of socialist thought work and psychotherapy that has emerged in a society that once denigrated psychotherapy as bourgeois ideology in Mao's era. Now it has been rehabilitated as a science that attends to the psychological well-being of the people and constructs "happy," "productive" subjects for the market economy. This rehabilitation is achieved in part through the retraining of grassroots party staff in psychotherapy, setting up the conditions for a recursive psychologizing of sociopolitical issues. This process does not replace but rejuvenates traditional communist thought work by infusing it with the scientism and professionalism now associated with psychotherapy. This is a politically charged process that births new subjects and legitimates certain emotions and outlooks, including happiness and self-reliance, that cohere with or are identified with state interests. Psychology mediates the production of subjecitities by rebuilding their identities around an emotional core that belies the socioeconomic dislocation they experience. Such subjects should engage in self-obsessive activities but be political passive. In addition, psychologization reconstructs workers as both consumers of psychological knowledge and self-reliant subjects who are ready to generate capital. In these ways psychology is implemented as a mode of control and as a resource that aims to heal individuals by revising any social, economic, and political attitudes they might harbor that are not deemed to be useful and productive in the new market economy.

Affect and Kindly Power

Unlike Western dichotomies such as psyche and soma, rationality and emotionality, psychosocial work in Changping intertwines an intellectual appreciation of self-knowledge with emotional experience of the self, thereby enlisting emotions as a powerful force for change (see also Yalom 1989). This intertwining of the emotional and the rational is also part of the dialectics of *biantong*.

Attention to affect and affective governance seems to be part of the lip service paid to socialism (or socialist ethics) in China today. Even though China is aggressively developing a market economy, it still claims to be a socialist state. Such contradictions emerge as Mao's ideologies are reapplied to contemporary psychotherapy; thought work is reshaped as "counseling" and the dialectic principle of *biantong* are manifested, for example, in current programs such as *song wennuan*. Although the ultimate goal of *song wennuan* is to "empower" the poor to become responsible, self-reliant subjects, its rhetoric highlights the warmth and care of the one-party state and its renewed commitment to "socialist" ethics through the practices of *renqing* (attention to human feelings) and counseling.

In the context of the party-state's emphasis on the construction of "a harmonious society" since 2004, psychotherapy has been adopted to alleviate the crippling effects of socioeconomic dislocation and attempt to reconstruct social harmony and social balance through people-centered goals that seek to enhance personal well-being and nurture sustainable development. Key to this vision of achieving a harmonious society is happiness. However, despite the party-state's effort to temper the competitive ethos of a growth-oriented market economy, the happiness mantra resonates with pillars of neoliberalism such as self-care and self-responsibility.

Indeed, the happiness the government promotes does not construct interpersonal relations that might create a sense of belonging and bring various groups into productive relations; instead, it invokes a mode of self-regulation that focuses on a good heart attitude and self-reflexivity.

The promotion of happiness celebrates the emotional, the psychological, and the potential; the political recedes into the background as the potential for sustained collective action is rechanneled into personal and psychological obsessions. This happiness is constructed not only as a set of rational, purposive calculations designed to enable people to accumulate social, cultural, and economic capital but also as a potentially compelling desire for a harmonic, illusory nation-state. Indeed, regulation through happiness and its promises is a mode of control over people's imaginations. The governing rationality of optimizing happiness elicits the desire for pleasure within subjects that is not readily accessible to critical evaluation (Tie 2004, 175) and minimizes opposition. The new psychotherapy replaces discipline imposed from above with the idea of individual responsibility for the self and thus the productive progress of society. However, in this process the so-called peaceful revolution is not depoliticized and amicable but a deeply political process imbued with negotiation, struggle, and contestation among different groups and within the self.

Within psychologization, emotions and potential carry out both the exercise of power and the creation of economic resources. Happiness promotion is a type of kindly power. The state has launched happiness campaigns and other social or welfare programs such as counseling and poverty relief to construct an atmosphere of optimism in the context of an economy in which jobs for the working class have been taken away and their livelihoods have been devastated. Destructive impulses are nevertheless softened under this veil of kindness. By offering psychological care to the unemployed, the government shows benevolence and kindness to the very groups who are displaced, impoverished, and distressed by state-led economic restructuring.

State-promoted psychotherapy with the most distressed group of workers being deployed in service of its promotion, constitutes a particular type of hegemony. The reigning political order is bending the therapeutic sector to its own purposes: attention to counseling and positive psychology provides the government with an opportunity to perform as a caring, therapeutic paternal state. Within this psycho-political economy, workers' misery provides employment opportunities for members of the managerial class and party staff to transform themselves into therapeutic practitioners who will sustain the cycle. The current government sees psychotherapy as a "positive" mode of intervention, a feasible model for reforming those on the margins of Chinese society. It constitutes a way of paying homage to socialism and of legitimating the party's continued existence in a market economy.

The therapeutic strategy reveals the flexibility and intensification of control by the Chinese state. Psychologization as it is implemented in China is not about the psyche but about the application of the Chinese notion of the heart, an all-encompassing concept that includes not only emotion and cognition but also morality and virtue. Chinese psychologists adopt an embodied, holistic approach to mental problems that seeks to regulate people's behavior, desires, and hidden capacities in order to harness their potential in the service of the state. This strategy came into being to deflect attention away from the state's inability to provide its people with adequate resources; instead, the state attempts to mobilize individuals to become responsible, entrepreneurial, productive subjects in the market economy.

The Politics of Potential

China's current system of governance targets the hidden capacities and energies of individuals and regulates their faculty of imagination. Psychology-oriented practices such as self-adjustment, self-reflexivity, and cultivating a positive heart-attitude mediate the dialectical relationship between *qianli* (positive potential) and *yinhuan* (negative potential). In this process, imagined potential propels and shapes actual practice and governance. It has become the driving force behind the training residents' committees in Changping offered to laid-off workers. This training counsels laid-off and underemployed workers to maximize their positive potential by pursuing a large variety of reemployment possibilities. The presumption is that this actualization of the positive will prevent the materialization of negative potential. This orientation is an example of the dialectics of *biantong*—the dialogic interaction and unity of opposites. Human potential is thus harnessed in the service of an expanding market. Beliefs about human potential also shape current modes of generating knowledge that is used to address social problems and govern community life. That is, the government not only rallies the resources of the victims of economic restructuring for the purpose of reordering the political sphere and expanding the economy, it also intensifies its control and exploitation by penetrating into people's hidden energies and capacities.

However, the growth of the service sector and the decline of redistributive state services in Changping has made it more difficult for members of the working class to make a living. Individuals circulate among different jobs and careers, and the conditions of their work change over time. In this bleak job market, the process of constant self-optimization becomes a cyclical norm because counselors perceive these former state workers to be the source of boundless potential and capacity. In reemployment training, counselors take the attitude that an individual's skills, traits, attitudes, values, beliefs, significant emotional events and experiences all contribute to his or her thinking and behavior. This information provides insight for both the counselor and the client about how much potential a person has in a given area and what needs to change in order for the client to achieve at their maximum level. The focus on psychologized modes of releasing positive potential also atomizes individuals and preempts organized resistance. The logic of governing is more oriented to actualizing potential and improving people's capabilities—that is, self-enhancement—than coercive measures, for example, in Mao's era. My attention to how potentiality and imagination play out in reemployment counseling increased my ethnographic sensibility to the assumptions and imagined potential of informants and those with whom they interact. In this aspect of the work, I contribute to the existing literature on the concept of *suzhi*.

Since the 1990s, the phantom of *suzhi* (quality) has been a dominant ideology in education and the training of workers in China (Yan H. 2003a; Anagnost 2004). Scholarly attention to *suzhi* has largely focused either on the training of rural migrant workers or on the education middle-class children receive to prepare them for university degrees or professional careers. However, since the mid-1990s, urban laid-off workers have also been included in this regime of *suzhi*. Transforming the skills and knowledge workers acquired in the service of the planned economy to new *suzhi* (qualities) suitable for the market economy requires training that focuses on correcting their attitudes about privatization and shaping workers' psychological traits so they can survive in a competitive market. Reemployment counseling programs not only provide laid-off workers with technical skills and knowledge but also aim to actualize their potential to meet the needs of the market in order to "relieve" their poverty and personal stress and minimize potential instability. However, because such training programs define unemployment as a self-correcting condition, they further disempower workers and devalue their skills and labor (Dunk 2002). In this sense, *peixun* (training, cultivation) and *suzhi* programs constitute a new regime of regulation: to acquire "citizenship" in this new regime, the working class has to be retrained and reregulated. A new politics of potential that promises a better and happier future has replaced communism's promise of a good life.

Biantong and Neoliberalism

Biantong, a basic principle of Chinese dialectics, treats occurrences and things not as static, superficial, and singular but as dynamic, dialogic, and historical. This principle accommodates intertwining temporalities, spatialities, meanings, and potentialities. The psycho-politics discussed in the book are an interplay of neoliberalism and the principle of *biantong*. *Biantong* is not only about how the past haunts the present and how the present informs the future but also about the intertwining of temporality and spatiality and the pairing of complementary ideas in conceptualization such that any issue can be seen from two opposing and dialectically interactive perspectives. For example, residents' committees and job counselors invoke the work ethics of the former work units and the virtues associated with the planned economy for the purpose of expanding the new capitalist market. This process asks individuals to internalize psychological knowledge in order to actualize or externalize their hidden capacities and potential and to reorient their heart attitude in order to maximize their positive energy. These transformations, which are not only spatial and temporal but are also personal, ideological, and psychological, are required of both laid-off workers and of party staff turned psychosocial workers. The privatization of state-owned enterprises and the emphasis on scientific psychosocial work has devalued their bureaucratic expertise and their prior contributions through ideological thought work. However, the state-led psychotherapeutic intervention has also provided these former party members with ample opportunities to make full use of their skills and experiences with traditional communist ideological orientations as they transform themselves from ideological workers to psychosocial workers.

Biantong as a basic dialectical principle is applied in various domains of social life. For example, invoking preexisting modes of subject formation is one of the default modes for reshaping subject formation in the reform era. In Chapter 2, I explored how the Mao-era principle "self-reliance" that was used to construct the collective subject of "the people" has been expanded into the principle of "four selves" that is being used in the reform era to raise the "self-consciousness" of marginalized women by enhancing their *xinli suzhi* (psychological or heart quality). In China, the new understandings of the self and its emotions triggered by the popularization of psychology clash and converge with existing norms and values, in the process generating new practices of subjectivization and therapy.

The application of *biantong* is particularly salient in state-led reemployment, counseling, and poverty relief programs that target the unemployed. These programs often adopt hybrid structures and foci that unite therapeutic and nontherapeutic discourses and old and new governing strategies. They provide the new urban poor with symbolic material support but also promote psychology-infused practices that aim to transform their emotions, heart attitudes, inner strength, and thought processes for a new market economy. The use of these social welfare programs also serves to extend the life of the "socialist" system.

However, by working with the principle of *biantong* and emphasizing the party's putative renewed socialist commitment to alleviating poverty and stress, these programs implicitly downplay their neoliberal market imperatives. The programs are key arenas for identity and power struggles ignited by the process of privatization. They define who participates, who is excluded, who benefits, and who is victimized and contribute to intensified social stratification. In their creative and strategic combination of market mechanisms and state socialism these programs exemplify China's transitional politics—socialist forms with neoliberal contents.

As neoliberalism emerges in China, it articulates dialectical principles embodied in the traditional principle of *biantong*. The Chinese version of neoliberalism is complex: it has roots in the West and in elements of Chinese tradition. Liu Rong, a professor of philosophy at Zhongshan

University, defends Deng Xiaoping's articulation of the "dialectical" way of "incorporating capitalism into socialism" in terms of *biantong*:

> The two systems [socialism and capitalism] under one state are *xiangfan xiangcheng* [contradictory yet complementary]; Deng's wisdom lies in his employing the dialectical method, *duli tongyi* [the unity of opposites], and viewing both contradictory relations and identical elements of the two systems, that is, unity, identity, sharing and agreeability, their mutual reliance, penetrating into each other, and cooperation. Under certain conditions, they complement and benefit from each other, glorifying and promoting each other. (quoted in Tian 2005, 175)

Liu interprets capitalism in China as a practice of neoliberalism that does not necessarily contradict socialism as a means to the end of building community. While Liu defends neoliberalism, he also criticizes the breakdown of organic communities based in work units. His analysis resonates with workers' critiques of the way privatization operates in Changping, where the collapse of work units and the absence of a comprehensive social support system has created new vulnerabilities for laid-off workers. Gary Sigley (2006) suggests that although China's embrace of neoliberalism is reflected in conceptual shifts from "government" (*zhengfu*) to "governance" (*zhili*) (see also Yu 2002), from detailed planning (*jihua*) to planning that steers (*guihua*), Chinese governmentality is still a hybrid of socialism and neoliberalism. That is, the Chinese system has adopted neoliberal practices while continuing some of the authoritarian principles that contributed to Mao's socialism.

Therapeutic Governance: Power and Knowledge

The Chinese government's attempt to adapt the logic of psychologization to the present moment is not the work of a strong state authority. Rather, it is a reflection of the state's inability to provide its people with adequate resources. Even though psychology may serve as a quick-fix solution in a difficult period, using psychology to manage social and economic issues obscures the possibility of more complex, responsible approaches to socioeconomic change. Power and knowledge are inseparable in the state-led therapeutic interventions that have taken place since the 1990s. Marginalized individuals act as both objects of and "experts" in psychotherapy, in the process supporting the state's political economy. This situation constitutes a compelling process for investigation of the question of who or what counts as "expert." Having been partially professionalized through a form of preliminary training, former party staff and residents' committee members confer their "expertise" in psychotherapy onto marginalized citizens. Their professionalization involves strategic engagement with thought work and the traditional dialectics of *biantong*. Different forms of knowledge and expertise (i.e., political expertise, bureaucratic skills, and psychotherapy) cross-pollinate in the professionalization process, resulting in different degrees of specialization in psychotherapy among professional counselors, party staff turned counselors, social workers, and housemaid or taxi counselors. New forms of managerial subjects are produced through the application of an odd mixture of the psychological disciplines, Confucianism, New Age training and others. This demonstrates a shift in governance from a focus on political ideology based on Marxism, Leninism, and Mao Zedong's thought to a focus on sciences and knowledge (or a more focused orientation toward meritocracy) in China.

In this process, local psychological knowledge confronts Western counseling and social work and the hierarchical transmission of validated knowledge from the top down that characterized the Mao era is being replaced by more diverse, more diffusive, and more interconnected sets of knowledge production and transmission. Various socioeconomic groups (former party staff turned psychosocial workers and informal counselors) with different access to psychological knowledge and politics have engaged different forms of "knowing." The psychological training of former party staff encourages them to make full use of their skills as ideological workers; laid-off workers are taught to revisit their experiences with unemployment and distress as a technique they can use as they counsel those who have experienced similar difficulties.

The recent emphasis on therapeutic or medical knowledge obscures the importance of capitalism in intensifying exploitation. Politicians use therapy to increase their popularity and legitimate their power and control over the lives of people to whom they offer "care" (Evans 2008). They use therapy to resolve social problems in the service of social harmony and in ways that are consonant with the demands of political legitimacy and personal fulfillment (Miller 1986; Miller and Rose 2008, 145). Therapy has thus become a pragmatic governing technology.

Gender and Class

The politics of gender and class are central to the unfolding economic restructuring in China. In the wake of gendered, mass unemployment, the pool of laid-off women and rural migrants fills the openings for domestic work, psychological care work, and informal counseling. Gender is a ground for testing and proving the efficacy of state-run socioeconomic transformation, and women are mobilized as shock absorbers. Women workers not only bore the heaviest brunt of economic restructuring and suffered the most from unemployment and poverty, they must now create a bridge between the old planned economy and the neoliberal market economy. They are expected to participate in promoting and performing psychotherapy and to cheerfully fill various service-sector jobs that carry them into downward mobility. The perception that women embody boundless positive potential is the basis of a strategy the state uses to manage the current unemployment and related mental health "crises." Indeed, gendered and psychologized reemployment expands a domestic sphere from which women had some distance in their prior work in work units and redefines the paid work that women can undertake "at home."

As psychological care laborers within the paradigm of a market economy, laid-off women are widely perceived to embody the feminine nurturing ideal that predisposes them to embrace the emerging therapeutic ethos. These women's psychological labor is exploited as a feminine virtue in order to promote psychotherapy and resolve social disorder in a postsocialist society. Hegemonic gendered exploitation is justified by the "happiness" the process of transformation purportedly brings to reemployed women. These transformations in work and outlook are reconstructed through media representations of women workers, for example, as "reemployment stars" that are intended to motivate others to follow similar paths.

Unemployed women are also mobilized to narrow the class gap that has been intensified by economic restructuring in China. These women are reemployed in jobs in which the role of counselor and female company are united, for example, as *peiliaos*. The creation of this new job was intended to elevate the status of laid-off women workers through their new training in positive psychology, but the overlap with traditions of female company and the traditional lack of respect for psychology that endures among the public has instead produced new vulnerabilities to gendered exploitation in the job market. However, the emphasis on gender in caring and (mental) health related work and the mobilization of marginalized women to take the middle-class subject position and to symbolically transcend class boundaries obscures the widening class gap. The focus on gender thus distracts people from a focus on new class stratification.

Gender is the channel for allocating resources, and the distribution of welfare is biased in China today. Laid-off men are often given priority in benevolent welfare programs (e.g., those designed for reemployment and poverty relief) because social instability is perceived to result from the masculine potential of men who lost their jobs during economic restructuring. Sustaining stability means pathologizing and governing masculinity (Yang 2010). Factory managers and residents' committee members have interpreted the unrest and protests of laid-off male workers as a crisis of masculinity. This so-called crisis among working-class men reframes the experience of class-based unemployment as gender relations or family concerns, thus downplaying class tensions.

Perceiving the unfolding economic restructuring in China as a revolution emphasizes the magnitude of the widespread dislocation that is occurring in this still purportedly socialist country. This book addresses the complexities of this "peaceful" revolution with special attention to its political nature. Through its focus on governing the emotions, hearts, and potential of those on the margins of society, the state attempts to exploit the innermost resources of workers for promoting capital production and advocating psychology. It also seeks to strengthen social stability and increase the participation of the people in the market economy through its mobilization of psychological processes. And the government seems to hope that this new strategy of governance through psychologization will ensure the continuation of these transformations.

Notes

Preface

1. This video can be viewed at http://v.youku.com/v_show/id_XMjM2NTk4NA==.html

2. Launched in 2004, *Psychology Talk Show* at CCTV 12 is the first TV counseling program in China to broadcast individual counseling live. Its founding counselors include Li Zixun, Yang Fengchi, Zhou Zheng, and Lei Ming. The show's motto is "open the door to one's soul, listen to inner stories, and advocate for a happy life." For a Chinese-language introduction of *Psychology Talk Show*, see baike.baidu.com/view/575827.htm (see also Yang 2013a).

3. Entrepreneurship in the context of reemploying laid-off workers in China since the mid-1990s refers to any endeavor workers undertook for self-reemployment without relying on the state, for being the "boss of themselves." To own a small food or vegetable stand in a local market or to open a hair salon or gift store is all called entrepreneurship.

Introduction

1. In 2000, the government changed the old residential committee (*jumin weiyuanhui*) to the new community residents' committee (*shequ jumin weiyuanhui*) by giving the latter more autonomy. They are based on a form of neighborhood organization and act as a linchpin between the state and residents (Ministry of Civil Affairs of the Government of China 2000). "Democratic" elections of the leadership of residents' committees are often held, but district governments and street agencies always play a key role in appointing or nominating leaders of these committees.

Even though many workers have been laid off from Beibiao, they still live in this community and their daily lives are regulated by the residents' committee, which has represented the state in governing those former workers since the watch factory was privatized. For many residents, "the government" refers to the community residents' committee or to a street agency, a government unit that is one level higher than the community residents' committee.

2. Some of the retraining in psychological counseling also aims for emotional rehabilitation to help laid-off workers get other kinds of jobs. I use the term laid-off workers (*xiagang gongren*) to refer to all people who were cast off from state-owned enterprises regardless of their status because this is the term they themselves used no matter if they were officially registered unemployed, early retirees or other statuses (see Solinger 2001 for the hierarchy of the laid-off and jobless, particularly their seven ranks). Solinger suggests that the government divides the unemployed into multiple categories in order to forestall them from engaging in unified mobilization (688).

3. In this book the term *psychotherapy* is used in a generic sense, meaning all types of psychotherapy such as client-centered therapy, cognitive-behavioral therapy, narrative therapy, postpsychological therapy, and so on. My use of the term reflects the synthetic approach many Chinese psychotherapists adopt.

4. After British psychologist Richard Wiseman's book *Rip It Up* was translated into Chinese as part of the psychological self-help movement, *zhengnengliang* became the most popular catchphrase in China in 2012. Wiseman suggests that a human body is an energy source; a person can bring forth a new self with more confidence and more energy by inspiring their internal positive potential.

5. This community was reportedly one of the 625 communities in China that have started procedures for building a safe community. These include mechanisms for maintaining the safety and health of residents and lowering the number of accidents and incidents that cause harm. China has a total of twenty-three International Safe Communities and 124 National Safe Communities ("China's Safe Communities," China News Net, October 20, 2009, http://www.safe community.org.cn).

6. Chinese phrases such as *zhiliang* (quality and quantity), *dongxi* (east and west), and *fanzheng* (negative and positive) all illustrate the unity of opposites.

7. Although Kipnis (2012) uses the notion of "the individual psyche" to discuss the process and nature of individualization and Chinese modernity, he offers a holistic approach to the notion of self in the Chinese context that is historically specific, embedded in society, embodied, and affective.

8. The themes of China's all-time bestselling work in translation, *Who Moved My Cheese?* coincide with the interests and concerns of the current Chinese government and corporations as they transition to a market economy. Companies mass-distribute copies of this book or distribute copies to those who face negative change at work.

9. *Laobing*, a pancake made of wheat flour, is the staple food in Changping. Here it symbolizes the full-time employment state workers expected before the transition to the market economy.

10. This notion of China's Dream focuses less on control and stability and more on mobilizing people to identify with government initiatives and visions. China's Dream is more affectively compelling than coercive. However, many Chinese Internet users view this dream as ambiguous and empty, enriching the party-state, not individuals (see also Steinmuller and Zhang 2014).

11. I did fourteen months of field research in Changping in 2002 and 2003 and then continued mainly in the summers of 2007, 2008, 2010, 2011, and 2013 for a total of ten additional months. I interviewed over 120 workers (those who were working and those who had been laid off), five directors of state-owned enterprises, twelve reemployment program managers, and thirty-six residents' committee members and psychosocial workers. I worked closely with six psychosocial workers in Changping and interviewed thirty residents' committee members from different

districts of Beijing who had attended training sessions on counseling, social work, and employee assistance programs.

12. Here "backyard garden" not only refers to its beauty as key to building the green belt surrounding the capital but also implies that it is a neglected space that still has the potential to bloom.

13. However, Solinger (2001) suggests that there is no way to count the actual number of the unemployed, which may be far larger than any official estimation because of the ambiguity and restriction of official definitions of unemployment, the use of a broad array of differentiating labels for the jobless, and different methods of calculation.

14. While all the unemployed who have gone through state-led reemployment training are subject to counseling, I focus on those who are retrained and reemployed as informal counselors. See the following links for both a Chinese and English definition of Peixun (training) baike.baidu.com/view/9787.htm, accessed March 3, 2013; and "Peixun, a Cutting Edge Training, Modern Self-Cultivation," Inside China, n.d., http://thinkingchinese.com/peixun-a-cutting-edgetraining-modern-self-cultivation, accessed March 3, 2013.

15. Proposed by President Hu Jintao and Premier Wen Jiabao in 2004, a harmonious society claims to be people-centered and socially and economically sustainable. Its key features include equity, freedom, and democracy.

16. This embodied and holistic notion of the heart differs from the Romantic tradition that distinguishes the heart from mind, rendering things of the heart as "the true, real seat of the individual self," and things of the mind as the superficial, social self (Lutz 1986, 296).

17. I thank one of the reviewers for this translation.

18. According to Nigel Thrift (2005, 7), all knowledge involves embodied performance (see also Boyer 2005; Harris 2007), or the expressive and productive potentials of the body that entrepreneurial capital increasingly attempts to harness. Indeed, psychology increases new forms of "commodities" and is bound up with new kinds of relations (i.e., counselor and clients) that are managed as a commercial resource.

19. Before 1997, suicide in this community was rare and was primarily limited to women.

20. Until the mid-1990s state-owned enterprises or work-units were the main providers of welfare and social security for urban citizens. Workers supposedly enjoyed lifetime employment and cradle-to-grave welfare. Work units regulated both work and residence. The life chances of workers were determined not by their position in the market but by their residence and employment status. Labor relations were characterized by worker dependence and managerial paternalism (Walder 1986; Lü and Perry 1997). This system is now fading. Instead of being viewed as a source of support for urban workers, it has recently been criticized by psychosocial workers in Changping for having negative effects on individual agency and productivity by increasing their dependency on the state.

21. Thought work (*sixiang gongzuo*) is an ideological ritual party authorities practiced at work units to control communication flows. Traditional Communist thought work was conducted in multiple and diverse ways, but it typically involved political study sessions or one-on-one ideological rituals through which the party staff transmitted policies and official ideologies to members of the rank and file (Rofel 1999; Brady 2008). Currently the party is losing direct control of the communication process because of wide access to the Internet, but efforts to shape workers' heart-mind continue (i.e., through censoring the contents of their online communication).

22. In China, social work was established as an academic discipline in 1987. There are 58 master and 250 bachelor programs of social work in Chinese universities and about 45,000 licensed social workers (Professor Zhang Mo, Beijing University of Labor Relations, personal communication, July 2011). Employee assistance programs, which originated in North America for the purpose of rehabilitating alcoholics, have expanded since the mid-1970s throughout the world to address emotional, family, and drug problems. Since 2001, employee assistance programs in China

have been playing an increasing role in training enterprise leaders in psychological diagnosis, vocational assistance, community assistance, and crisis management (Shi 2011).

23. For example, through her TV lectures and books on the *Analects*, celebrity scholar Yu Dan psychologizes Confucian doctrines and claims to offer a soothing "chicken soup" for Chinese souls. However, given the hierarchy embedded in Confucian doctrines, such psychologization can help naturalize intensified social stratification (Yu 2006; Zhang Y. 2014). Liu Yuli (2008) and others invoked precepts of Confucian moral psychology as a resource for relieving psychological and emotional disorders, which they viewed as social and moral dilemmas.

24. Literature on psychiatric power in Japan contradicts the presumed self-centric, antisocial nature of therapeutic societies. In her study of the widespread embrace of the American notion of codependency in Japan, Borovoy (2005) finds that Japanese conceptualize pathology as a social dilemma rather than a personal deviation. Similarly, Kitanaka (2012) notes that Japanese tend to locate the causes of depression and suicide in the social environment rather than in the individual.

25. The trend toward psychologization has also been implemented through state-organized movements since 1996, such as the *xinlixue jin shequ* (Psychology Enters Communities) program, through which psychologists, counselors, social workers and members of residents' committees began working in urban communities. Similarly, psychologists and psychotherapists disseminate knowledge of mental health and ways of identifying and preventing mental illness among urban residents in the *quanmin jianxin yundong* (National "Heart" Health Movement). Within this framework, a magazine called *Liaoba* (Chatting Bar) was established in 2006 that provides a platform where people can share their psychological disorders and personal dilemmas (Zheng 2009, 174–175).

26. The development of human potential runs throughout Marx's work. In *Capital* (1977), human potential is defined as purposeful and creative human activity that transforms nature into useful objects. For Marx, much of this potential is distorted by capitalism, denied to workers, and turned against them. Human nature could be freed to achieve its true potential through socialism and communism when alienation, private property, and other obstacles that block potential are eliminated.

27. It includes three interacting elements: the client, the therapist, and the therapy process. The client is valued for her worth and potential and is seen not just as who she is but as what she may become. The therapist acts as a facilitator in the client's growth process; she puts her own self aside and enters into the world of the client's perception as much as possible (Rogers 1995, 35).

28. In the wake of mass layoffs, Chinese media have often represented suspects in serious crimes as laid-off workers who were recently released from mental hospitals. Such portrayals of mental illness as the cause of unemployment (rather than the other way around) not only rationalize the association between unemployment and mental illness but also undermine the possible political motivations of unemployed workers for their "criminal" acts (Zhao 2008; Yang 2010).

29. Here I adopt Chinese scholars' distinction, since the mid-1990s, between government and governance (Yu 2002: 194). While government (*zhengfu*) refers to the party-state apparatus, operating top-down through orders, statutes, bureaucracy, and coercion, governance (*zhili*) refers to the relationships between the government, corporations, and communications, operating both top-down and bottom-up, through collaboration, coordination, negotiation, social networking, neighborhoods, identity, and consensus (Yu 2002: 195). Governmentality in a Foucauldian sense refers to fostering life or governing life. Instead of coercion and saying no to people's desires, it acknowledges and channels people's desires (Zhang 2011a).

30. China's more recent emphasis on benevolence and harmony is also part of a revival of Confucianism in politics and everyday life. Confucianism has become a filler for the moral vacuum created by the declined acceptance of communist ideology and rapid market development (Bell 2008).

31. Speaking bitterness was an ideological genre in Mao's era through which the subaltern were encouraged to speak their suffering and bitterness in the old bad society before liberation. By

encouraging the subaltern to speak bitterness, the Communist Party attempted to construct ideal socialist subjects who conformed to the new socialist order (Rofel 1999).

32. Psychology is also part of the "scientific concept of development" in China, which relies on continued economic growth as a means of advancing the market economy. This approach builds political and spiritual civilization in China. For a Chinese explanation of *Kexue fazhan guan* (Scientific concept of development), see http://news.xinhuanet.com/ziliao/2005-03/16/content_2704537.htm, accessed on August 28, 2013.

33. Women workers have experienced layoffs at a disproportionate rate. A survey by the State Statistical Bureau of 15,600 households in 71 cities across China in 1997 revealed that women constituted 62.8 percent of laid-off workers while accounting for less than 39 percent of the total urban workforce (Wang 2003).

34. Reemployment stars—laid-off women who are reemployed in the service sector—are invited to speak at official media outlets about their reemployment experience and psychological transformation from depression and distress to happiness and self-fulfillment (Dai 2004; Yang 2007).

35. In 2011, in a neighboring district of Daxing, a man who was reportedly antisocial and depressed, killed six members of his family, including his six-year-old son.

1. Happiness and Self-Reflexivity as Therapy

1. Since *siyouhua* (privatization) is a taboo word in the official discourse in China, within the factory, *gaizhi* (reform the system) was typically used. However, workers invoked *siyouhua* directly when they criticized management or the government.

2. Dr. Shi Kan (2011) also edited the first Chinese textbook on employee assistance programs. He used this textbook to train Chinese CEOs at the People's University in August 2011. He helped organize the second annual meeting of the Chinese Employee Assistance Programs Association held in Beijing on August 16, 2004 with the theme "Strength of the Heart Means New Growth" (*xin de liliang, xin de chengzhang*).

3. Happiness is also commodified, part of the marketing strategy by the party-governed media to use happiness to stimulate consumption, for example, as in Coca Cola's 2009 Open Happiness Campaign in China.

4. Sara Ahmed (2008) suggests that there is a happiness turn not only in academic disciplines such as history, psychology, architecture, and economics (in anthropology, see Mathews 2006 and Johnston 2012), but also in governance and international arenas.

5. TV series such as *pinzu Zhangdamin de xingfu shenghuo* [The happy life of talkative Zhangdamin], *Yangguang de kuaile shenghuo* [Yangguang's happy life], and *laoda de xingfu* [The happiness of the eldest brother], and movies such as *gaoxing* [Gladness] all treat underprivileged characters and settings.

6. Management at Beibiao noted three major waves of unemployment in urban China that had impacted the factory's operations. The first came in 1958, when the factory was established, which was the first year of the Great Leap Forward (1958–1960) launched by Mao Zedong. During the mass mobilization of labor, this factory recruited workers from rural areas. In 1962, those who had entered cities in 1958 had to return to their native places, a move referred to as "62 *ya*," or "forced return in 1962." The second wave was *youhua zuhe* (optimization grouping) at state enterprises in the early 1980s, when women were the first to be excluded from efficient work teams and placed in the service sector of state enterprises. The last wave started in the mid-1990s, resulting from widespread privatization and economic restructuring.

7. The crisis is real, directly linked as it must be with the socioeconomic dislocation described above. But it is also a discursive construct on the part of state and experts that supports the use of psychology (via counseling, psychiatry, or social work) as a solution to social problems.

8. The government's message is that workers' problems come not from the state but from their own failure to adapt to the market and that workers ought to accept market-based logic when examining their own lives (Blecher 2002, 298–299).

9. For example, in 2010, two international conferences on positive psychology were held in Beijing to disseminate the knowledge of positive psychology and apply it to the Chinese situations: the China International Conference on Positive Psychology at Tsinghua University and the International Conference on Positive Psychology and Education at Beijing Normal University. Timothy So, a scholar from the University of Cambridge, also founded the Global Chinese Positive Psychology Association as a forum for international collaborations on the application of positive psychology in China.

10. This is different from Mao's time, when happiness was derived from politics and from the elevation of the collective over the self (McGrath 2009).

11. Reemployment Service Centers as part of the national reemployment project were implemented at state enterprises from 1998 to 2003 to help laid-off workers find new jobs.

12. The lecture was originally delivered to middle school students in Beichuan after the 2008 earthquake in Sichuan Province and then made into a DVD. Bi Shumin's best-selling books such as *zhengjiu lufang* [Saving the breasts] *or nv xinli shi* [Female counselors] focus on women and promote psychological introspection and emotional management.

13. Similarly, a movie called *Gao Xing*, which describes the life of Liu Gaoxing, a garbage collector in Xi'an City, promotes a notion of gratitude as a way of enhancing optimism, energy, and happiness and of leading people to act virtuously. Liu thanks each of his organs every day for keeping him healthy and productive. This emphasis on optimism and gratitude romanticizes the poverty and suffering of a marginalized group.

14. Basic precepts of eco-psychology are often invoked in advertisements for eco-tourism and counseling in China. For example, a "forest shower" (*senlin yu*)—walking in the forest—is considered therapeutic because it enables nature's energy and self-correcting balance to flow through the heart to promote wellbeing.

15. Many Chinese psychologists have only a general college degree and some on-the-job experience (Clay 2002). There is a national certification program for both counselors and psychologists, but most professionals are not certified, as it is not always required for employment. Social work was established as an academic discipline in China in 1987; to date there are 58 master's-level programs and 250 bachelor's-level programs of social work in Chinese universities. There are about 45,000 licensed social workers in China (Professor Zhang Mo, personal communication, July 2011).

2. "We Help You Help Yourself"

1. See the link to the skit in Zhao Benshen's collection of comedies—"*xinbing*" (the Heartache), http://v.ku6.com/show/wGO2DosD-MtsXa5A.html, accessed on October 20, 2013.

2. Residents' committees derive from the Guomindang's (the Chinese Nationalist Party) *baojia* system of urban administration and control. All families were integrated into a *baojia* network, and each unit within a *baojia* had a designated leader who liaised with local authorities and public security officials (Schurmann 1968, 369). The Chinese Communist Party also considered such grassroots organization essential for the control and reintegration of the urban population in its government and thus used residents' committees to replace the *baojia* system.

3. See Organic Law of the People's Republic of China on Urban Residents' Committees (1989) http://www.npc.gov.cn/englishnpc/Law/2007-12/12/content_1383916.htm, accessed on August, 21, 2014.

4. "Views for Advancing the Construction of Urban Residents' Communities," (*Mingzhengbu zai quanguo tuijin chengshi shequ jianshe de yijian*) or Central Document 23, Beijing: Minzhengbu, 2000

5. By 2004, there were about 2,500 community residents' committees in the urban areas of Beijing.

6. Community residents' committees function as a mode of social control. In the Beibiao community this can be seen in the committee's anti-Falungong campaigns and in the methods used to contain the 2003 SARS epidemic.

7. Scientific socialism, which originated in Marx's writings, has developed in a complex way in China since Mao's era. At the grassroots level of urban residential communities in Changping, scientific socialism is often equated with the more propagandized notion of *kexue fazhanguan* (scientific concepts of development). These concepts, which were proposed at the Third Plenary Session of the Sixteenth National Congress of the Communist Party in China in 2003, show the new state leadership's deeper, innovative understanding of the connotations, essence, and nature of China's development. For a detailed description of this concept, read an English translation at "Scientific Concept of Development & Harmonious Society," www.china.org.cn/english/congress/227029.htm.

8. *Dang'an*, a defining feature of the all-encompassing socialist work-unit system, refers to the classified entextualization of an individual's everyday existence for various disciplinary, regulatory, and bureaucratic purposes. This is kept by the party and includes reports from one's superiors, but individuals cannot access or verify what is documented in their own *dang'an* (Anagnost 1997; Hoffman 2010; Yang 2011b).

9. Leifeng died in 1962. On March 5, 1963, Chairman Mao Zedong called upon the whole country to learn from Leifeng. The spirit of Leifeng has often been deployed to attest to the value of various social and political pursuits, but it means different things at different historical moments. In general, the spirit of Leifeng refers to authenticity, kindness, and beauty and to serving others wholeheartedly. See a slideshow on "Living Leifeng" at http://news.xinhuanet.com/photo/2012-02/29/c_122770298.htm. Other materials on "How to learn from comrade Leifeng" (*xiang Leifeng tongzhi xuexi*) are available from Chinese Web sites such as http://news.sohu.com/s2012/leifeng, accessed on December 21, 2012.

10. *Suzhi* is roughly translated as "quality." It refers to a combination of education, health, upbringing, social skills, and responsibility. It was not a neologism, but it was appropriated by the party in the 1980s as a way of justifying its emphasis on population control as part of economic reform. This policy stressed *renkou suzhi* (population quality) rather than *renkou shuliang* (population quantity). Improving citizens' *suzhi* constitutes a new mode of modern subject production whose goal is to build a powerful nation in the post-Mao era. This idea represents a shift in state policy from regulating births to raising the quality of the population as a whole. By the early 1990s, population quality had become a key term in the party-state's policy statements and directives to cadres, and the notion began to circulate more broadly as a general explanation for everything that held the Chinese nation back from achieving its rightful place in the world (Yan H. 2003a; Anagnost 2004).

11. A preliminary counseling license requires candidates to take two exams based on two books: one is an introduction to Western psychological counseling and the other concerns basics in counseling techniques.

12. In this fable, the old man finds that his only horse is missing. His neighbors come to show sympathy, but the old man is not upset and says instead, "Who knows if this is a curse or a blessing in disguise?" One year later, his horse unexpectedly returns home with a younger horse. When the old man's neighbors come to congratulate him, he says, without visible emotion, "Who knows whether it is a curse or a blessing in disguise?" The old man's son, who loves horse-riding, one day falls from the horse and breaks his leg. Again, neighbors arrive to show sympathy. "Who knows whether it is a curse or a blessing in disguise?" the old man repeats. Later, war breaks out. All the young men are sent to the battlefield and many are killed. But because of his broken leg, this old man's son is spared from recruitment and survives.

13. The factory's party committee discovered a diary written by the murdered woman documenting her efforts to prevent Li from interacting with boyfriends and having a heterosexual relationship. This discovery was used as part of the evidence, along with the petition, to press the court to release Li sooner. This was reportedly the first public homosexual murder in contemporary China.

3. Sending "Warmth" and Therapy

1. The privatization of state-owned enterprises widens income gaps and generates both absolute and relative poverty. For example, through management buy-outs managers easily scoop state assets into their own pockets under various guises, while workers have no access to such "windfall" opportunities.

2. The guaranteed basic minimum income system was set up in 1995. One hundred cities established a minimum income threshold ranging from 96 to 170 RMB per month (US$15.64 to US$27.69 as of September 2014) (Rocca 2003, 91).

3. China's Ministry of Civil Affairs manages poverty-relief work and organizes donations. By 2002, about 21,000 regular donation sites had been established (*China Daily*, January 29, 2003, 1). The wave of unemployment has enabled the party to showcase the continuity of its socialist commitment, which is highlighted in the names assigned to programs such as *yangguang* (sunshine) reemployment programs and the poverty-relief programs of *song wennuan*, which compares the party to the sun shining upon the unemployed and sending the warmth of the party to the poor.

4. The other dimension of the therapeutic state refers to a certain class of experts and the procedures they use to address psychological or physical problems (Cohen 1990; Kleinman and Kleinman 1997; Nolan 1998; Szasz 2001).

5. The severing fee (*maiduan*) and early retirement offered to workers as compensation was based on the years of their service to the factory plus 1,000 or 2000 yuan (US$163 or US$326 in September 2014). The amount varied based on the revenue of the factory (Yang 2011).

6. For example, in a rural village of northern China, a woman's anger toward a peddler who had cheated one of her neighbors not only displayed *renqing* or sympathy for the cheated villager but also extended or reproduced *guanxi* (social connections) between the woman and her neighbor (Kipnis 1997, 28).

7. The affect/emotion split originates in psychoanalysis and distinguishes third-person from first-person representations of feeling. Affect refers to feelings described from an observer's perspective and emotion refers to feelings that "belong" to the speaker "I" (S. Ngai 2005, 25). Massumi (2002) and Grossberg (1992) claim a stronger distinction between affect and emotion in terms of a subjective/objective divide and narrative/nonnarrative opposition, but Ahmed (2004) and Ngai (2005) use affect and emotion interchangeably, both encompassing cognition and bodily sensation (see Yang 2014 for an overview).

8. *Kuqiong* has had different meanings at different historical moments in China. During the Great Leap Forward (1958–1960) and the three-year famine (1960–1962), *kuqiong* was viewed as politically "incorrect" (Walder 1986). Instead, during these periods, the "wind of exaggeration" (*fukua feng*, or bragging) was encouraged to compensate for the failures of the socialist system.

9. Filial piety is unquestioning obedience to parents. In Changping, the biggest failure to fulfill filial piety is childlessness.

10. The concept of filial piety shows the intricate relationship between the state and the family. The superior-subordinate roles defined by the virtue of filial piety govern not only familial relationships but also relationships within the state and between state and society. This forms a political order in which the government micromanages the individual (Yang 1988, 416).

11. *Song wennuan* is not only performed before festivals but also at times when people experience special difficulties such as serious accidents, illness, or death.

4. Thought Work and Talk Therapy

1. In this chapter I use the terms *narrative* and *story* interchangeably.

2. Ellis (1991, 1993) proposed that people become unhappy and develop self-defeating habits because of unrealistic or faulty beliefs. Most of these beliefs originate from three core unrealistic ideas: 1) I must perform well to be approved of by others; 2) You must treat me fairly—if not, then it is horrible and I cannot bear it; 3) Conditions must be developed my way and if not, I cannot stand to live in such a terrible and awful world. These premises can lead to grief and suffering. Disputing irrational beliefs based on these premises; reframing them by viewing situations from a more positive angle; and using problem solving, role-playing, modeling, humor, or bibliotherapy are all possible modes of addressing beliefs that contribute to psychological stress or mental problems.

3. Thought work was often interpreted as a "truth event" in the name of Chairman Mao or the party. It was often a well-structured one-on-one interaction or interrogation, and participants seldom changed their footing over the course of their speaking. This fixed ideological procedure facilitated the universalization of a concrete historical juncture that reflected the interest of a particular class (the Communist Party in this case).

4. Ideology can take many forms and can be adjusted to various practical circumstances. States traditionally maintain power by means of performance-based legitimacy or ideology. Most states use a combination of these approaches to maintain political power. Deng Xiaoping's slogan "seize with both hands" emphasizes both approaches as the means for continuing the party's power: simultaneously strengthening and developing the Chinese economy and maintaining the party's tradition of propaganda and thought work (Brady 2008, 199).

5. In China, people have traditionally embraced an integrative view of the world, which brings about the concept of holism, meaning that all things are inseparable from their opposite and that relationships are interdependent. For example, the Chinese character for human *ren* consists of the character for man and the character for two. Even more clear is the expression *ren zhi ren ye*. The first character means man and the third character means humanity (the other two *zhi* and *ye* are grammatical particles). That is, what constitutes a person's self is its interaction with others (Worm 2010, 218). Self-cultivation is a precondition for the individual to enter into the larger networks that Chinese society was and is built around.

6. According to Althusser (1971), this type of agency is not innate or given. Rather, it is acquired within the structure of established social practices that impose on individuals a particular role of subject. The subject may have freedom, but that freedom is constrained by the historical, hegemonic, and ideological contexts within which the subject functions.

7. The therapeutic ideals of rational emotive behavior therapy are happiness, harmony, and growth. While this therapy uses cognitive strategies to help clients, it also focuses on emotions and behaviors. In addition to identifying and disputing irrational beliefs, therapists also target the emotional responses that accompany "problematic" thoughts.

8. If there is no counselor, the client talks to himself or herself or to the air; this can still lead to a cure. Another example of this is how Christians or people with other religious faiths get inspiration or a new understanding of their problems through prayer. In this sense, clients' talk contributes to their own cure.

9. Training sessions on social work sponsored by the Chinese Ministry of Civil Affairs were delivered at Beijing Techonology University in Beijing in July 2011.

10. Another possible manifestation of *jianbing ren* is in social relationships. During communism and the early reform years most people were bound to a work unit (*danwei*) or to the

extended family, thus making their social realm quite small and homogeneous, whereas today people do not have the same social stability. They need to create social ties in many directions. They make many superficial friendships to find job opportunities. As one's social network becomes larger, the essence of each relationship becomes shallower (see Ruan et al. 1997; and "Jianbing Ren, 'Pancake People,' a Chinese Version of a Global Phenomenon," Thinking Chinese, n.d., http://thinkingchinese.com/jianbing-ren-pancake-people-chinese-version-global-phenomenon, accessed on July 22, 2013).

11. Even though Beibiao has been privatized since 2004, one of the conditions for the purchase the Beijing Light Industry Bureau set is that the factory must continue to produce watch parts and continue to hire the remaining work force. This is why, to many workers, Beibiao remains more or less the same "state-owned" factory.

12. The philosophy of *nande hutu* is embedded in a famous passage by Zheng Banqiao: *Congming nan, hutu nan, you congming er zhuanru hutu geng nan. Fang yizhao, tui yibu, dang xia xin an, fei tu houlai fu bao ye* [Being bright is not easy. But it's also difficult being muddled. If you start out being bright, it is even harder to be muddled. Let go! Step back! If you want to have present peace of mind, don't anticipate future rewards] (Matthyssen 2009).

5. *Peiliao* and Psychological Labor

1. In Shanghai, *peiliao* requires formal training in psychology; obtaining a license requires 400 hours of academic study and training in social psychology, education psychology, crisis intervention skills, and psychological care techniques. However, the training that Li Ying offered *peiliao* was a largely reduced program, a way to demonstrate to potential employers that these laid-off women did get training and were qualified for what they were doing.

2. *Peiliao zhiyi zhengshi huo pi, bei zhi yi daozhi bianxiang seqing.* "The profession of 'Peiliao' was officially approved, but could lead to pornography or sex work." The People's Net, February 20, 2010. http://news.sohu.com/20100220/n270305395.shtml, accessed on October 20, 2013. The following video deals with similar topics to *peiliao* and counseling in Chinese: *Zhong dian gong* "Paid-by-the-hour housemaid-counselor" Chinese New Year Gala, CCTV 2000, http://v.qq.com/cover/w/wl3gxn5b6ih7snt/5Ny4RiuD6mm.html, accessed on September 20, 2013.

3. This echoes the poststructural approach to class and gender, which considers the cultural and historical construction of these two categories (Scott 1988). Emphasizing the constructed or constitutive nature of class, Joan Scott argues that class is deeply gendered and that gender provides a way of articulating and naturalizing differences and class inequality (60; see also Ortner 1991).

4. Yan Hairong (2003) observes that employers want their domestic workers to have clean hands and feet, and desire to hire a maid who is not inclined to theft or other criminal conduct.

5. The Beibiao Residents' Committee deems residents (especially women) who are evaluated based on their filial piety as *xiao xing*.

6. For analysis of the training elite urban women offered rural girls in interpersonal skills and office politics, see Chang 2008.

6. Job Burnout or Suppressed Anger?

1. The novel was later made into a film titled *da chuan qi* (Out of Breath). See *Xiangpi Ren* (modeling clay people). *Xindeng xinli zixun* (the Light of the Heart Psychological Counseling) http://www.xindengxinli.com/News_show.aspx?id=238, accessed on July 16, 2013.

2. Read about "*Xiangpi Ren*" (modeling clay people) in Chinese: http://bbs.nciku.cn/space.php?uid=11570&do=thread&id=7906, accessed on July 16, 2013.

3. A 2012 news article reported that the number of deaths caused by overwork (*guolao si*) in China—600,000 per year or 1,600 per day—has exceeded that of Japan. The report also suggests that *guolao si* is actually caused not by overwork but by health problems triggered by overwork, an analysis that downplays the structural forces that necessitate overwork and cause deaths. For the Chinese report, see Guo Lao Si (Death because of overwork). http://business.sohu.com/20130712/n381438143.shtml?adsid=1, accessed on July 15, 2013.

4. In this city, taxi companies are often formed as follows: individuals borrow money to buy cars, they sell or rent cars to drivers, and then they use the money levied from drivers to pay back their borrowed money and make more money. http://book.sohu.com/20130605/n378068402_2.shtml.

5. Even as mass transit options have expanded and the number of miles of paved roads has increased in the past two decades, the number of vehicles in China has grown three times faster than road capacity. In 2010, Beijing drivers added 2,000 new cars to the city's streets every day, contributing to the nearly five million vehicles in the city (Shank 2012). On June 10, 2013, Beijing traffic administration had to raise the cost of taxi fares from the starting price of 10 yuan within three kilometers to 13 yuan, and from 2 yuan per kilometer to 2.3 yuan per kilometer for longer trips. See Beijing Chuzu hangye xin guiding (New Regulations in Beijing's Taxi Industry). http://business.sohu.com/20120610.shtml, accessed on July 7, 2013.

6. Allocation of apartments to employees of state-owned enterprises was a long-standing practice during the pre-reform period. The quality of relations between management and workers in an enterprise is determined largely by whether or not workers' housing needs have been satisfied. In the 1990s, commodification of housing stock became a reform policy and enterprises began selling apartment units that had been built by work units to their employees at subsidized prices. The commodification of work-unit housing has turned many state-sector workers into private property owners (C. K. Lee 2007). However, not all workers can afford to purchase their apartments, and some remain tenants and pay monthly rent to the local housing bureau. By 2000, rent in the public sector had increased to levels that some working-class families can no longer afford.

7. China's Ministry of Health has also offered free psychological counseling to migrant workers, many of whom are taxi drivers in cities. Labor disputes, complaints, and arrears in wages have afflicted migrant workers, and their psychological distress has aroused increasing concern. This pilot project that was initiated in 2010 covers at least 80 percent of migrant workers in sixty-five cities of twenty-nine provinces. More than 80 percent of migrant workers will undergo at least one psychological counseling session to improve their adaptability ("Free Therapy Offered to Migrant Workers," *People's Daily*, September 5, 2010, 5).

8. Taxi star is a title Beijing taxi companies give to superior drivers who have no record of traffic rule violations, have received no or minimum complaints from customers, and have received letters or phone calls of thanks from passengers because of their suicide prevention efforts and other good deeds.

9. See Krieger 2009 on the efficacy of television psycho-education. Krieger discusses how knowledgeable Beijing taxi drivers were about counseling because of the influence of television and radio counseling in China.

10. During the National Congress meetings in Beijing in 2012, for example, car handles that were close to passengers' seats in taxis were disabled to prevent people from distributing anti-government posters through open doors, and those who purchased chef knives during that period had to register them officially. The latter measure was intended to preempt possible violence (Author's field notes, 2012).

11. *Shangfang* is a unique communist petition system through which senior state leaders or superior institutions present a benevolent face to people who have been wronged by local officials

and deprived of the chance for a fair hearing or trial. This system aims to redress injustice and defuse unrest. However, in the context of a rapidly escalating number of grievances and mass discontent during the tumultuous transition to a market economy, the system has become inefficient.

12. At the Beibiao factory, *naoshi* is a more masculine practice than *majie* and connotes criminality and serious disturbance.

13. In a 2001 speech, former president Jiang Zemin gave official approval to the status of entrepreneurs. Jiang proposed that entrepreneurs from the nonpublic sector of society should join workers, farmers, intellectuals, cadres, and soldiers as the fundamental elements of the socialist Chinese nation (Li 2001). In 2004, the Constitution was amended to protect private property rights, further legitimating the status of the new rich.

14. Even though former party staff have been "marginalized" and their authority has diminished as they have joined residents' committees, they are still given priority for training in counseling, social work, or employee assistance programs. In general, they are better off than most ordinary workers in the market economy.

References

Agamben, Giorgio. 1998. *Homo Sacer: Sovereign Power and Bare Life*. Stanford, CA: Stanford University Press.

——. 1999. *Potentiality: Collected Essays in Philosophy*. Stanford, CA: Stanford University Press.

Ahmed, Sara. 2004. *The Cultural Politics of Emotion*. London: Routledge.

——. 2008. "The Happiness Turn." *New Formations* 63: 7–14.

——. 2010. *The Promise of Happiness*. Durham, NC: Duke University Press.

Althusser, Louis. 1971. *Lenin and Philosophy*. New York: Monthly Review Press.

Anagnost, Ann. 1997. *National Past-times: Narrative, Representation, and Power in Modern China*. Durham, NC: Duke University Press.

——. 2004. "The Corporeal Politics of Quality (Suzhi)." *Public Culture* 16, no. 2: 189–208.

Aneshensel, Carol S. 1992. "Social Stress: Theory and Research." *Annual Review of Sociology* 18: 15–38.

Bakhtin, Mikhail. 1986. *The Dialogic Imagination: Four Essays*. Austin, Texas: University of Texas Press.

Bateson, Gregory. 2000. *Steps to an Ecology of Mind*. Chicago: University of Chicago Press.

Beijing Reemployment Project Leadership Office. 2002. *Reemployment Assistance Pamphlet*. Beijing: Beijing Reemployment Project Leadership Office.

Bell, Daniel A. 2008. *China's New Confucianism: Politics and Everyday Life in a Changing Society*. Princeton, NJ: Princeton University Press.

Benewick, Robert, Irene Tong, and Jude Howell. 2004. "Self-Governance and Community: A Preliminary Comparison between Villagers' Committees and Urban Community Councils." *China Information* 18, no. 1: 11–28.

Berlant, Lauren. 2004. *Compassion: The Culture and Politics of an Emotion*. New York: Routledge.

Bi, Shumin. 2008. *Notes on Psychological Counseling*. Beijing: China Youth Press.

Blackman, Lisa. 2008. "Is Happiness Contagious?" *New Formations* 63: 15–32.

Blecher, Marc. 2003. "Hegemony and Workers' Politics in China." *China Quarterly* 170 (June): 283–303.

———. 2004. "The Working Class and Governance." In *Governance in China*, ed. Jude Howell, 193–206. Lanham, MD: Rowman & Littlefield.

Borovoy, Amy. 2005. *The Too-Good Wife: Alcohol, Codependency, and the Politics of Nurturance in Postwar Japan*. Berkeley: University of California Press.

Bottici, Chiara, and Benoit Challand. 2010. *The Politics of Imagination*. New York: Birkbeck Law Press.

Boyer, Dominic. 2005. "The Corporeality of Expertise." *Ethnos: Journal of Anthropology* 70, no. 2: 243–266.

Brady, Anne-Marie. 2008. *Marketing Dictatorship: Propaganda and Thought Work in Contemporary China*. Lanham, MD: Rowman & Littlefield Publishers.

Bricken, William. 1991. "Training in Virtual Reality." In *Proceedings of the 1st International Conference on Virtual Reality*, 46–48. London: Meckler International.

Brinkman, Svend. 2011. *Psychology as a Moral Science: Perspectives on Normality*. New York: Springer.

Brockmann, Hilke, Jan Delhey, Christian Welzel, and Hao Yuan. 2008. "The China Puzzle: Falling Happiness in a Rising Economy." *Journal of Happiness Studies* 10: 387–405.

Brodie, Janine. 2002. "The Great Undoing: State Formation, Gender Politics and Social Policy in Canada." In *Western Welfare in Decline: Globalization and Women's Poverty*, ed. Catherine Kingfisher, 90–110. Philadelphia: University of Pennsylvania Press.

Brook, Timothy, and Hy V. Luong. 1997. *Culture and Economy: The Shaping of Capitalism in Eastern Asia*. Ann Arbor: University of Michigan Press.

Brownell, Susan, and Jeffrey Wasserstrom. 2002. "Introduction." In *Chinese Femininities and Masculinities: A Reader*, ed. Susan Brownell and Jeffrey Wasserstrom, 1–46. Berkeley, Los Angeles and London: University of California Press.

Bugliani, Adriano. 2011. "From Soul to Mind: Psychology and Political Imagination." In *The Politics of Imagination*, ed. Chiara Bottici and Benoit Challand, 73–85. New York: Birbeck Law Press.

Butler, Judith. 1993. *Bodies That Matter: On the Discursive Limits of "Sex."* London and New York: Routledge.

———. 1997. *The Psychic Life of Power: Theories in Subjection*. Stanford, CA: Stanford University Press.

Canetti, Elias. 1984. *Crowds and Power*. Translated by Carol Stewart. New York: Farrar, Straus and Giroux.

Carr, Summerson E. 2011. *Scripting Addiction: The Politics of Therapeutic Talk and American Sobriety*. Princeton, NJ: Princeton University Press.

Castells, Manuel. 1997. *The Power of Identity: the Information Age: Economy, Society and Culture* Volume II. Oxford: Wiley-Blackwell.

Catalano, Ralph, and David C. Dooley. 1983. "Health Effects of Economic Insecurity: A Test of the Economic Stress Hypothesis." *Journal of Health and Social Behavior* 24, no.1: 46–60.

Chamberlain, Lori. 1989. "Bombs and Other Exciting Devices, or the Problem of Teaching Irony." *College English* 51, no. 1: 29–40.

Chambers, Robert. 1990. "Irony and the Canon." *Profession* 90: 18–24.

Chang, Doris F., Huiqi Tong, Qijia Shi, and Qifeng Zeng. 2005. "Letting a Hundred Flowers Bloom: Counselling and Psychotherapy in the People's Republic of China." *Journal of Mental Health Counseling* 27, no. 2: 104–116.

Chang, Gordon G. 2001. *The Coming Collapse of China*. New York: Random House.

Chang, Lesley T. 2008. *Factory Girls: From Village to City in a Changing China*. New York: Spiegel & Grau.

Chen, Feng. 1997. "The Dilemma of Eudaemonic Legitimacy in Post-Mao China." *Polity* 29, no. 3: 421–439.

Chen, Jie, Chunlong Lu, and Yiyin Yang. 2007. "Popular Support for Grassroots Self-Government in Urban China: Findings from a Beijing Survey." *Modern China* 33, no. 4: 505–528.

Chen, Nancy N. 2003. *Breathing Spaces: Qigong, Psychiatry and Healing in China*. New York: Columbia University Press.

Chen, Zewei. 2010. Resolving the Pain/Threats Posed by Mental Illness. *Outlook Weekly* (May 31): 36–37.

Cho, Mun Young. 2012. "Dividing the Poor." *American Ethnologist* 39, no. 1: 187–200.

——. 2013. *The Specter of "The People": Urban Poverty in Northeast China*. Ithaca, NY: Cornell University Press.

Chriss, James L. 1999. *Counseling and the Therapeutic State*. New York: Aldine de Gruyter.

Clarke John. 2004. *Changing Welfare, Changing States: New Directions in Social Policy*. London: Sage.

Clay, Rebecca A. 2002. "Chinese Psychology." *Monitor on Psychology* 33, no. 3: 64.

Comaroff, Jean, and John J. Comaroff. 2001. "Millennial Capitalism: First Thoughts on a Second Coming." In *Millennial Capitalism and the Culture of Neoliberalism*, ed. Jean Comaroff and John L. Comaroff, 1–56. Durham, NC: Duke University Press.

Conrad, Peter. 1992. "Medicalization and Social Control." *Annual Review of Sociology* 18, no. 1: 209–232.

Cook, John J. 1964. "Silence in Psychotherapy." *Journal of Counseling Psychology* 11, no. 1: 42–46.

Crespo, Suarez, and Amparo Serrano. 2010. "The Psychologisation of Work, the Deregulation of Work and the Government of Will." *Annual Review of Critical Psychology* 8: 43–61.

Dai, Jinhua. 1996. "Redemption and Consumption: Depicting Culture in the 1990s." *Position* 4, no. 1: 127–143.

——. 2002. "Invisible Writing: The Politics of Mass Culture in the 1990s." In *Cinema and Desire: Feminist Maxism and Cultural Politics in the Work of Dai Jinhua*, ed. Jing Wang and Tani Barlow. 213–234. London and New York: Verso.

——. 2004. "Class and Gender in Contemporary Chinese Women's Literature." In *Holding Up the Half Sky: Chinese Women Past, Present and Future*, ed. Tao Jie, Zheng Bijun, and Shirley L. Mow, 289–302. New York: The Feminist Press.

Davidson, Arnold I. 1987. "Sex and the Emergence of Sexuality." *Critical Inquiry* 14, no. 1: 16–48.

Davis, Elizabeth. 2012. *Bad Souls: Madness and Responsibility in Modern Greece*. Durham, NC: Duke University Press.

Derleth, James, and Daniel R. Koldyk. 2004. "The *shequ* Experiment: Grassroots Political Reform in Urban China." *Journal of Contemporary China* 13, no. 41: 747–777.

Derrida, Jacques. 1982. "Difference." In *Margins of Philosophy*, translated by Alan Bass, 3–27. Chicago: University of Chicago Press.

Desjarlais, Robert, and C. Jason Throop. 2011. "Phenomenological Approaches in Anthropology." *Annual Review of Anthropology* 40, no. 1: 87–102.

De Vos, Jan. 2011. "The Psychologization of Humanitarian Aid: Skimming the Battlefield and the Disaster Zone." *History of the Human Sciences* 24, no. 3: 103–122.

Dirlik, Arif. 1989. "Introduction." In *Marxism and the Chinese Experience: Issues in Contemporary Chinese Socialism*, ed. Arif Dirlik and Maurice Meisner, 3–26. New York: M. E. Sharpe.

——. 1997. *The Postcolonial Aura: Third World Criticism in the Age of Global Capitalism*. Boulder, CO: Westview Press.

——. 2007. *Global Modernity—Modernity in the Age of Global Capitalism*. Boulder, CO: Paradigm Publishers.

Dolan, Paul, Tessa Peasgood, and Mathew White. 2008. "Do We Really Know What Makes Us Happy? A Review of the Economics Literature on the Factors Associated with Subjective Well-Being." *Journal of Economic Psychology* 29, no. 1: 94–122.

Dooley, David C., and Ralph Catalano. 1984. "Why the Economy Predicts Help-Seeking: A Test of Competing Explanations." *Journal of Health and Social Behavior* 25, no. 2: 160–176.

Durkheim, Emile. 1982. *The Rules of Sociological Method and Selected Texts on Sociology and Its Method*. Edited by Steven Lukes. Translated by W. D. Halls. New York: MacMillan.

Dunk, Thomas. 2002. "Remaking the Working Class: Experience, Consciousness and the Industrial Adjustment Process." *American Ethnologist* 29, no. 4: 878–900.

Dwivedi, Kedar Nath. 1997. *The Therapeutic Use of Stories*. London and New York: Routledge.

Dwivedi, Kedar Nath, and Damian Gardner. 1997. "Therapeutic Perspectives and Clinical Approaches." In *The Therapeutic Use of Stories*, ed. Kedar Nath Dwived. London: Routledge.

Eghigian, Greg. 2004. "The Psychologization of the Socialist Self: East German Forensic Psychology and Its Deviants, 1945–1975." *German History* 22, no. 2: 181–205.

Eghigian, Greg, Andreas Killen, and Christine Leuenberger. 2007. *The Self as Project: Politics and the Human Sciences in the Twentieth Century*. Chicago: University of Chicago Press.

Ellis, Albert. 1967. "Rational-Emotive Psychotherapy." In *Counseling and Psychotherapy*, ed. Dugald Arbuckle, 78–95. New York: McGraw Hill.

——. 1973. *Humanistic Psychotherapy: The Rational-Emotive Approach*. New York: Julian Press.

——. 1991a. *Reason and Emotion in Psychotherapy*. New York: Carol.

——. 1991b. "The Revised ABC's of Rational-Emotive Therapy." *Journal of Rational-Emotive and Cognitive-Behavior Therapy* 9, no. 3: 139–172.

——. 1993. "Reflections on Rational-Emotive Therapy." *Journal of Consulting and Clinical Psychology* 61: 199–201.

Emerson, Caryl. 2006. "Building a Responsive Self in a Post-Relativistic World: The Contribution of Mikhail Bakhtin." In *The Self: Beyond the Postmodern Crisis*, ed. Paul C. Vitz and Susan M. Felch, 25–44. Wilmington, DE: ISI Books.

Epston, David, and Michael White. 1995. "Consulting Your Consultants: A Means to the Co-Construction of Alternative Knowledges." In *The Reflecting Team in Action*, ed. S. Friedman. New York: Guilford Press.

Evans, Harriet. 2008. "Sexual Bodies, Sexualized Identities and the Limit of Gender." *China Information* 22, no. 2: 361–386.

Evans, Tim. 2008. "Rise of the Therapeutic State: New Challenges for Twenty-First Century Medicine." *Economic Affairs* 28, no. 4: 22–26.

Farquhar, Judith. 1994. *Knowing Practice: The Clinical Encounter in Chinese Medicine*. Boulder, CO: Westview Press.

Feng, Youlan. 1956. *Zhongguo Zhexue shi* [The History of Chinese Philosophy]. Hong Kong: Tai Ping Yang Tu Shu Gong Si (The Pacific Books Company).

Feng, Jicai. 1996. *Ten Years of Madness: Oral Histories of China's Cultural Revolution*. San Francisco: China Books.

Fewsmith, Joseph. 2001. *China since Tiananmen: The Politics of Transition*. New York: Cambridge University Press.

Finance Editorial Board (*caijing zazhi bianjibu*) 2002. Concerns of Unemployment (shiye zhiyou). In Transitional China (Zhuanxing Zhongguo), 377–390. Beijing: Shehui kexue wenxian chubanshe (Social Sciences Documentation Publishing House).

Ford, Peter. 2007. "Modern China, Eye on Mental Health." *Christian Science Monitor*, November 13. http://www.csmonitor.com/2007/1113/p06&01/-woap.html, accessed May 2009.

Foucault, Michel. 1972. "The Discourse on Language." In *Archaeology of Knowledge*, translated by A. M. Sheridan Smith, 215–237. New York: Pantheon.

——.1977. *Discipline and Punish: The Birth of the Prison*. Knopf Doubleday Publishing Group.

——. 1978. *The History of Sexuality, Volume I: An Introduction*. New York: Pantheon Books.

——. 1982. "The Subject and Power." In *Michel Foucault: Beyond Structuralism and Hermeneutics*, ed. Hubert Dreyfus and Paul Rabinow. Chicago: University of Chicago Press.

——. 1991. *The Foucault Effect: Studies in Governmentality*, ed. Graham Burchell, Colin Gordon, and Peter Miller. London, Toronto, Sydney, Tokyo and Singapore: Harvester Wheatsheaf.

——. (1997) 2008. *Mental Illness and Psychology*. Translated by Alan Sheridan. Berkeley: University of California Press.

Frank, Jerome D. 1961. *Persuasion and Healing: A Comparative Study of Psychotherapy.* Baltimore, MD: Johns Hopkins University Press.

———. 1974. "Psychotherapy: The Restoration of Morale." *American Journal of Psychiatry* 131, no. 3: 271–274.

Fraser, Nancy. 1987. "Women, Welfare and the Politics of Need Interpretation." *Hypatia* 2, no. 1: 103–121.

———. 1994. "A Genealogy of Dependency: Tracking a Key Word in the U.S. Welfare State." *Signs: Journal of Women in Culture and Society* 19, no. 2: 309–336.

———. 1995. "From Redistribution to Recognition? Dilemmas of Justice in a 'Post-Socialist' Age." *New Left Review* 212 (July/August): 68–93.

Freudenberger, Herbert, and Geraldine Richelson. 1983. *Burn-Out: The High Cost of High Achievement.* London: Random House.

Fromm, Erich. 1947. *Man for Himself: An Inquiry into the Psychology of Ethics.* New York: Rinehart.

Furedi, Frank. 2004. *Therapy Culture: Cultivating Vulnerability in an Uncertain Age.* London: Routledge.

Gabbard, Krin, and Glen O. Gabbard. 1999. *Psychiatry and the Cinema.* 2nd ed. Arlington: American Psychiatric Press.

Giddens, Anthony. 1991. *Modernity and Self-Identity: Self and Society in the Late Modern Age.* Cambridge: Polity Press.

Goffman, Erving. 1979. "Footing." *Semiotica* 25, nos. 1/2: 1–29.

Good, Mary-Jo DelVecchio, Sandra Hyde, Sarah Pinto, and Byron Good. 2008. *Postcolonial Disorders.* Berkeley: University of California Press.

Greenberg, Leslie S. 2004. "Emotion-Focused Therapy." *Clinical Psychology and Psychotherapy* 11, no. 1: 3–16.

Greenberg, Leslie S., and Sandra C. Paivio. 1997. *Working with Emotions in Psychotherapy.* New York: Guilford Press.

Greenberg, Leslie S., and Jeremy D. Safran. 1987. *Emotion in Psychotherapy.* New York: Guilford Press.

———. 1989. "Emotion in Psychotherapy." *American Psychologist* 44, no. 1: 19–29.

Grossberg, Lawrence. 1992. *We Gotta Get Out of This Place: Popular Conservatism and Postmodern Culture.* New York: Routledge.

Gordo, Angel and Jan De Vos. 2010. "Psychologism, Psychologising and Depsychologisation." *Annual Review of Critical Psychology* 8: 3–7.

Gu, Xiulian. 2001. *Zaitan Xiagong Nugong Zaijiuye Wenti* (Discuss the Reemployment of Laid-off Women Workers). China Women's News, Feb 13, p. 1

Gui, Yong, Joseph Y. S. Cheng, and Weihong Ma. 2006. "Cultivation of Grassroots Democracy: A Study of Direct Elections of Residents' Committees in Shanghai." *China Information* 20, no. 1: 7–31.

Gutwirth, Marcel. 1993. *Laughing Matter: An Essay on the Comic.* Ithaca, NY: Cornell University Press.

Hall, David L., and Roger T. Ames. 1998. *Thinking through the Han: Self, Truth and Transcendence in Chinese and Western Culture.* Albany: State University of New York Press.

Han, Buxin, and Zhang Kan. 2007. "Psychology in China." *Psychologist* 20: 734–736.

Hanser, Amy. 2008. *Service Encounters: Class, Gender and the Market for Social Distinction in Urban China*. Stanford, CA: Stanford University Press.

Hanying Cidian [A Chinese-English Dictionary]. 1995. Rev. version. Beijing: Foreign Language Teaching and Research Press.

Hardt, Michael. 1999. "Affective Labor." *Boundary 2* 26, no. 2: 89–100.

Harris, Mark. 2007. *Ways of Knowing: New Approaches in the Anthropology of Experience and Learning*. New York and Oxford: Berghahn.

Harris, Russ. 2007. *The Happiness Turn: How to Stop Struggling and Start Living*. Auckland, New Zealand: Exisle Publishing.

Heelas, Paul, and Andrew Lock. 1981. *Indigenous Psychologies: The Anthropology of the Self*. London: Academic Press.

Henderson, Lynne N. 1987. "Legality and Empathy." *Michigan Law Review* 85, no. 7: 1574–1653.

Higgins, Louise T., Gareth Davey, Xiang Gao, Richang Zheng, Zijun Ni, and Lijun Lang. 2008. "Counselling in China: Past, Present and Future." *Psychology and Developing Societies*. 20, no. 1: 99–109.

Hill, Clara E., Barbara J. Thompson, and Nicholas Ladany. 2003. "Therapist Use of Silence in Therapy: A Survey." *Journal of Clinical Psychology* 59, no. 4: 513–524.

Hinton, William. 1966. *Fanshen: A Documentary of Revolution in a Chinese Village*. New York: Vintage.

Hippler, Thomas. 2011. "The Politics of Imagination: Spinoza and the Origins of Critical Theory." In *The Politics of Imaginationi*, ed. Chiara Bottici and Benoit Challand, 55–72. New York: Birbeck Law Press.

Ho, Sang Lok. 2006. "'The Three Happiness' and Public Policy." In *Happiness and Public Policy: Theory, Case Studies and Implications*, ed. Yew-Kwang Ng and Lok Sang Ho, 47–66. New York:Palgrave Macmillan.

Ho, David Yau-Fei, and Chi-Yue Chiu. 1998. "Collective Representations as a Metaconstruct: An Analysis Based on Methodological Relationalism." *Culture and Psychology* 4, no. 3: 349–369.

Hochschild, Arlie R. 1983. *The Managed Heart: Commercialization of Human Feeling*. Berkeley: University of California Press.

——. 2003. *The Commercialization of Intimate Life: Notes from Home and Work*, 104–118. Berkeley: University of California Press.

Hoffman, Lisa. 2006. "Autonomous Choices and Patriotic Professionalism: On Governmentality in Late-Socialist China." *Economy and Society* 35, no. 4: 550–570.

——. 2010. *Patriotic Professionalism in Urban China: Fostering Talent*. Philadelphia, PA: Temple University Press.

Hou, Zhijin, and Zhang Naijian. 2007. "Counselling Psychology in China." *Applied Psychology: An International Review* 56, no. 1: 33–50.

Hsu, Francis L. K. 1985. "The Self in Cross-Cultural Perspective." In *Culture and Self: Asian and Western Perspectives*, ed. Anthony J. Marsella, George DeVos and Francis L. K. Hsu, 24–55. New York: Tavistock.

Hu, Angang, Cheng Yonghong, and Yang Yunxin. 2002. *Kuoda Jiuye Yu Tiaozhan Shiye: Zhongguo Jiuye Zhengce Pinggu (1949–2001)* [To Expand Employment and Challenge Unemployment: Evaluation of China's Employment Policies (1949–2001)]. Beijing: Zhongguo Laodong Shehui Baozhang Chubanshe.

Huang, Hsuan-ying. 2014. "The Emergence of the Psycho-boom in Contemporary Urban China." In *Psychiatry and Chinese History*, ed. Howard Chiang, 183–204. London: Pickering & Chatto.

Hurst, William. 2004. "Understanding Contentious Collective Action by Chinese Laid-Off Workers: The Importance of Regional Political Economy." *Studies in Comparative International Development* 39, no. 2: 94–120.

——. 2009. "The Power of the Past: Nostalgia and Popular Discontent in Contemporary China." In *Laid-off Workers in a Workers' State: Unemployment with Chinese Characteristics*, ed. Thomas Gold, William Hurst, Jaeyoun Won, and Li Qiang, 115–134. New York: Palgrave-MacMillan.

Hurst, William, and Kevin J. O'Brien. 2002. "China's Contentious Pensioners." *China Quarterly* 170 (June): 345–360.

Hutcheon, Linda. 1995. *Irony's Edge: The Theory and Politics of Irony*. London: Routledge.

Illouz, Eva. 2008. *Saving the Modern Soul: Therapy, Emotions, and the Culture of Self-Help*. Berkeley: University of California Press.

Jaggar, Alison M. 1989. "Love and Knowledge: Emotion in Feminist Epistemology." In *Women, Knowledge, and Reality: Explorations in Feminist Philosophy*, ed. Ann Garry and Marilyn Pearsall, 129–156. Boston: Unwin Hyman.

Jing, Qicheng, and Fu Xiaolan. 2001. "Modern Chinese Psychology: Its Indigenous Roots and International Influence." *International Journal of Psychology* 36, no. 6: 408–418.

Johnson, Spencer. 1998. *Who Moved My Cheese? An Amazing Way to Deal with Change in Your Work and in Your Life*. New York: Putnam Adult.

Johnston, Barbara Rose. 2012. "Introduction to Happiness." *American Anthropologist* 114, no. 1: 6–7.

Kernan, Antonie, and Jean-Louis Rocca. 2000. "Social Responses to Unemployment and the New Urban Poor: Case Study in Shenyang City and Liaoning Province." *China Perspectives* 27: 35–51.

Kessler, Ronald C., and Jane D. McLeod. 1985. "Social Support and Mental Health in Community Samples." In *Social Support and Health*, ed. S. Cohen and S. L. Syme, 219–240. New York: Academic Press.

Kingfisher, Catherine. 2002. *Western Welfare in Decline: Globalization and Women's Poverty*. Philadelphia: University of Pennsylvania Press.

Kingfisher, Catherine, and Michael Goldsmith. 2001. "Reforming Women in the United States and Aotearoa/New Zealand: A Comparative Ethnography of Welfare Reform in Global Context." *American Anthropologist* 103, no. 3: 714–732.

Kipnis, Andrew, ed. 1997. *Producing Guanxi: Sentiment, Self, and Subculture in a North China Village*. Durham, NC: Duke University Press.

——. 2012. *Chinese Modernity and the Individual Psyche*. New York: Palgrave Macmillan.

Kitanaka, Junko. 2012. *Depression in Japan: Psychiatric Cures for a Society in Distress*. Princeton, NJ: Princeton University Press.

Kleinman, Arthur. 1986. *Patients and Healers in the Context of Culture: An Exploration of the Borderland between Anthropology, Medicine, and Psychiatry*. Berkeley: University of California Press.

———. 1988. *The Illness Narratives: Suffering, Healing, and the Human Conditions*. New York: Basic Books.

———. 1991. *Rethinking Psychiatry: From Cultural Category to Personal Experience*. New York: Free Press.

———. 2010. "The Art of Medicine: Remaking the Moral Person in China: Implications for Health." *Lancet* 375, no. 9720: 1074–1075.

———. 2011. "Foreword." In *Governance of Life in Chinese Moral Experience: The Quest for an Adequate Life, ed*. Everett Zhang Yuehong, Arthur Kleinman and Tu Weiming, xi–xiv. London: Routledge.

Kleinman, Arthur, and Byron Good. 1985. "Introduction: Culture and Depression." In *Culture and Depression*, ed. Arthur Kleinman and Byron Good, 1–33. Berkeley: University of California Press.

Kleinman Arthur, and Joan Kleinman. 1997. "The Appeal of Experience, the Dismay of Images: Cultural Appropriation of Suffering in Our Times." In *Social Suffering*, ed. Arthur Kleinman, Das Veena, and Margaret Lock. Berkeley: University of California Press.

Kleinman, Arthur, Yunxiang Yan, Jing Jun, Sing Lee, Everett Zhang, Pan Tianshu, Wu Fei, and Guo Jinhua. 2011. *Deep China: The Moral Life of the Person*. Berkeley: University of California Press.

Kong, Shuyu. 2014. "Melodrama for Chang: Gender, Kuqingxi and the Affective Articulation of Chinese TV Drama." In *The Political Economy of Affect and Emotion in East Asia*, ed. Jie Yang, 116–134. London: Routledge.

Kraus, Richard Curt. 1977. "Class Conflict and the Vocabulary of Social Analysis in China." *China Quarterly* 69 (March): 54–74.

Krieger, Josh. 2009. "Manufacturing Psychological Understanding: How China's First National Psychotherapy TV Show Teaches Viewers the Psychological Narratives of Chinese Family Problems." PhD diss., The Wright Institute.

Kulick, Don. 1998. "Anger, Gender, Language Shift and the Politics of Revelation in a Papua New Guinean Village." *Pragmatics* 2, no. 3: 281–296.

Ledoux, Joseph. 1998. *The Emotional Brain: The Mysterious Underpinnings of Emotional Life*. New York: Touchstone.

Lee, Ching Kwan. 2000. "The 'Revenge of History': Collective Memories and Labor Protests in Northeastern China." *Ethnography* 1, no. 2: 217–237.

———. 2007. *Against the Law: Labor Protests in China's Rustbelt and Sunbelt*. Berkeley: University of California Press.

Lee, Haiyan. 2006. "Nannies for Foreigners: The Enchantment of Chinese Womanhood in the Age of Millennial Capitalism." *Public Culture* 18, no. 3: 507–529.

———. 2007. *Revolution of the Heart: A Genealogy of Love in China, 1900–1950*. Palo Alto, CA: Stanford University Press.

Levitt, Heidi M. 2001. "The Sounds of Silence in Psychotherapy: The Categorization of Clients' Pauses." *Psychotherapy Research*, 11, no. 3: 295–309.

Lewis, Patricia. 2008. "Emotion Work and Emotion Space: Using a Spatial Perspective to Explore the Challenging of Masculine Emotion Management Practices." *British Journal of Management* 19, supplement S1: 130–140.

Li Minsheng. 2001. "Entrepreneurs from Non-Public Sector Hail Jiang's Speech." *Beijing Review* 31: 11–13.

Liang Yue. 2002. *China Women's News*, September 24, 3.

Lieblich, Amia, Dan P. McAdams, and Ruthellen Josselson. 2004. *Healing Plots: The Narrative Basis of Psychotherapy*. Washington, DC: American Psychological Association.

Liu, Dehuai. 1995. "Dangqian zhongguo qiye zuzhi de chuantong tezheng" [The Traditional Characteristics in Contemporary Chinese Enterprises]. *Shehuixue Yanjiu* (Sociological Research) 5 (1995).

Liu, Yuli. 2008. *Xintai Gaibian Mingyun* [Heart-Attitude Changes One's Fate]. Beijing: Guojia Xingzhen Xueyuan Yinxiang Chubanshe (Audio-Visual Press of China's National Administrative Academy).

Louie, Kam. 1991. "The Macho Eunuch: The Politics of Masculinity in Jia Pingwa's 'Human Extremities.'" *Modern China* 17, no. 2: 163–187.

Lü, Hsiao-po, and Elizabeth Perry, eds. 1997. *Danwei: The Changing Chinese Workplace in Historical and Comparative Perspective*. London: M. E. Sharpe.

Lutz, Catherine A. 1988. *Unnatural Emotions: Everyday Sentiments on a Micronesian Atoll and Their Challenge to Western Theory*. Chicago: University of Chicago Press.

Lyman, Peter. 1981. "The Politics of Anger." *Socialist Review* 11, no. 3: 55–74.

———. 2004. "The Domestication of Anger: The Use and Abuse of Anger in Politics." *European Journal of Social Theory* 7, no. 2: 133–147.

Madigan, Stephen. 2011. *Narrative Therapy*. Washington, DC: American Psychological Association.

Mao Zedong. 1957. "On the Correct Handling of Contradictions among the People." Speech at the Eleventh Session (Enlarged) of the Supreme State Conference, February 27, 1957. http://marxistphilosophy.org/CorrectHandling.pdf, accessed on March 21, 2013.

———. 1968. *Mao Zedong Xueji* [Selected Works of Mao Zedong]. Beijing: Renmin Chubanshe.

Markus, Hazel R., and Shinobu Kitayama. 2003. "Culture, Self and the Reality of the Social." *Psychological Inquiry* 14, nos. 3/4: 277–283.

Martin, Emily. 2007. *Biopolar Expeditions: Mania and Depression in American Culture*. Princeton, NJ: Princeton University Press.

Marx, Karl. 1976. *Capital: A Critique of Political Economy*. Vol. 1. Trans. B. Fowkes. Harmondsworth: Penguin Books.

Maslach, Christina, Wilmar B. Schaufeli, and Michael P. Leiter. 2001. "Job Burnout." *Annual Review of Psychology* 52, no. 1: 397–422.

Massumi, Brian. 2002. *Parables for the Virtual*. Durham, NC: Duke University Press.

———. 2007. "Potential Politics and the Primacy of Preemption." *Theory and Event* 10, no. 2.

Matthews, Gordon. 2006. "Happiness and the Pursuit of a Life Worth Living: An Anthropological Approach." In *Happiness and Public Policy*, ed. Yew-Kwang Ng and Lok Sang Ho, 147–168. Hampshire, UK: Palgrave Macmillan.

Matthyssen, Mieke. 2009. "*Nande Hutu*, 'It's Not Easy to Be Muddleheaded': A 'Strategy' for a Harmonious Society." Paper presented at the 108th annual meeting of American Anthropological Association, Philadelphia, December 4.

Matthyssen, Mieke. 2012. "*Nande Hutu* and 'the Art of Being Muddled.'" PhD diss., University of Ghent.

McLeod, John. 2004. "The Significance of Narrative and Storytelling in Postpsychological Counseling and Psychotherapy." In *Healing Plots: The Narrative Basis of Psychotherapy*, ed. Amia Lieblich, Dan P. McAdams, and Ruthellen Josselson, 11–27. Washington, DC: American Psychological Association.

McElhinny, Bonnie S. 1995. "Challenging Hegemonic Masculinities: Female and Male Police Officers Handling Domestic Violence." In *Gender Articulated: Language and the Socially Constructed Self*, ed. Kira Hall and Mary Bucholtz, 217–243. New York: Routledge.

——. 2003. "Fearful, Forceful Agents of the Law: Ideologies about Language and Gender in Police Officers' Narratives about the Use of Physical Force" *Pragmatics* 13, no. 2: 253–284.

——. 2007. *Words, Worlds, Material Girls: Language, Gender and Global Economies*. Berlin: Mouton de Gruyter.

——. 2010. "The Audacity of Affect: Gender, Race, and History in Linguistic Account of Legitimacy and Belonging." *Annual Review of Anthropology* 39: 309–328.

McGrath, Jason. 2009. "Communists Have More Fun! The Dialectics of Fulfillment in Cinema of the People's Republic of China." *World Picture* 3. http://www.world picturejournal.com/WP_3/McGrath.html. Accessed January 13, 2013.

McLaughlin, Kenneth. 2010. "Psychologisation and the Construction of the Political Subject as Vulnerable Object." *Annual Review of Critical Psychology* 8: 63–79.

McLeod, John. 2004. "The Significance of Narrative and Storytelling in Postpsychological Counseling and Psychotherapy." In *Healing Plots: The Narrative Basis of Psychotherapy*, ed. Amia Lieblich, Dan P. McAdams and Ruthellen Josselson, 11–28. Washington DC: American Psychological Association.

Mencius. 2004. *Mencius*. Rev. ed. Trans. D. C. Lau. New York: Penguin Books.

Miller, Peter. 1986. "Psychotherapy of Work and Unemployment." In *The Power of Psychiatry*, ed. Peter Miller and Nicolas Rose, 143–176. Cambridge: Polity Press.

Miller, Peter, and Nikolas Rose. 1991. "Programming the Poor: Poverty, Calculation and Expertise." In *Deprivation, Social Welfare and Expertise*, ed. J. Lehto. Helsinki: National Agency for Welfare and Health.

——. 1994. "On Therapeutic Authority: Psychoanalytic Expertise Under Advanced Liberalism." *History of the Human Sciences* 7, no. 30: 29–64.

——. 2008. *Governing the Present: Administering Economic, Social and Personal Life*. Cambridge: Polity.

Ministry of Civil Affairs of the People's Republic of China. 2000. "Minzhengbu guanyu zai quanguo tuijin chengshi shequ jianshe de yijian" [Views for advancing the construction of urban residential communities]. http://www.mca.gov.cn/ article/ content/WJYL_SQJS/200491101216.tml, accessed November 11, 2011.

Moore, Henrietta L. 1994. *A Passion for Difference: Essays in Anthropology and Gender*. Cambridge: Polity Press.

Munn, Nancy. 1986. *The Forms of Gawa: A Symbolic Study of Value Transformation in a Massim (Papua New Guinea) Society*. Cambridge: Cambridge University Press.

Munro, Robin. 2002. *Dangerous Minds: Political Psychiatry in China Today and Its Origins in the Mao Era*. New York: Human Rights Watch and Geneva Initiative on Psychiatry.

Ng, Emily. 2009. "Heartache of the State, Enemy of the Self: Bipolar Disorder and Cultural Change in Urban China." *Culture, Medicine, Psychiatry* 33, no. 3: 421–450.

Ng, Yew-Kwang, and Lok Sang Ho. 2006. *Happiness and Public Policy*. Hampshire, UK and New York: Palgrave Macmillan.

Ngai, Pun. 2005. *Made in China: Women Factory Workers in a Global Workplace*. Durham, NC: Duke University Press.

Ngai, Pun, and Chris King-chi Chan. 2008. "The Subsumption of Class Discourse in China." *Boundary 2* 35, no. 2: 75–91.

Ngai, Sianne. 2005. *Ugly Feelings*. Cambridge: Harvard University Press.

Ngeow, Chow Bing. 2012. "The Residents' Committee in China's Political System: Democracy, Stability, Mobilization." *Issues and Studies* 48, no. 2: 71–126.

Nietzsche, Friedrich. 1968. "Good and Bad," "Good and Evil." In *Geneaology of Morals*, translated by Walter Kaufman. New York: Modern Library.

Noddings, Nel. 2000. "Two Concepts of Caring." In *Philosophy of Education Yearbook 1999*, ed. Randall Curren, 36–39. Urbana, IL: Philosophy of Education Society.

Nolan, James L., Jr. 1998. *The Therapeutic State: Justifying Government at Century's End*. New York: New York University Press.

Ochs, Elinor. 1989. "Introduction." In "The Pragmatics of Affect," ed. Elinor Ochs, special issue of *Text* 9, no. 1.

O'Hanlon, Bill, and James Wilk. 1997. *Shifting Contexts: The Generation of Effective Psychotherapy*. New York: The Guilford Press.

Ong, Aihwa, and Li Zhang. 2008. "Introduction: Privatizing China: Powers of the Self, Socialism from Afar." In *Privatizing China: Socialism from Afar, ed*. Li Zhang and Aihwa Ong, 1–19. Ithaca: Cornell University Press.

Ortner, Sherry B. 1991. "Reading America: Preliminary Notes on Class and Culture." In *Recapturing Anthropology: Working in the Present*, ed. Richard G. Fox, 163–190. Santa Fe, NM: School of American Research Press.

Ots, Thomas. 1994. "The Silenced Body—the Expressive Leib: On the Dialectic of Mind and Life in the Chinese Cathartic Healing." In *Embodiment and Experience: The Existential Ground of Culture and Self*, ed. Thomas J. Csordas, 116–136. Cambridge: Cambridge University Press.

Ou, Shuyi. 2003. "Dr. Xu's Pysch-Hotline Counseling in Beijing." *China Daily*, January 21, 10.

Pawelczyk, Joanna. 2011. *Talk as Therapy: Psychotherapy in a Linguistic Perspective*. Boston: Walter de Gruyter.

Pearlin, Leonard I. 1983. "Role Strains and Personal Stress." In *Psychosocial Stress: Trends in Theory and Research*, ed. H. B. Kaplan, 3–32. New York: Academic.

Pearlin, Leonard I., and Morton A. Lieberman. 1979. "Social Sources of Emotional Distress." *Research on Community Mental Health* 1: 217–248.

Pennebaker, James W. 1997. "Writing about Emotional Experiences as a Therapeutic Process." *Psychological Science* 8, no. 3: 162–166.

People's Daily. 2001. "WHO Survey on Mental Health in China." *People's Daily*, December 15. www.peopledaily.com.cn, accessed on December 12, 2010.

Phillips, Michael R., Xianyun Li, and Yanping Zhang. 2002. "Suicide Rates in China, 1995–1999." *Lancet* 359(March 9): 835–840.

Platt, Tristan, with Pablo Quisbert. 2007. "Knowing Silence and Merging Horizons: The Case of the Great Potosi Cover-Up." In *Ways of Knowing: New Approaches in the Anthropology of Experience and Learning*, ed. Mark Harris, 113–138. New York: Berghahn.

Polsky, Andrew J. 1991. *The Rise of the Therapeutic State*. Princeton, NJ: Princeton University Press.

Power, Nina. 2010. "Potentiality or Capacity?—Agamben's Missing Subjects." *Theory and Event* 13, no. 1.

Pupavac, Vanessa. 2002. "Pathologizing Populations and Colonizing Minds: International Psycosocial Programs in Kosov." *Alternatives* 27: 489–511.

Qian, Mingyi. 1994. *Xinli Zixun yu Xinli Zhiliao* [Psychological Counseling and Psychotherapy]. Beijing: Beijing University Press.

Qian Mingyi, Craig, W. Smith, Zhonggeng Chen, and GuoHua Xia. 2002. "Psychotherapy in China: A Review of Its History and Contemporary Directions." *International Journal of Mental Health* 30, no. 4: 49–68.

Richburg, Keith B. 2011. "China Tries to Cure a Happiness Deficit." *Washington Post*, May 15. http://www.washingtonpost.com/world/asia-pacific/china-tries-to-cure-a-happiness-deficit/2011/05/10/AFUtIL4G_story.html, accessed on July 8, 2011.

Roberman, Sveta. 2013. "All That Is Just Ersatz: The Meaning of Work in the Life of Immigrant Newcomers." *Ethos* 41, no. 1: 1–23.

Roberts, Janine. 1994. *Tales and Transformations: Stories in Families and Family Therapy*. London: W. W. Norton.

Rocca, Jean-Louis. 2003. "Old Working Class, New Working Class: Reforms, Labor Crisis and the Two Faces of Conflicts in Chinese Urban Areas." In *China Today: Economic Reforms, Social Cohesion and Collective Identities*, ed. Taciana Fisac and Leila Fernandez-Stembridge, 77–104. London: RoutledgeCurzon.

Rofel, Lisa. 1999. *Other Modernities: Gendered Yearnings in China after Socialism*. Berkeley: University of California Press.

———. 2007. *Desiring China: Experiments in Neoliberalism, Sexuality, and Public Culture*. Durham, NC: Duke University Press, 2007.

Rogers, Carl. 1951. *Client-Centered Therapy*. Boston: Houghton Mifflin.

———. 1995. *On Becoming a Person: A Therapist's View of Psychotherapy*. New York: Houghton Mifflin Harcourt.

Rogers, Carl, and John Wood. 1974. "Client-Centered Theory: Carl Rogers." In *Operational Theories of Personality*, ed. Arthur Burton, 211–249. New York: Brunner/Mazel.

Rose, Nikolas. 1989. "Individualizing Psychology." In *Texts of Identity*, ed. John Shotter and Kenneth Gergen, 64–72. London: Sage.

———. 1996. *Inventing Our Selves: Psychology, Power and Personhood*. Cambridge: Cambridge University Press.

———. 1999. *Powers of Freedom: Reframing Political Thought*. Cambridge: Cambridge University Press.

Rosen, Stanley. 1994. "Chinese Women in the 1990s: Images and Roles in Contention." In *China Review*, ed. Maurice Brosseau and Lo Chi Kin, 1–28. Hong Kong: Chinese University of Hong Kong Press.

Ruan, Danching, Linton C. Freeman, Xinyuan Dai, Yunkang Pan, and Wenhong Zhang. 1997. "On the Changing Structure of Social Networks in China." *Social Networks* 19, no. 1: 75–89.

Rudnyckyj, Daromir. 2010. *Spiritual Economies: Islam, Globalization, and the Afterlife of Development*. Ithaca, NY: Cornell University Press.

Russell, Andrew, and Ian R. Edgar. 1998. "Research and Practice in the Anthropology of Welfare." In *The Anthropology of Welfare, ed*. Ian R. Edgar and Andrew Russell. London: Routledge.

Ryle, Gilbert. (1949) 1984. *The Concept of Mind*. Chicago: University of Chicago Press.

Sabbadini, Andrea. 1991. "Listening to Silence." *British Journal of Psychotherapy* 7, no. 4: 406–415.

Schneider, Jo Anne. 2001. "Introduction: Social Welfare and Welfare Reform." *American Anthropologist* 103, no. 3: 705–713.

Schram, Stuart R. 1989. *The Thought of Mao Tse-Tung*. New York: Cambridge University Press.

Schurmann, Franz. 1968. *Ideology and Organization in Communist China*. Berkeley: University of California Press.

Scott, Joan. 1988. "On Language, Gender and Working-class History." In *Gender and the Politics of History*, 53–67. New York: Columbia University Press.

Shank, Megan. 2012. "King of the Road." In *Chinese Characters: Profiles of Fast-Changing Lives in a Fast-Changing Land*, ed. Angilee Shah and Jeffrey Wasserstrom, 103–113. Berkeley: University of California Press.

Shi, Kan. 1999. *Zhiye zhidao de lilun and yingyong* [Job Guidance: Theory and Practice]. Beijing: Beijing Xicheng Qu Zhiye Zhidao Shiyan Jidi.

———. 2011. *Yuangong yuanzhu shi* (Employee Assistants). Beijing: Zhongguo jiuye peixun jishu zhidao zhongxin (China's Employment and Training Guidance Center) and Guojia yuangong yuanzhushi kecheng fazhang zhongxin (National Employee Assistant Pedegogy Development Center).

Sigley, Gary. 2006. "Chinese Governmentalities: Government, Governance, and the Socialist Market Economy." *Economy and Society* 35, no. 4: 487–508.

Smart, Alan. 1993. "Gifts, Bribes, and Guanxi: A Reconsideration of Bourdieu's Social Capital." *Cultural Anthropology* 8, no. 3: 388–408.

Smith, Benjamin. 2005. "Ideologies of the Speaking Subject in the Psychotherapeutic Theory and Practice of Carl Rogers." *Journal of Linguistic Anthropology* 15, no. 2: 258–272.

Smith, Joanna Handlin. 2009. *The Art of Doing Good: Charity in Late Ming China*. Berkeley, CA: University of California Press.

Smith, Roger. 1997. *The Norton History of the Human Sciences*. New York: W. W. Norton.

Smyth, Russell, and Xiaolei Qian. 2008. "Inequality and Happiness in Urban China." *Economics Bulletin* 4, no. 24: 1–10.

Solinger, Dorothy. 2001. "Why We Cannot Count the Unemployed." *China Quarterly* 167: 671–688.

———. 2006. "The Creation of a New Underclass in China and Its Implications." *Environment and Urbanization* 18, no. 1: 177–193.

———. 2009. "The Phase-Out of the Unfit: Keeping the Unworthy Out of Work." In *Work and Organizations in China after Thirty Years of Transition*, ed. Lisa Keister, 307–336. Bingley, West Yorkshire: Emerald.

Song, Jesook. 2006. "Family Breakdown and Invisible Homeless Women: Neoliberal Governance during the Asian Debt Crisis in South Korea, 1997–2001." *positions: east asia cultures critique* 14, no. 1: 37–65.

Spelman, Elizabeth V. 1989. "Anger and Insubordination." In *Women, Knowledge, and Reality: Explorations in Feminist Philosophy*, ed. Ann Garry and Marilyn Pearsall, 263–274. Boston: Unwin Hyman.

Steinmuller, Hans, and Zhang Yuanbo. 2014. *Gambling on the Chinese Dream*. New Left Project, May 1, 2013. http://www.newleftproject.org/index.php/site/article_comments/gambling_on_the_chinese_dream, accessed on October 10, 2014.

Stratherm, Marilyn. 1999. *Property, Substance and Effect: Anthropological Essays on Persons and Things*. London: Athlone Press.

Sundararajan, Louise. 2005. "Happiness Donut: A Confucian Critique of Positive Psychology." *Journal of Theoretical and Philosophical Psychology* 25, no. 1: 35–60.

Sun Lung-kee. 1983. *Zhongguo Wenhua De "Shengceng Jiegou"* [The Deep Structure of Chinese Culture]. Hong Kong: Jixianshe.

Sun, Wanning. 2009. "Mapping Space for the Maid: Metropolitan Gaze, Peripheral Vision and Subaltern Spectatorship in Urban China." *Feminist Media Studies* 9, no. 1: 57–71.

Svendsen, Mette N. 2011. "Articulating Potentiality: Notes on the Delineation of the Blank Figure in Human Embryonic Stem Cell Research." *Cultural Anthropology* 26, no. 3: 414–437.

Szasz, Thomas S. 1963. *Law, Liberty, and Psychiatry: An Inquiry into the Social Uses of Mental Health Practices*. New York: Macmillan.

———. 2001. "The Therapeutic State: The Tyranny of Pharmacy." *Independent Review* 5 no. 4: 485–521.

Taylor, Charles. 2004. *Modern Social Imaginaries*. Durham: Duke University Press.

Taussig, Mark, and Rudy Fenwick. 2011. *Work and Mental Health in Social Context*. New York: Springer.

Thin, Neil. 2008. "Why Anthropology Can Ill Afford to Ignore Well-Being." In *Pursuits of Happiness: Well-Being in Anthropological Perspective*, ed. Gordon Mathews and Carolina Izquierdo, 23–44. New York: Berghahn.

Thrift, Nigel. 2005. *Knowing Capitalism*. London: Sage.

Tian, Chenshan. 2005. *Chinese Dialects: From Yijing to Marxism*. Lanham, MD: Lexington Books.

Tie, Warwick. 2004. "The Psychic Life of Governmentality." *Culture, Theory, and Critique* 45, no. 2: 161–176.

Urciuoli, Bonnie. 2008. "Skills and Selves in the New Workplace." *American Ethnologist* 35, no. 2: 211–228.

Vanheule, Stijn, An Lievrouw, and Paul Verhaeghe. 2003. "Burnout and Intersubjectivity: A Psychoanalytical Study from a Lacanian Perspective." *Human Relations* 56, no. 3: 321–328.

Venn, Couze. 2007. "Cultural Theory, Biopolitics and the Question of Power." *Theory, Culture and Society* 24, no. 3: 111–124.

Vigh, Henrik. 2011. "Vigilance: On Conflict, Social Invisibility, and Negative Potentiality." *Social Analysis* 55, no. 3: 93–114.

Vitz, Paul C. 1994. *Psychology as Religion: The Cult of Self-Worship*. Grand Rapids, MI: William B. Eerdmans Publishing Company.

Walder, Andrew G. 1984. "The Remaking of the Chinese Working Class, 1949–1981." *Modern China* 10, no. 1: 3–48.

———. 1986. *Communist Neo-Traditionalism: Work and Authority in Chinese Industry*. Berkeley: University of California Press.

Walker, Nancy A. 1990. *Feminist Alternatives: Irony and Fantasy in the Contemporary Novel by Women*. Mississippi: University Press of Mississippi.

Wang, Guangwu, and Zheng Yongnian. 2008. *China and the New International Order*. London: Routledge.

Wang, Xiuqiu. 2008. *Ganbian Qiangwan Ren Yisheng de Xinli Jianya Fa* [The Psychological Practice on De-stressing That Will Benefit All Your Life]. Haikou, Hainan Province: Nanhai Shubanshe.

Wang, Zheng. 2003. "Gender, Employment and Women's Resistance." In *Chinese Society: Change, Conflict and Resistance*, ed. Elizabeth J. Perry and Mark Selden, 159–182. New York: Routledge Curzon.

Warnecke, Tonia. 2011. "Gender and the Welfare State in China." *International Journal of Business and Globalisation* 6, no. 1: 44–53.

Warr, Peter. 1987. *Work, Unemployment, and Mental Health*. Oxford, UK: Oxford University Press.

Weber, Max. 1978. *Economy and Society*. Berkeley: University of California Press.

Wen, Jiabao. 2003. Press conference speech. March 18. Women's Newspaper, p. 1.

White, Craig A. 2001. "Cognitive Behavioral Principles in Managing Chronic Disease." *Western Journal of Medicine* 175, no. 5: 338–342.

White, Michael. 1995. *Re-Authoring Lives: Interview & Essays*. Adelaide, Australia: Dutch Centre Publications.

White, Michael, and David Epston. 1990. *Narrative Means to Therapeutic Ends*. New York: Norton.

Won, Jaeyoun. 2004. "Withering Away of the Iron Rice Bowl? The Re-Employment Project of Post-Socialist China." *Studies in Comparative International Development* 39, no. 2: 71–93.

Wong, Linda. 1998. *Marginalization and Social Welfare in China*. New York: Routledge.

Wong, Linda, and Bernard Poon. 2005. "From Serving Neighbors to Recontrolling Urban Society: The Transformation of China's Community Policy." *China Information* 19, no. 3: 413–442.

Woodward, Susan L. 1995. *Socialist Unemployment: the Political Economy of Yugoslavia, 1945–1990*. Princeton, NJ: Princeton University Press.

Worm, Verner. 2010. "Chinese Personality: A Center in a Network." In *Mentality and Thought: North, South, East and West, ed*. Per Durst-Anderson and Elisabeth F. Lange, 215–231. Frederiksberg: Copenhagen Business School Press.

Wu, Fulong, and Ningying Huang. 2007. "New Urban Poverty in China: Economic Restructuring and Transformation of Welfare Provision." *Asia Pacific Viewpoint* 48, no. 2: 168–185.

Xu, Bing. 2003. *China Women's News*. January 4.

Xu, Gary, and Susan Feiner. 2007. "Meinu Jingji/China's Beauty Economy: Buying Looks, Shifting Value and Changing Place." *Feminist Economics* 13, nos. 3/4: 307–323.

Yalom, Irvin. 1989. *Love's Executioner and Other Tales of Psychotherapy*. London: Penguin Books.

Yan, Hairong. 2003a. "Neoliberal Governmentality and Neohumanism: Organizing Suzhi/Value Flow through Labor Recruitment Networks." *Cultural Anthropology* 18, no. 4: 493–523.

———. 2003b. "Spectralization of the Rural: Reinterpreting the Labor Mobility of Rural Young Women in Post-Mao China." *American Ethnologist* 30, no. 4: 576–594.

Yan, Yunxiang. 1996. *The Flow of Gifts: Reciprocity and Social Networks in a Chinese Village*. Stanford, CA: Stanford University Press.

———. 2003. *Private Life under Socialism: Love, Intimacy, and Family Change in a Chinese Village, 1949–1999*. Stanford, CA: Stanford University Press.

———. 2011. "The Changing Moral Landscape." In *Deep China: The Moral Life of the Person*, ed. Arthur Kleinman, Yunxiang Yan, Jing Jun, Sing Lee Everett Zhang, Pan Tianshu, Wu Fei, and Guo Jinhhua, 36–77. Berkley: University of California Press.

Yang, Jie. 2007. "'Reemployment Stars': Language, Gender and Neoliberal Restructuring in China." In *Words, Worlds, Material Girls: Language, Gender and Global Economies*, ed. Bonnie McElhinny, 73–102. Berlin: Mouton de Gruyter.

———. 2010. "The Crisis of Masculinity: Class, Gender and Kindly Power in Post-Mao China." *American Ethnologist* 37, no. 3: 550–562.

———. 2011a. "*Nennu* and *Shunu*: Gender, Body Politics and the Beauty Economy in China." *Signs: Journal of Women in Culture and Society* 36, no. 2: 333–357.

———. 2011b. "The Politics of the Dang'an: Spectralization, Spatialization, and Neoliberal Governmentality in China." *Anthropological Quarterly* 84, no. 2: 507–534.

———. 2013a. "Fake Happiness: Counseling, Potentiality and Psycho-Politics in China." *Ethos* 41, no. 3: 291–311.

———. 2013b. "The Politics of Huanghua: Gender, Metaphors and Privatization." *Language and Communication* 33, no. 1: 63–68.

———. 2014. "The Politics of Affect and Emotion: Potentiality, Imagination and Anticipation." In *The Political Economy of Affect and Emotion in East Asia*, 1–28. London: Routledge.

Yang, Mayfair Meihui. 1988. "The Modernity of Power in the Chinese Socialist Order." *Cultural Anthropology* 3, no. 4: 408–427.

———. 1999. *Spaces of Their Own: Women's Public Sphere in Transnational China*. Minneapolis: University of Minnesota Press.

Yu, Dan. 2006. *Yu Dan's Reflections on Analects*. Beijing: Zhonghua Shuju.

Yu, Keping. 2002. "Toward an Incremental Democracy and Governance: Chinese Theories and Assessment Criteria." *New Political Science* 24, no. 2: 181–99.

Zhang, Everett Yuehong. 2005."Rethinking Sexual Repression in Maoist China: Ideology, Structure, and the Ownership of the Body." *Body and Society* 11, no. 3: 1–25.

———. 2011a. "Introduction: Governmentality in China." In *Governance of Life in Chinese Moral Experience: The Quest for an Adequate Life*, ed. Everett Zhang Yuehong, Arthur Kleinman, and Tu Weiming, 1–30. London: Routledge.

———. 2011b. "China's Sexual Revolution." In *Deep China: The Moral Life of the Person*, ed. Arthur Kleinman, Yunxiang Yan, Jing Jun, Sing Lee, Everett Zhang, Pan Tianshu, Wu Fei, and Guo Jinhua, 106–151. Berkeley, CA: University of California Press.

Zhang, Guihua, and Luo Zhaohong. 1996. *Shichang jingji shiqi de funu gongzuo* [Women's Work in the Market Economy]. Beijing: Hongqi Chubanshe.

Zhang, Li. 2014. "Bentuhua: Culturing Psychotherapy in Postsocialist China." *Culture, Medicine, and Psychiatry* 38, no. 2: 283–305.

Zhang, Li, and Aihwa Ong. 2008. *Privatizing China: Socialism from Afar*. Ithaca, NY: Cornell University Press.

Zhang, Yanhua. 2007. *Transforming Emotions through Chinese Medicine: An Ethnographic Account from Contemporary China*. Albany: State University of New York Press.

———. 2014. "Crafting Confucian Remedies for Happiness in Contemporary China: Unraveling the Yu Dan Phenomenon." In *The Political Economy of Affect and Emotion in East Asia*, ed. Jie Yang, 31–44. London: Routledge.

Zhang, Yi. 2002. *Guoyou qiye de jiazuhua* [The Familialization of State-Owned Enterprises]. Shehui kexue wenxian chubanshe.

Zhao Yuezhi. 2002. "The Rich, the Laid-Off, and the Criminal in Tabloid Tales: Read All about It." In *Popular China: Unofficial Culture in a Globalizing Society*, ed. Perry Link, Richard Madsen, and Paul Pickowicz, 111–136. London: Rowman & Littlefield.

———. 2008. *Communication in China: Political Economy, Power and Conflict*. Toronto: Rowman & Littlefield.

Zheng, Jun. 2009. *Xinli zhuren de di san zhong shili* [The Third Force for Psychological Assistance]. Shanghai: Huadong Shifang Daxue Chubanshe [The Northeast Normal University Press].

Zheng, Tiantian. 2009. *Red Lights: The Lives of Sex Workers in Postsocialist China*. Minneapolis: University of Minnesota Press.

Zhong, Xueping. 2000. *Masculinity Besieged? Issues of Modernity and Male Subjectivity in Chinese Literature of the Late Twentieth Century*. Durham: Duke University Press.

Zhou, Jiawang. 2003. "Juweihui zhixuan bili gao, Beijing shequ minzhu zhengzhi da jinbu" [The Percent of Direction Election of Residents' Committees Is Increasing, Beijing's Community Democracy Is Making Progress]. *Beijing Wanbao* [Beijing Evening News], October 22.

Zizek, Slavoj. 1994. *The Metastases of Enjoyment: Six Essays on Woman and Causality*. London: Verso.

INDEX